CASE STUDIES IN CULTURAL ANTHROPOLOGY

GENERAL EDITORS

George and Louise Spindler

STANFORD UNIVERSITY

CHINA'S URBAN VILLAGERS

Changing Life in a Beijing Suburb

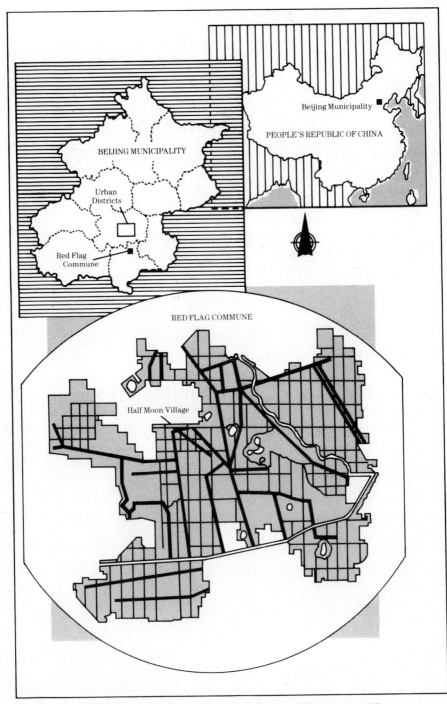

Beijing Municipality and Half Moon Village in 1979

CHINA'S URBAN VILLAGERS
Changing Life in a Beijing Suburb

Second Edition

NORMAN A. CHANCE

University of Connecticut

Harcourt Brace College Publishers

Fort Worth Philadelphia San Diego
New York Orlando Austin San Antonio
Toronto Montreal London Sydney Tokyo

Publisher	Ted Buchholz
Acquisitions Editor	Chris Klein
Senior Project Editor	Christine Caperton
Copyeditor	D. Teddy Diggs
Production Manager	Tom Urquhart
Art & Design Supervisor	Vicki McAlindon Horton

Cover photograph: A woman holding a child.

Library of Congress Cataloging-in-Publication Data
Chance, Norman A. (Norman Allee), 1927–
    China's urban villagers: changing life in a Beijing suburb / by
Norman A. Chance.—2nd ed.
    (Case studies in cultural anthropology)
    Includes bibliographical references and index.
    1. Peking (China)—Social life and customs. 2. Villages—China-
-Peking. I. Title. II. Series.
DS795.2.C48 1991
   306'.0951'156—dc20   90–43198
ISBN: 0-03-031333-3

Requests for permission to make copies of any part of the work should be mailed to Copyrights and Permissions Department, Harcourt Brace Jovanovich, Inc., 8th Floor, Orlando, FL 32887. Address editorial correspondence to 301 Commerce Street, Suite 3700, Fort Worth, TX 76102. Address orders to 6277 Sea Harbor Drive, Orlando, FL 32887, 1-800-782-4479, or 1-800-433-0001 (in Florida).

Printed in the United States of America
  4 016 9 8 7 6 5 4

Harcourt Brace Jovanovich, Inc.
The Dryden Press
Saunders College Publishing

To My Three Fine Sons

Stephen, Christopher, and Jonathan

Foreword

Norman A. Chance

Norman Chance is Professor of Anthropology at the University of Connecticut. Born in Lynn, Massachusetts, he received his initial training in anthropology at the University of Pennsylvania prior to receiving his Ph.D. from Cornell University in 1957. After spending five years at the University of Oklahoma, he accepted a teaching appointment at McGill University in Montreal, Canada, eventually becoming the founder and first director of the Programme in the Anthropology of Development. In 1968, he returned to the United States to establish a new Department of Anthropology at the University of Connecticut, where he continues teaching today.

Among his many academic activities, he has held postdoctoral research fellowships from Harvard University, the Russell Sage Foundation, and the Arctic Institute of North America. Fieldwork has been conducted in the American Southwest, subarctic Canada arctic Alaska as well as China. He has served on numerous national and international committees, panels, and boards, including those of the National Academy of Sciences, the National Research Council, the American Association for the Advancement of Science, the American Anthropological Association, and the Arctic Institute of North America. He has written several case studies in this series, the most recent being *The Inupiat and Arctic Alaska* (1990), along with other publications.

Norman Chance first became interested in China while teaching a seminar on Third World development at McGill University. In the spring of 1972, he was invited by the People's Republic of China (PRC) Embassy in Ottawa to give a series of lectures on American education at five well-known Chinese universities. This was followed six years later by a second trip to China in which he served as the leader of a delegation of teachers and population planners. Then, in the fall of 1979, together with Fred Engst and several other Americans, he was invited by the officials of a large state farm on the outskirts of Beijing Municipality to live and work in Half Moon Village, located within their district. The ethnographic data obtained from this unique experience serves as a focal point for the analysis of the collective life of the village described in this case study.

Fred Engst*

Fred Engst was born and grew up in China. His American parents, Sid Engst and Joan Hinton, initially went to China in the 1940s to work with the United Nations Relief and Rehabilitation Administration. Deciding to remain, they spent over 40 years as agricultural specialists, living and working in both rural and urban areas of the country. After completing his schooling in the 1960s, Fred Engst became an electrician at a state factory in Beijing. In 1974, he came to the United States. After working for several years in a large factory in Philadelphia, he attended Temple University, eventually graduating with a degree in economics. Presently, he is is a graduate student in the Department of Economics at Rutgers University, New Brunswick.

On several occasions during the 1980s, Fred Engst revisited Beijing and other regions of China. In 1988, he returned and spent 10 months at a state farm in Beijing Municipality as an Assistant to the Deputy of Farm Management. During this time, he undertook research on agricultural developments in several suburban districts of the city, including the area first studied with Norman Chance and others in 1979. In July 1989, he again returned to China as a consultant for a large American corporation seeking to expand its enterprises in the PRC. On this occasion, shortly after the violent suppression of the Beijing student-led uprising in Tiananmen Square, he briefly revisited Half Moon, bringing this book up-to-date on events occurring in the village.

*Coauthor of Chapter 9

ABOUT THIS CASE STUDY

The first edition of this case study of Half Moon Village within Red Flag Commune was largely based on three visits by Norman Chance to the People's Republic of China. Periods of residence and participant observation in the village include time spent in agricultural field labor as well as sharing in the social and cultural life of the people. Fifty in-depth interviews were also conducted with a

wide range of personnel including peasants, factory workers, students, local leaders, government officials, and intellectuals. Few field researchers have been able to
learn enough about modern China and its complex history to write knowledgeably
about more than one small aspect of it. That aspect, for Norman Chance, is a
mid-sized village in a large commune in the shadow of China's capital city. Half
Moon Village is an understandable and relatively manageable unit for study from an
anthropological, ethnographic point of view. That this case study is credible is
attested to not only by Dr. Chance's professional status as an experienced anthropologist but also by extensive reviews by other students of modern China and by
qualified individuals in the People's Republic who gave their assistance while the
manuscript was taking shape.

This second edition includes a new chapter (Chapter 9) on a decade of dramatic
change that took place in Half Moon Village and Beijing Municipality between
1979 and 1989. The massive protest by students and other city residents in and
around Tiananmen Square in 1989 are described and the larger socioeconomic and
political antecedents analyzed. This analysis makes these events more understandable as the consequence of long-term tensions rather than as an explosion of the
moment. Fred Engst, the coauthor of Chapter 9, has deep and prolonged experience
in China, enabling him to contribute an invaluable perspective to the discussion.

The study is remarkable for its combination of two quite unlikely themes: One is
the effort to analyze socialist political and economic processes aimed at developing
viable solutions to the country's pressing problems. The other is a study of family
and kin, the nature of sex roles and marriage, the events and contexts of socialization, and going to school. This combination makes the case study much more than it
could have been were only one of these themes emphasized. Without the direct
observation in the field and participant interaction with the people—two constant
features of the anthropological approach—the latter theme would not have
appeared.

The style of presentation in this case study contributes to readability and
understanding. The author not only draws on his own direct observations in telling
anecdotes that enliven the pages and evoke images but also he uses dialogue
extensively, permitting the people themselves to tell about their lives and circumstances as closely to their own way as translation and the ethics of field research
permit. The reader feels close to the concerns of everyday life as well as to the
issues of socialism at the grass-roots level in modern China.

There are few countries in the world today about which Americans are more
curious than the People's Republic of China. And there is no country about which
we have more misinformation, more hazy understandings, and gross mis-
understandings. This case study is a step in the direction of improving our knowledge and understanding.

It is also a demonstration of the capabilities of anthropology as an approach to
the study of complex societies. Though Half Moon is only one of many villages in
China, knowing about it permits us to form some relevant perspective on the
complex whole of which it is a part. If relations between the People's Republic and
the United States improve, we may acquire enough comparative material from other

village studies to make firmer judgments about the whole. For the present, we are fortunate to have this study of a village in the vicinity of a large urban center—one that is neither the poorest nor the richest, nor the most backward, nor most progressive of its kind.

GEORGE AND LOUISE SPINDLER
Editors
Calistoga, California

Preface

Fieldwork is a hallmark of anthropology. Living with the people—experiencing their work, social patterns, thought, and values—is one characteristic that often distinguishes our approach from that of other social sciences. Yet, since 1949, on-the-scene rural studies of China's mainland by Western anthropologists or other social analysts have been almost nonexistent.

Even within China itself, few government-sponsored ethnographic and sociological investigations have been made available to the public. The actual teaching of cultural anthropology was abandoned in 1952 (Whyte and Pasternak 1980:148), not to be revived until the mid-1980s. The resulting loss of a generation of scholars trained in comparative investigation and social science methodology is only just now being realized as academic institutions seek to reestablish cultural anthropology, sociology, psychology, and similarly oriented disciplines into their curricula.

From the early 1950s through the Cultural Revolution of the 1960s and 1970s, such fields of inquiry were perceived as reactionary and therefore unworthy of recognition in a revolutionary society committed to socialist transformation. Instead of making a distinction between the development of anthropological knowledge and the uses to which it would be put, Chinese leaders of the time placed the whole subject matter outside the bounds of political acceptability. They assumed that such intellectual activity challenged the views of Marx and Lenin and opened the door to new forms of neo-colonialism.

The slowness with which cultural anthropology and related fields have returned to the academic fold is only partly due to established priorities and the limited availability of trained teachers and researchers. Although the Chinese Academy of Social Sciences has emphasized the importance of these subjects in strengthening the country's drive toward modernization, some government leaders still express concern about the possible emergence of a scholarly elite committed to challenging the present political direction of Chinese polity in the name of "objective" social science—demonstrating once again that "objectivity" cannot be separated from politics and its impact on human beings.

Needless to say, questions of objectivity in the development and utilization of knowledge are raised in the United States and other countries too. A well-known American example was the heated debate carried on by members of various social (and physical) scientific societies on the role of their professions in the Vietnam War. Still, social research in the United States received continuing recognition and support, whereas in China it has only recently reemerged within universities and institutes. The fact that relatively little anthropological research has been undertaken in rural China in recent years—whether by Chinese social scientists or others—is one reason to encourage more in-depth village studies. Chinese peasant-farmers represent one-fifth of the world's population. It would certainly behoove the other four-fifths to learn more about them. Nevertheless, paucity of knowledge is not the only reason for studying rural China.

Beginning in the 1950s and continuing to the present, a dramatic increase has taken place in the comparative study of rural economic development. Many years ago, when I first began teaching a seminar on the topic, I kept coming across references to China's alternative "model" (see Frolic 1978). Why is it, I asked myself at the time, that China—the most ancient of civilizations—had stimulated such great interest among Western social scientists as well as intellectuals of the increasingly independent Third World? Was it the case, as many sympathetic analysts proposed, that China had found a more humane way of developing, one geared toward communal enrichment rather than greed?

Could underdeveloped countries like China improve their standard of living without succumbing to the myriad problems of expanding urbanization, with its attendant dislocation and unemployment; heavy industrialization, with its height-ened exploitation of the rural sector; increased economic dependence on outside capital, with the all-too-frequent inflationary spiral that accompanies it; and the subtler but powerful cultural blandishments of Western consumer-oriented society? In the 1970s, some knowledgeable economists, historians, and China specialists thought so (see Gurley 1971; Stavrianos 1975; Nee and Peck 1975). Others, such as Simon Leys, were far more critical of China's post-1949 development, calling Mao Zedong's efforts to create a socialist society "essentially totalitarian and feudal bureaucratic" (Leys 1977:xi).

Having become deeply concerned about the seeming inability of Western-based development programs to meet the needs of the people to whom they were directed, I wanted to learn more. I hoped that a firsthand visit to China would provide some enlightenment and perhaps even a few tentative answers. At least it was worth a try.

In 1971, following the advent of "ping-pong diplomacy" (in which the Chinese government invited an American table-tennis team to play in Beijing), the process of renewing formal ties between China and the United States was begun. I im-mediately applied to the Chinese Embassy in Ottawa to undertake a brief study of changing educational patterns resulting from the policies, then being implemented, of the Cultural Revolution. Having recently become head of an anthropology department, I was particularly interested in academic administration and felt that I could learn something from China's seemingly innovative efforts in this regard. Given the existing political climate, it was also clear that more in-depth field research by an American anthropologist was out of the question. At that time, even a one- or two-month field trip to China was uncommon (see Schell 1977).

The following spring, I learned from the embassy that my proposal had indeed been approved and, furthermore, that I was expected to give a series of lectures on American education at several Chinese universities. Shortly thereafter, in April and May 1972, together with Nancy Chance, also an anthropologist, I had the rather heady experience of traveling to five major cities and many towns and villages throughout China. Visits were made to various universities, colleges, and research and minority institutes, interviewing faculty, administrators, and students and in other ways gathering initial data on the impact of the "Great Proletarian Cultural Revolution" on the social and educational life of the Chinese people.

As one of the first American anthropologists to visit China in over twenty years, I soon found myself being treated as an "honored guest"—an experience perhaps best described as "un-humbling"—complete with an overwhelming array of culinary delights, flashbulb lights, and breathtaking sights. Introduced to many of the country's scientific leaders in the Academy of Sciences and other key educational institutions, I was quickly presented with an overview of China's recent academic innovations. Almost impossible to achieve in the politically rarified atmosphere of the capital city, however, was an insight into the educational system from the perspective of students, teachers, administrators, and other participants not so imbued with official policy.

Nevertheless, I did have several lively discussions with faculty members of the Beijing Central Institute of Minorities, including the anthropologist Fei Xiaotong. Fei, an internationally known social scientist trained in England and the United States, had only recently reestablished ties with Westerners after having undergone a long period of intellectual isolation in China's countryside following his active criticism of the government (Fei, Wu, and Lin 1973; Fei 1980; and McGough 1979). Invited to give a formal lecture on "Minority Life in America" to the student body of the Institute, I soon found myself engaged in a four-hour discussion that dramatically illustrated how limited East-West scholarly contact had been in the past two decades and, also, how different were our perspectives on the relationship between minority and majority cultures.

After leaving the capital for politically less intense areas of the country, I was able to undertake some preliminary research of the sort that had originally brought me to China—though, of course, not all that I had hoped to do. Still, this first trip helped me to appreciate China's immense historical complexity that has led some in the past to describe the country as "unfathomable," "unpredictable," or "unknowable."

However, on returning to the United States, I was soon asked to put aside the complexities in favor of simple generalizations. That is, as one of the few academic visitors to China at the time, I was immediately (and temptingly) called upon to draw large-scale conclusions based on a modicum of experience. Indeed, symptoms of "instant expertise" were showing up in many literary and scholarly circles at that time.

Actually, it was rather easy to report on the positive aspects of China's development effort, given the ease of access to those models and experiments deemed successful by the initiators and participants. Many people, including myself, were impressed with Mao Zedong's strategy of reducing economic inequalities through the immense collective effort of the people (Chance 1973). It was the failures—the economic, political, and personal failures that were barely glimpsed, if seen at all—and this knowledge was necessary to gaining any well-rounded picture of contemporary China. Unfortunately, all other requests to return to China for more in-depth anthropological investigation were either ignored or rejected. Obviously, I had to settle for what had already been accomplished. Looking back on these years, I now realize that my initial evaluation of China was based more on what I had hoped was occurring than on what was actually happening—hardy a scientific appraisal. As a result, my interpretations were often more illusory than real.

Six years later, I joined millions of other Americans in observing a significant turnaround in China's internal government policies. External relations too were changing as the country decided to open the door wider to foreign visitors. In just a few years, over a quarter of a million tourists had savored the country's cultural fare. Government and scientific delegations began formal talks culminating in a proliferation of exchanges, including a few of an educational and scholarly nature. In August and September 1978, I led a delegation of academic and professional people to Beijing and Northeast China, where we focused on education, population control, and related issues. Changes in the six years since my first visit were striking. The revolutionary fervor of the late 1960s and early 1970s had dissipated significantly as post-Mao China sought to quell old conflicts and instill a new sense of purpose directed toward realizing the "Four Modernizations" in agriculture, industry, science and technology, and defense. Talks with village leaders, agricultural specialists, population planners, educators, and health professionals suggested that, at least for the moment, a new openness was in the air and that prospects for the kind of wide-ranging discussion and expression of varied opinion necessary to sound anthropological field research might well become possible in the not-too-distant future.

As changing international affairs continued to draw China and the United States closer together, culminating in the establishment of diplomatic relations, Fred Engst and Nancy Chance submitted to the Chinese government a proposal that an opportunity be provided for a small group of Americans of differing socioeconomic, occupational, and racial backgrounds to live and work with the Chinese people for several months in the fall of 1979. Approval was eventually given. The group then took up residence in a small village within the borders of a large state farm on the outskirts of Beijing City and within the municipality. A month and a half later, the group spent several weeks working in a textile factory in adjacent Hebei Province, interspersed with travel to other cities, rural areas, and a brief stay in a banner village in Inner Mongolia. A major part of this book draws extensively on research undertaken in this suburban Beijing village during the fall of 1979, including one additional month that Nancy Chance and I spent in China after the conclusion of the group trip. Between September and December of that year, I taped and transcribed over 50 detailed interviews conducted with young, middle-aged, and older men and women from a wide range of backgrounds, including peasant leaders, factory workers, students, teachers, paraprofessional "barefoot doctors," and many others who I felt could help in putting together a picture of changing life in a North China village.[1]

This data was then compared with earlier information I had accumulated on life in this same Beijing Municipality state farm dating back to the spring of 1972, with data gathered on a short trip to the farm headquarters and outlying agricultural and

---

[1]These and other interviews all required the use of a translator. However, in the chapters that follow, accounts of dialogues with villagers seldom make reference to this fact. This was done for literary convenience, so as not to distract the reader by having to introduce an interpreter at each instance. Obviously, Fred Engst and others who helped with translation were essential to the success of this phase of the research.

industrial sectors in the summer of 1978, and with other information received from Chinese and Americans who had lived and worked in the area during this time— including several Beijing exchange scholars to the United States who had once resided in nearby villages as "educated youth." The first edition of this book, published in 1984, was largely based on this ethnographic material.

Throughout the 1980s, as important economic, social, and political changes continued to sweep across China, I was regularly asked by teachers, students, and others if I could update this book on events occurring in the small region of the Beijing suburbs I had come to know in 1979. Unfortunately, since I had refocused my attention on other areas of anthropological inquiry, all such requests had to be denied.

However, Fred Engst, an active participant in the 1979 research, maintained his close ties with China. Born and raised there, he had worked for several years in a state factory in Beijing while his parents, Sid Engst and Joan Hinton, were serving as agricultural specialists at a nearby state farm. Coming to the United States in 1974, he eventually became a graduate student in economics at Rutgers University, after many years working as an electrician in a large factory in Philadelphia and attending Temple University part time.

In 1984, while on a return trip to Beijing, he visited workers from his old factory and peasants in the village where we had undertaken our earlier research, as well as renewed ties with other friends and relatives. Several years later, he again returned to the area for a longer stay. After spending one month in 1987 at a state farm in Beijing Municipality, he was invited to come back for another ten months in 1988, at which time he served as an Assistant to the Deputy of Farm Management. His major responsibilities entailed economic research on agricultural developments in several surburban districts of the municipality, including the region where he and I had briefly lived nine years before.

Finally, in the early summer of 1989, Fred Engst again returned to China as a consultant for a large American corporation seeking to expand its interests in the PRC. He arrived in Beijing shortly after the violent conclusion of the student-led prodemocratic and anticorruption protest in and around Tiananmen Square. His earlier associations and friendships in Beijing were immensely helpful, enabling him to observe and assist in interpreting the people's response to this tragic event—including those people living in the general area described in this book. Following discussions between the two of us, I decided that with Fred Engst's active assistance, it would be not only possible but also of significant educational value to produce a new edition of this book. By tracing the impact of key economic reforms undertaken in a suburban area of Beijing Municipality beginning in the late 1970s and continuing through the 1980s, readers could gain additional insight into some of the serious problems facing China today.

Equally important, this new edition could illustrate how the economic *and* political events of recent years led many of China's urban workers and suburban farmers to actively condemn the actions of those leaders who sought to maximize privileges for themselves and their families at the expense of others whom they were expected to serve. Students from Beijing have held many demonstrations in Tiananmen Square in recent decades in support of more open leadership, improved educational facilities, and greater freedom of expression and against foreign domination and economic control. But what really brought the Tiananmen Square protest of 1989 to its tragic conclusion were Chinese workers and their profound outrage at the rampant inflation and corruption then occurring with their country—conditions that seriously threatened the people's livelihood and challenged their sense of social justice. It was only after the workers actively joined the protest that the government became truly fearful.

Thus, it is not surprising that an important theme expressed by the suburban Chinese described in the concluding chapter of this book is resistance—not in direct opposition to socialism per se but against a government and party that in recent times chose to put its own interests ahead of those of the Chinese people. In the early years of the People's Republic, the Communist party was the major force leading the struggle for economic improvement, enhanced social equality, and greater political empowerment of its predominantly peasant population. But the protest movement of May and June 1989, supported by thousands of Chinese from all walks of life, demonstrated to everyone that the party and the government no longer had a mandate of leadership. What the future holds for China remains to be seen. But the lessons of the recent past, from which much can be learned, are there for all to see.

N.A.C.

North Hatley, Quebec

Acknowledgments

Early fieldwork on which much of this book is based was conducted by Norman Chance berween the years 1972 and 1979, more specifically in April and May 1972, August and September 1978, and most important, September through December 1979. Analysis of economic reforms occurring in the 1980s stems from research undertaken by Fred Engst in the spring of 1984, the summer of 1987, the fall, winter, and spring of 1988, and the summer of 1989. Much of the data was obtained in villages located within a large, well-known state farm approximately 25 miles from the capital city of Beijing. In the 1970s, this farm was commonly referred to as a commune.

It should be noted at the outset that the names of individual Chinese, as well as those names associated with the state farm, commune, village brigades, and other localities, are fictitious, to protect the privacy of the people involved. Needless to say, their anonymity should not be construed to mean that their efforts were not appreciated.

Of the numerous people providing assistance, I am particularly grateful for the support of the director and staff of the state farm and commune where much of the research was undertaken, as well as the leaders of the several villages that were studied. All gave considerably more than was either required or expected.

In addition, I wish to express appreciation to the villagers themselves, who were so helpful in home, field, factory, and school by answering continual questions, correcting mistakes, and responding to census forms and questionnaires. Several students from the First Foreign Languages Institute and other educational in-stitutions in Beijing were also of assistance, aiding in interviewing, translating, and gathering statistical data. In different ways, all these individuals illustrate why it is that anthropologists so often speak positively about the experience of living with the people they wish to learn from and come to understand—that is, the sharing of one's life with others promotes a common cause.

Many people have stimulated my interest and knowledge of China, including Professor Paul T. K. Lin, the past director of the East Asian Studies Centre at McGill University; William Hinton, the author of the classic ethnography *Fanshen* (1966), one of the early detailed studies of revolutionary change in a Chinese Village; Sid Engst and Joan Hinton; and Fred Engst, who was a co-leader of the 1979 "work-study" delegation of which I was a member. He was also a key translator for most of the in-depth interviews conducted in the villages of the state farm where we were located. Given my lack of Chinese language skills, his frequent assistance in translation was invaluable. Also, the latter section of the book dealing with economic reforms in the 1980s draws so extensively on his research and writing that it is offered under our joint authorship.

Also to be acknowledged are David and Isabel Crook, who before their retirement were faculty members of the English Language Section of the Beijing First Foreign Languages Institute and were the authors of several volumes pertaining to the North China village of Ten Mile Inn (1959, 1966, 1979); Cliff DuRand, Cindy Engst, Daniel Sipe, and other members of the 1979 delegation who assisted in gathering field data; and most of all, Nancy F. Chance, co-leader of the 1979 trip, co-worker with me for over forty years, and the person who first introduced me to the intellectual adventure called anthropology.

Of the North American scholars and friends whose suggestions and criticisms of earlier chapters and drafts of this book have helped clarify my thinking, I particularly want to thank Robert Dewar, Norma Diamond, Chris Gilmartin, Frank Kehl, Julia Kwong, Vera Schwarcz, Mark Selden, and Peter Seybolt. Further appreciation is expressed to Cliff DuRand for sharing his analysis of village economic life, to Nancy Chance for sharing her research on education and women, and to Stephen C. Chance for his line drawings.

Similar acknowledgment is due to three young Chinese scholars from Beijing who, while attending the University of Connecticut as graduate students in the 1980s, graciously shared their knowledge and experience with me. They are Zang Junhong and Yang Haiping (Anthropology) and Jia Liling (Political Science).

Appreciated also is the aid of the Chinese People's Association for Friendship with Foreign Countries, whose invitation and arrangements for the 1972 and 1979 field trips were essential; the China Travel Service; and the University of Connecticut Research Foundation for the generous financial support offered during the years 1972–74 and 1979–83.

Changes and additions in this second edition have also been greatly assisted by the detailed comments and suggestions of Nancy Chance, Fred Engst, and William Hinton.

To Chris Caperton, a special note of appreciation for her skillful editing and sheperding the book through the production phase.

Finally, I want to thank George and Louise Spindler, editors of the Case Studies in Cultural Anthropology, for the many suggestions they offered while this book was being written. Their insightful blend of constructive criticism and continuing encouragement was always helpful and much appreciated.

Contents

CASE STUDIES IN CULTURAL ANTHROPOLOGY

GENERAL EDITORS

George and Louise Spindler

STANFORD UNIVERSITY

CHINA'S URBAN VILLAGERS

Changing Life in a Beijing Suburb

Introduction

Who built the seven towers of Thebes?
The books are filled with the names of kings.
Was it the kings who hauled the craggy blocks
of stone? . . .
In the evening when the Chinese wall was finished.
Where did the masons go? . . .

Bertolt Brecht

A little more than one billion people live in China—more than one-fourth of the world's population. Of that number, 80 percent are men and women who seek their subsistence largely from the soil in an agrarian pattern that has changed rather slowly for much of the past 2000 years, from the abolition of an ancient form of feudalism in the third century B.C. to the penetration of Western capital and culture in the nineteenth century.

Beginning in the 1920s and continuing through the 1950s and 1960s, the pace of change increased significantly as China's villagers became involved in a massive revolutionary transformation that produced a sufficiently impressive increase in their standard of living to eventually draw recognition from other Third World countries and even from the West. Still, China's development is very limited, as any visitor who has passed beyond the usual tourists sights can quickly attest. Just how limited is it? If we compare the level of agricultural productivity in China with that of the United States, the comparison is striking: whereas one American farmer can feed almost one hundred city dwellers, it takes the intensive labor of between three and four peasants to feed one urbanite in China. With little more than 11 percent of China's land arable and with the need to feed over four times the American population, it is no wonder that the country is striving to determine how best to modernize its agricultural sector.

Note too the different use of the words *farmer* and *peasant*. The distinction is important. Farmers produce primarily for others, exchanging what they make for quite different goods and services, often at the national and even international level. Peasants, on the other hand, produce mostly for themselves—for their own use—and only secondarily for others through the medium of local and regional markets, rent, taxes, and the like. In China today, members of the agricultural work force are changing from peasant to farmer, producing both for their own use and for exchange. What part peasant and what part farmer? It varies greatly, not only between

1

Women field workers in Half Moon Village.

regions but between towns and even villages. In most instances where grain is the major agricultural crop, a rough indicator of the degree of transition from peasant to farmer is the amount of grain kept and the amount sold.[1]

Another significant measure of the difference between old and new China is seen in the increasing number of peasants now working in village sideline enterprises and larger state-owned industries and factories that are rapidly emerging in semi-urban areas surrounding China's big cities. Young men and women, peasants in upbringing and outlook but occupationally workers with newly acquired technical skills, represent a potentially vibrant force in the development of China. This dialectic of cyclical and developmental change, of persisting in old ways while at the same time being increasingly involved in the larger modern society, is not limited to China's rural population. It sums up the dilemma of contemporary peasants the world over. One important difference in China, however, is the active role played by peasants in revolutionizing the countryside to better their own economic and social conditions.

THE RISE OF REVOLUTION

What social conditions led to the assumption of power by China's revolutionary leaders? Although such a complex question cannot be addressed here (see Bianco 1971), two historical factors should be stressed, since they continue to have an important bearing on the daily life of the peasants described in this book. One is the impact of foreign capital, technology, and occupation on China for over 100 years. The other is the social turmoil occurring in the country during that time, generated in part by that foreign contact.

For many centuries, China was ruled by powerful dynasties. But in the mid-

---

[1]In the early 1980s, of the 300 million tons of food grain produced each year by the peasantry, approximately 250 million were self-consumed (Vermeer 1982).

1800s, following defeat by the British Empire in the so-called Opium War, Qing dynasty officials were forced to open China's ports to foreign trade, including the importation of opium; to consent to customs tariffs fixed by treaty; to grant extraterritoriality (the right of foreign consular officers to try their own nationals in China); and to agree to other unequal treaties that dealt crippling blows to the country's sovereignty and economy. The eventual collapse of the dynasty and the rise of a new Republic of China under Sun Yat-sen and the Kuomintang (KMT) Party in 1911 instilled hope for a stronger centralized government. However, its success was hampered by many factors.

Foreign capital severely disrupted the internal economy, promoting inflationary spirals, which then forced large rent increases. For peasants and others unable to pay, this meant land foreclosure. Taxes and surtaxes rose, not only dramatically but also, from the villager's point of view, inequitably.[2] The introduction of Western technology into an expanding urban textile industry brought a sharp decline in the need for rural handicrafts, with a resulting further loss in peasant income. Problems of corruption in the government and the military increased the unpredictability of rural life.

Large landowners began moving out of villages for the more attractive life of nearby towns and cities. This disrupted traditional economic relations between landlord and peasant, an arrangement once based on a clearly recognized pattern of reciprocity. Lawlessness increased. Finally, as perceived by Chiang Kai-shek, the leader of the KMT government after the death of Sun in 1925, the most serious threat of all was the rapid rise of the Chinese Communist Party (CCP), first organized in 1921. However, to Chiang's constant frustration, numerous attempts by the KMT military to rid the country of these "bandits" were unsuccessful.

For China's villagers, on the other hand, increasing impoverishment and threat of famine led some to accept the proposal of the CCP that only by following its policies, summed up in the slogan "Land to the Tiller," could the vast majority improve their lives. Mostly illiterate and lacking contact with the outside world, these rural people knew little about socialism. But they did know that their existing world held few benefits for them. And so the Communist party's rural ranks continued to grow.

Then, in the mid-1930s, after the Japanese occupied Manchuria in Northeast China, promoted the "autonomy of Inner Mongolia," and threatened much of China's Northern Plain, Communist leaders changed their strategy, urging that past differences between the KMT and the CCP be put aside in favor of a "United Front" against Japan's military expansion. Under great difficulty, the alliance held until the defeat of Japan in 1945, when the question of who was to lead postwar China again returned to the fore. The result of that civil conflict is now well known. The KMT was simply unable to gain sufficient support from the people to achieve its goal. By

---

[2]Chesneaux reported that in Sichuan Province in 1933, peasants were forced to pay taxes in advance up to the year 1971. Actually, such taxes reflect a much deeper inequality pervading at least part of China's countryside at that time. For example, a study undertaken in Wuxi (near Nanjing) found that in 1929, poor peasants, composing 69 percent of the population, owned less than 14 percent of the land, whereas landlords, representing 6 percent of the population, owned 47 percent (Chesneaux 1973:78–79). Other scholars have questioned the pervasiveness of such inequities within peasant villages (see Myers 1970).

the autumn of 1949, Mao Zedong's Communist forces had achieved victory. It was a time of exhaustion. But it was also a time of dramatic opportunity.

THE NATURE OF CHINESE SOCIALISM

October 1 is celebrated in China as National Day. On this date in 1949, in front of a huge crowd of supporters in Tiananmen Square in Beijing, Mao Zedong, Chairman of the Chinese Communist Party, proclaimed the establishment of the People's Republic of China. Its first task was an all-out effort to remove the national ills that had led to the stigma of being called "the sick man of Asia." This was to be accomplished by a revolutionary transformation in the economic and social relations of the country, resolving long-festering internal problems caused by a combination of foreign intervention and social decay. Mao predicted that out of this massive upheaval would emerge a highly productive socialist society whose collective endeavor could enable the people to significantly raise their standard of living and whose political structure could provide them with the tools to more fully determine their own lives. This book is largely concerned with how Chinese peasants, living in a small village on the outskirts of Beijing, have responded to that challenge.

Among the rural issues first addressed by the CCP leaders following their assumption of power, the question of land reform was central. In those areas of the country not previously under their political control, the government immediately initiated a massive new program aimed at completely restructuring land ownership. Millions of needy peasants, including those described in this book, participated. Those whose lives of hardship had been economically dominated by landlords, large or small, began reversing the relationship—taking the latter's property and redistributing it to the poor and landless.

By the mid-1950s, many peasants throughout northern China had joined elementary agricultural producers' cooperatives (APCs). These cooperatives, organized under the leadership of the party, comprised 20 or more households, which shared labor, land, and small tools for their common benefit. In Chapter 2, we will learn more on how these cooperatives were formed, who supported them, and who opposed them.

In nearby Beijing, small-scale industries were also turned into economic cooperatives. Larger private industrial holdings were purchased by the state, the previous owners often receiving salaried positions in the enterprises plus 5 percent annual income on the surrendered property for a period of 10 years. Foreign-owned industries had already been nationalized.

As can be imagined, the changes brought about by this transformation were considerable. The whole structure of economic relations between peasant and landlord, on the one hand, and between urban worker and proprietors of large industries, on the other, was altered dramatically. However, among private-business leaders, high-level managers, and bureaucratic officials outside the party, political support for these economic efforts was less than enthusiastic. Yet their expertise was needed to administer the country's economic, educational, and local governmental institutions, which had been disrupted by years of war.

This posed a serious problem for China. Some party officials urged that further changes be delayed. By allowing existing developments to mature, more traditionally minded leaders, workers, and peasants could be incorporated into the process. Others differed. In 1955, Mao Zedong, then president as well as party chairman, concluded that the process was moving too slowly. Indeed, it was tottering along "like a woman with bound feet." Progress could always be undermined. It was better that the momentum be maintained.[3]

Until this time, party leaders had generally agreed that the low-level APCs, based on the voluntary participation of members, were the stepping-stones to a fully functioning socialist society in the rural areas (see Shue 1980). The steps involved in this transitional process moved from private ownership through mutual aid teams to elementary and advanced cooperatives and concluded with collective and state ownership of the key means of production. In this manner, it was reasoned, the continued poverty of many peasants, rooted in inequitable ownership of land, animals, tools, and machinery, could be reduced and eventually eliminated, and the reallocation of resources through state planning could be initiated.

In Half Moon Village, a community we will look at in depth throughout this book, poor peasant families usually joined the cooperatives, viewing them as economically beneficial. However, when several "middle" peasant families were encouraged to join, they refused, preferring to work their own land with their own tools and their own labor. (Landlords and rich peasants were initially excluded from participation.) How important was it to draw these middle-level peasants into the cooperative? If the APC leaders were patient and moved more slowly in setting up the cooperatives, could these households—with better land and tools—be persuaded to join their poorer brethren? Or, reminiscent of old women with bound feet, was it more likely that they would hardly move at all? Even worse, might they set up roadblocks, thereby limiting the success of others?

This type of response occurred in Half Moon Village when the head of a more well-to-do family refused to allow the members of a mutual aid team (a precursor of the APCs) to construct an irrigation ditch across his land. The man recognized that the proposed water system would enhance the productivity of the team, perhaps at his own expense. The response was repeated after the formation of more advanced cooperatives several years later.

Problems of a quite different order were faced by local party cadres newly placed in positions of leadership. Most cadres were villagers themselves, with relatives and friends in the area. Occasionally, the responsibility to implement a party or government policy conflicted with their views and those of friends. Should one's action always be guided by party policy determined "from above"? What if one's evaluation of local conditions leads to a different conclusion? Such dilemmas were common in Half Moon Village then, and they still are today.

In one incident to be discussed later, we find party members being informed by agricultural officials in Beijing that the peasants in their village should begin

---

[3]Actually, in the late 1940s and early 1950s, Mao himself warned of overeagerness and "left opportunism" in completing the socialist transformation in rural areas (Mao 1949:367 and 419). His views changed in the mid-1950s (Mao 1955:394–404).

implementing "triple cropping" during the next planting season. Local leaders passed on the plan to the villagers, even though some of them felt it was basically unsound. The villagers definitely opposed it. Learning how the problem was resolved helps us understand day-to-day relations within the party and between the party and the people. Furthermore, it provides a practical illustration of a rather complex political process—the relationship between centralized planning and democratic decision-making. On several occasions throughout the book, we will address this important topic.

While villagers attempted to resolve day-to-day problems posed by the societal changes of the mid-1950s, China's national leaders grappled with a far more difficult issue: What direction should the country take after the conclusion of land reform and the establishment of elementary cooperatives? Was an increasingly more collectivized labor force the key to advancing the country's economic development and—through that effort—the people's social well-being and standard of living? Specifically, should the government urge the consolidation of the APCs into larger, more advanced units, thereby expanding the cooperative base still further? Or, was the mechanization of the country's productive forces a necessary precondition for advancing the social cooperation of its members toward a more fully socialist society? That is, should the society focus its limited energies on rapidly expanding its urban industrial infrastructure and (to a lesser extent) its agricultural technology in the countryside?[4]

The two approaches were intimately linked, both collectivization and mechanization being seen as necessary steps in the socialist development of China. Still, the question remained: which should receive the greater emphasis? Under Mao's leadership, the party and government opted for an acceleration of rural collectivization—a "Socialist Upsurge in the Countryside"—in which mutual aid teams and low-level cooperatives (still a minority throughout the country) were to be combined into larger, more advanced units.

PROBLEMS OF DEVELOPMENT

Problems stemming from this effort to accelerate the process of socialist ownership were substantial. For the poorer peasantry, representing between 60 and 70 percent of northern China's rural population, so too were the benefits.[5] Owning the least (or nothing at all), these people had the most to gain by furthering collectivization, since under the advanced APCs, ownership of land and other means of production ceased being a factor in income distribution. At that moment a turning point was

---

[4]A good illustration of the latter perspective that mechanization is a necessary prerequisite for socialist development in agriculture is contained in a book written by an American who served as a teacher at a state-run tractor driver training school in Hebei Province. When the school first opened in 1953, the director announced to his new students: "Our task is to build islands of socialism in a vast sea of individual farming. We are the ones who will have to show the way for the whole country" (Hinton 1970:45–46).

[5]In some areas surrounding Beijing, including Half Moon Village, the figure ran as high as 80 percent.

reached. From now on, how hard the members worked, rather than what they owned, was to be the deciding factor in the distribution of collective income.

When production was high, well-to-do peasants also gained; but when it was low, they benefited less. In addition, such peasants occasionally found that their contribution of land and other goods did not result in the compensation promised earlier by local party officials. Finally, in 1957–58, increasing pressure was placed on them to join the larger, more advanced cooperatives—a policy that contrasted sharply with the more voluntary nature of earlier efforts (Selden 1982). Such a shift in strategy not only increased conflicts between the peasants but also raised important questions about the extent of their participation in building a new socialist society.

After the ownership of land and other means of production was placed in the hands of the collective, new issues of socialist construction moved to the fore. There have been both successes and failures in these efforts. Successes include the widespread mechanization of simple stationary tools owned by community members; the building of extensive irrigation canals shared by different brigades; a rural health system that during the collective period provided care for every rural villager at a cost of less than 50¢ per individual per year; an educational system that assured eight years of schooling for all resident children; and tall shade trees that line today's roadways between villages like Half Moon and Little River—trees planted 35 years ago as part of a cooperative intervillage reforestation project.

Failures are represented by the continuation in office of those highly prejudiced bureaucratic officials who look down on peasants as hardly able to care for their own affairs, let alone contribute knowledge and experience toward improving the larger society. Failures are also seen in hundreds of now faded revolutionary slogans staining village walls, slogans—such as "Carry the Revolution under the Dictatorship of the Proletariat through to the End"—whose tendentious meaning probably eluded the painters as well as those peasants who still pass by these relics of an earlier era on their way to work. Additionally, such failures sometimes appear in more poignant form, as in the life story of an "educated youth" who came to Half Moon Village after trying to help develop a state farm in a province far to the northeast, or in the furious denunciation of a local party cadre by a young woman who was unfairly passed over for a factory job in favor of the official's niece.

Underlying these conflicts is a fundamental problem in the building of a socialist society—the issue of human nature. If greediness is at the heart of human nature, then the whole idea of socialism is nothing more than a utopia. If, on the other hand, human nature involves a dialectical tension between self-interest *and* social interests, then self-interest can become secondary to the interests of the larger group. Anthropological studies of various societies demonstrate that pure greediness in human behavior is deviant indeed. Rather, individual motivation is strongly shaped by the social and cultural environment. If greed is encouraged and rewarded, it would be considered foolish not to act in a similar fashion. By contrast, if friends and associates strive to act in a helpful, cooperative manner, selfish actions on the part of an individual would likely lead that person to feel ashamed. Even within the competitive, individualistic orientation of Western society, one regularly finds selfless actions by individuals who are willing to risk their personal security for a given cause. Thus, in discussing greed and selflessness, the question is not human nature but rather the dominant behavior expected in normal circumstances. For socialism to succeed requires that those in leadership positions place the interests of the majority ahead of their own. When that process fails, corruption, abuse of power, demoralization, and stagnation quickly follow. Mao Zedong expected that after 20 years of struggle in wars of liberation, Communist party members at all levels would "serve the people" while constructing a new socialist society. Yet, the history of China's socialist revolution demonstrates just how difficult it is for that goal to be implemented.

In the 1950s, the party enjoyed overwhelming support from the working people for its program of socialist transformation and construction. During this time, corruption and abuse of power by party officials were also quite limited. For example, one important theme introduced shortly after the advanced APCs was Mao's call for a mass mobilization of the people to make a "Great Leap Forward." This national campaign of 1958–59 was undertaken partly to raise grain and steel output and in other ways increase the country's economic development. In its rural manifestation, it also encouraged peasants to transform their lives by mobilizing local resources and labor in constructing water conservation and reforestation projects and in setting up small sideline industries to process crops and to manufacture farm tools. The profits created by these self-reliant efforts could then be used to mechanize agriculture, thereby freeing peasant labor for small-scale industrial development.

Furthermore, the Great Leap provided the impetus for one of the most intriguing social experiments in human history—a nationwide consolidation of the country's newly formed advanced APCs into 42,000 communes. At this time, the *xiang,* or township, encompassing a population of 20,000 or more, was the lowest level of rural public administration. With the formation of communes, agricultural and small industrial enterprises came under their control, as did commerce, the militia, education, health, and other human services. The commune soon subsumed the political administration of the *xiang* under its jurisdiction as well. Although reduced in size and revised in form, both economically and politically, communes continued in rural China for 25 years. However, as we will learn shortly, critics of Mao charged that the failures of the Great Leap, including those associated with the communes, far outweighed its successes.

The decade of the 1950s was clearly one in which different ideas of how to build socialism emerged within the party. As a result, Mao found his economic policies increasingly opposed, first by party leaders such as Peng Dehuai (then Minister of Defense) and shortly thereafter by others such as Liu Shaoqi and Deng Xiaoping. Many party officials at this time felt that they had sacrificed enough—that it was time for them to reap some benefit from the revolution. Questioning whether the people could be motivated by the cause of socialism, they stressed the role of personal incentives in the workplace and farms. This in turn was used to justify the increasing privileges sought by party officials themselves. Thus, by the early 1960s, China's development became focused on increasing economic productivity through means more conventional than Mao's revolutionary strategy of collectively oriented mass mobilization, utilizing the spirit of hard work and plain living.

Becoming increasingly concerned about the possible resumption of power by a bureaucratic elite within the party itself, not unlike what he perceived had happened in the Soviet Union, in 1965–66 Mao launched his last big campaign: "The Great Proletarian Cultural Revolution." Its stated aim was to replace ingrained bourgeois, bureaucratic values with socialist ones and remove from power those individuals— "class enemies"—who would turn China away from its socialist path. In the minds of many critics such as Liu and Deng, it was also an attempt by Mao to remove from the party leadership any individuals who might challenge his authority.

However, since Mao enjoyed great prestige among the Chinese people, his opponents within the party seldom challenged him directly. Rather, they opposed him by carrying his views to ridiculous extremes, often portraying him like a god in the process. All of this intensified interparty conflicts, especially during the Cultural Revolution—at which time the struggles within the party were brought out into the open. Increasingly, hypocrisy became the norm, the most corrupt and abusive party officials often claiming to be Mao's most loyal supporters. While attacking others for a lack of dedication to socialism, they actively pursued their own political goals. The struggle became so intense and factionalized that China soon found itself on the brink of all-out civil war. Schools and universities were closed down. Many young students, undirected and restless, traveled freely throughout the country, using Mao's instruction to "use the society as the classroom" as their justification. Millions of urban youth initially volunteered and later were required to relocate to rural villages and isolated border areas to work and "learn from the peasants." Although economic production continued, the party and government reached an impasse and were barely able to function. Arguments over the correct socialist course of action raged. By 1967, Mao was forced to bring the politically well-disciplined People's Liberation Army (PLA) into leadership positions in many institutions to restore order.

Over the next nine years, until Mao's death in 1976, the Chinese people were called upon to participate in a series of related campaigns reflected in such slogans as "Criticize Lin Biao and Confucius" and "Grasp Revolution and Promote Production" (which basically meant: while pursuing revolution, don't forget production). Many people in cities and the countryside had already turned away from such strident efforts, preferring to live out their lives far removed from the warlike turmoil. Others, unable to escape, were caught up in accusations, charges, and countercharges, leading all too frequently to public humiliation, beatings, and death. It was only after Mao's death in 1976 and the arrest of several party leaders associated with the Cultural Revolution—referred to as the "Gang of Four"—that China's leaders rejected active political movements in favor of an economically focused modernization program.

Despite the many pitfalls, a sizable minority in China looked more positively at the Cultural Revolution's goals, such as the effort to challenge commandist, centralized, bureaucratic controls; the bringing of improved medical care to the villages; the expansion and development of primary education; the recruitment of peasants and workers into technical and higher education; reforms such as "combining work and study," which aimed to stimulate people of all ages to think for themselves and examine and test well-established theories in practice; and finally, the challenge to Confucian-inspired cultural patterns that continued to place women in a subservient status in village life. These people acknowledged that the extrem-

Harvesting corn with a hand scythe, Half Moon Village.

ism of the Cultural Revolution had brought chaos to the country and personal tragedy to many. But they distinguished that result from what they thought the revolution was meant to achieve or should have achieved.

As interparty struggle intensified, the spread of corruption and the abuse of power by party officials multiplied. Not even an extraordinary effort like the Cultural Revolution could rid the party of the corrupt officials. With its failure and Mao's death, Deng Xiaoping and other opposition leaders in the party finally assumed control. Shortly thereafter, corruption became endemic, ultimately leading to the massive demonstrations in Beijing in the spring of 1989 and the brutal suppression that followed.

Deng Xiaoping, an astute politician, did not reveal his political program immediately. At first he seemed interested only in correcting the numerous ultraleft policies that had emerged during the Cultural Revolution. He showed more flexibility in the relationship between individual and collective economic development, including the promotion of family and individual enterprises outside the collective sphere. He seemed more open-minded in testing how best to increase the standard of living. He tentatively explored how to encourage a more decentralized, grass-roots democracy in the decision-making process at the local level. Older cadres, earlier removed from their positions in the party and government, returned, while some of those more closely associated with Mao and his ideas were transferred. Furthermore, most working people appeared glad to see the demise of the sharp political battles that had led to such conflict and factionalism.

By slowly subverting Mao's strategy of socialist development, Deng was able to isolate his supporters in the party. By glorifying the slogan that "It is all right for some to get rich first," he found a ready audience in and out of the party for what he wanted to do: privatize much of China's economy. Armed with a vast network of personal ties and endowed with political power that few dared challenge, senior party members quickly turned themselves into entrepreneurs. By offering peasant-farmers new economic freedoms and providing workers with larger bonuses, they bought wide support for their reform. The dream of getting rich quick soon resulted in ever-expanding cycles of price hikes and inflation. This was another crucial factor eventually leading to the massive demonstration in Tiananmen in 1989.

This brief portrayal of China's efforts to establish a socialist society provides a necessary backdrop to the unfolding of daily life in Half Moon Village in the late 1970s—the subject of Part One: "Collective Life." Chapters 1 and 2 describe the people of Half Moon in 1979, the setting in which they lived, and the history that brought them there. Two old peasants tell of early hardships, how land reform and the agricultural cooperative movement brought new opportunities to their lives, and how village sons and daughters eventually were able to find employment in small sideline industries and in larger factories emerging on the outskirts of Beijing. We find that Half Moon was only one of 116 villages composing Red Flag Commune, a particularly large collective unit and state farm with a total population of over 85,000. Attention is given also to the important role of the Chinese Communist Party: how it was organized, how it provided leadership in village and local affairs, and how it dealt with two of China's age-old problems—bureaucracy and nepotism.

In Chapter 3, the focus is on work: how families made their living in private household, collective brigade, and state-owned enterprises. We learn how income was generated and distributed in field and factory, what was appealing about employment in state factories, and why it was so difficult for rural villagers to obtain jobs in the state sector. And in both field and factory, we gain insight into the kinds of conflicts that divided leaders and the people from each other and how they went about trying to resolve them. This is followed by a discussion of how alternative forms of employment were developed, including small village sidelines. An analysis of how three villages addressed this question illustrates quite clearly that distinct paths of socialist economic development could be followed even within the same commune—an important reminder for those tending to view socialist society as monolithic.

Chapters 4, 5, 6, and 7 take quite a different tack, presenting a view of the village from an ethnographic life-cycle perspective, tracing the process of growing up, going to school, getting married, having a family, and growing older. In contrast to the dramatic political and economic transformation described earlier, this section of the book highlights what anthropologists and other students of China have so often emphasized in the past—the importance of the family in village life.[6]

Part Two, "Changing Political Economy," addresses important economic reforms undertaken by the government beginning in 1979 and continuing throughout the next decade. We find, for example, that any decision to further mechanize the production of field crops immediately raises the question of what to do with the peasant work force. We also watch as dramatic changes in government policy unfold, such as the reestablishment of peasant markets; the increased shifting of responsibility for rural production to smaller economic units like the family household; and the decollectivization of communes and village brigades. What advantages were gained by these changes? What problems occurred? Which villagers supported the changes and which ones were opposed? Why did some struggle to maintain collective enterprises while others welcomed the shift in government policy? In what way were traditional family ties reinforced by the policy of breaking up work groups into smaller units? And also, what happened when the responsibility system emphasizing greater household productivity was combined with the population planning program emphasizing the limiting of births to only one per family? Not surprisingly, in this latter instance the policy found little support among those Half Moon residents still closely tied to the land.

In the last section of Chapter 9, negative effects of the 1980s economic reforms are summarized, in particular, those having to do with the devastating cycle of inflation and the equally severe problems of corruption, which by this time had become common among party cadres and government officials at every level. The resistance to these developments by suburban Beijing residents eventually culminates in their support for the Tiananmen Square protests of May and June 1989, led by Beijing's university students and joined by people throughout the city. A final visit to the village following the June 4 massacre provides a brief glimpse of how local party leaders, workers, and farmers differ in their perception of that incident and its implications for the future. The chapter concludes with a commentary on bureaucracy, "democracy," and equality and on how the link between these three social attributes are mediated by continuing class conflict.

As we come to know the people of Half Moon Village—first in 1979 and then more recently—one point becomes increasingly clear: they are "urban villagers" in a geographical sense only. Culturally they represent a complex mixture of old and new; some are retaining their family ties and lifeways largely intact, while others are finding themselves actively drawn in to the economic and social network of the city. Does this mean they bear a close resemblance to the millions of other peasants living on the edge of cities throughout the Third World? No, not really. Actually, as we will learn shortly, the differences are quite striking.

---

[6]Numerous studies of Chinese village life have been written since the late 1800s. Those pertaining to the pre-1949 period include Smith (1899), Fei (1939), Yang (1945), Lin (1947), and Gamble (1954). Those focusing on post-1949 Chinese mainland include Yang (1959), Myrdal (1963), Crook and Crook (1959; 1966; 1979), Hinton (1966; 1983), Chen (1973), Bennett (1978), Chan, Madsen, and Unger (1984), Huang (1989), Siu (1989), and Potter and Potter (1989). Three outstanding films have also appeared about daily life in Long Bow Village, the location of William Hinton's two books on the subject (see Hinton and Gordon 1986).

PART ONE

COLLECTIVE LIFE

HALF MOON VILLAGE

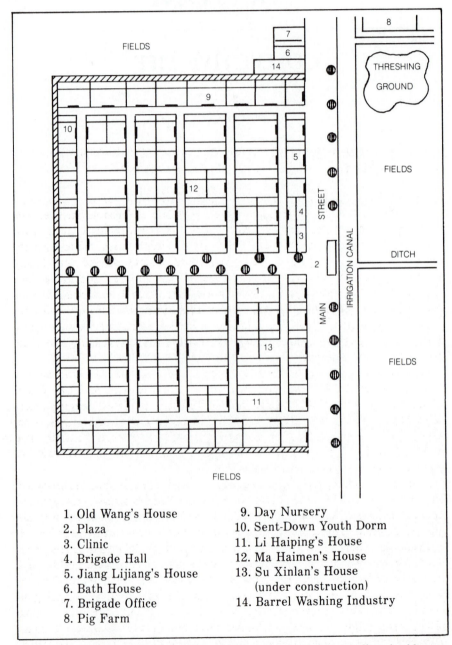

FIELDS

THRESHING GROUND

FIELDS

DITCH

FIELDS

FIELDS

STREET

IRRIGATION CANAL

MAIN

FIELDS

1. Old Wang's House
2. Plaza
3. Clinic
4. Brigade Hall
5. Jiang Lijiang's House
6. Bath House
7. Brigade Office
8. Pig Farm
9. Day Nursery
10. Sent-Down Youth Dorm
11. Li Haiping's House
12. Ma Haimen's House
13. Su Xinlan's House (under construction)
14. Barrel Washing Industry

Half Moon Village, including plaza, clinic, nursery, brigade office, bathhouse, and other service centers.

1/The Meeting

A BRIEF DISCUSSION

Taking one look at the pale gray December sky, the wiry rooster stood up, breathed in deeply, and proceeded to inform all those within earshot that it was indeed time to stir.

Across the courtyard in a small bedroom, Mother Wang lay quietly on her *kang,* listening as the rooster's crow faded into the background. Opening her eyes, she took in the familiar features of the room. To her right, dominating the rest of the furniture, was a tall wooden cupboard, stained a dull shade of red. On top, a dusty old cloth suitcase, unopened in years, served as a locker stuffed with family mementos, a few civil records, and other papers. Adjacent to the cupboard and flush against the interior yellow-painted wall stood a glass-covered dresser, the drawers filled with sewing utensils. Underneath the glass top, a panorama of black-and-white photos of relatives and friends served as a constant reminder of earlier Spring Festivals (Chinese New Year) and other holiday occasions when family members were apt to come together.

Firmly, but with a certain gentleness so as not to disturb her husband, the woman laid back the worn quilt covering the bed and rose to her feet. Lao Wang, whose responsibilities didn't require such an early rise, continued sleeping peacefully. Standing upright, Mother Wang felt a sharp twinge of rheumatic pain in her ankles—one more reminder of increasing age. How many years now had she risen early to prepare the morning meal for her family? Too many, she had said just yesterday to her neighbor down the lane.

Taking her worn blouse, faded blue pants, and quilted jacket from the bed where they had been used for extra warmth during the night, she donned them quickly. Then, slipping her feet into two dark-colored cloth shoes buckled on the side, she glanced at herself in the dresser mirror before heading toward the central living area of the house. Brushing aside a long rectangular piece of plain cloth hanging from the doorframe, she stepped into the larger room and from there to the yard beyond. At the far end of the house, near the courtyard gate, she reentered the building through a kitchen door, turned on a small overhead light, and began preparing the morning meal. First she removed bits of kindling and wood from a nearby box, placed them upright in a small brick-lined stove, and fired the stack with a match. Then, placing a soot-smudged iron pot on the metal grill above the fire, the woman poured several cups of water, from a nearby bucket, into the darkened container. In the background, through the thin kitchen wall, she heard the voice of her eldest daughter calling other family members to rise. Standing quietly, waiting for the water to warm, she slowly combed her short graying hair. As the liquid reached the boiling point, Mother Wang took some recently ground cornmeal from a metal container and added it and a few pickled vegetables to the pot, creating a cornmeal porridge. This, together with some steamed bread, would serve as the morning meal.

Hearing a noise outside the kitchen window, the woman watched as her son, Hubao, and his sister Huzeng headed across the courtyard to the family chicken pen. After vigorously brushing their teeth, the two young people dispensed the remaining saliva and paste over a low wooden fence to the waiting creatures below. The ritual was soon repeated by the elder son, Hulan, and his wife, Chao Liling, and finally by sleepy-eyed Lao Wang.

Within minutes, the five family members had entered the kitchen. Saying little, they scooped porridge from the pot into bowls, squatted down on small stools in a rough circle, and proceeded to slurp down their breakfast in acceptable Chinese fashion. On finishing, the sons and daughters excused themselves to complete various chores before departing for work. Only Old Wang, now wide awake, hung back, helping his wife clean up. Once finished, he went outside and chatted briefly with Hulan. Then, after climbing on his ancient bicycle, he headed through the courtyard gate toward the nearby district administrative headquarters, where he worked as a janitor.

At the opposite end of the house from the kitchen, I too had heard the morning call of the rooster, but unlike Mother Wang, I chose not to get up until most of the household members had gone off to work. After washing, I heard a familiar voice calling my name through the door. Looking out the window, I recognized Zhou Xing talking by the pigsty with Mother Wang, who was pointing a hand in the direction of my room.

"Xiao Zhou, I'm here," I called, slipping on a jacket and stepping out into the yard.

Zhou, a friend from the Beijing First Foreign Languages Institute with a good comprehension of English, had first helped in translating and interviewing during the early autumn. Now, several months later, he had offered to help me finish the household survey. He was quite intrigued by what he called my *shehui diaocha,* or "social investigation." For my part, his continuing help was most appreciated. Today, I had some special information for him.

"Zhou, there is going to be an important meeting of all field workers this afternoon following work. It was announced over the loudspeaker last night by Jiang Lijiang, the party secretary. What do you think it's about?"

Frowning slightly, Zhou shook his head once, conveying the information that we might have to wait until late afternoon to determine the agenda. During the extremely busy fall harvest season there had been little time to hold such a gathering. Only now that the fall vegetable and rice crops were in and the winter wheat planted could such a meeting be called—most likely to report on the success of the overall production and on how the results of the various work teams compared with the village quotas established in the spring in consultation with commune and municipal leaders.

As Mother Wang walked over to where we were standing, he asked her the question on both our minds.

"Do you have any idea why a meeting is being held this afternoon?"

"Jiang Lijiang is calling it?" responded Wang, the voice inflection allowing the remark to be interpreted as either a question or a statement of fact.

"Yes," said Zhou.

"Perhaps he will tell the people to work harder and maybe report on the results of the fall harvest."

"Are you going?" I asked.

Her response was noncommittal. However, she did forewarn us that if we planned to go, we should be prepared for the meeting to start late.

Actually, I was rather curious to know whether Mother Wang planned to be there. She had recently retired, at age 50, from working in the fields. Now she was much involved in the forthcoming birth of her first grandchild to the wife of her eldest son, Hulan. As a retired field worker, she was no longer expected to attend such occasions, although she could do so if she wished. I thought she might go if for no other reason than to keep up with the local news.

The afternoon gathering could offer a more unusual opportunity as well. It had to do with Jiang Lijiang, the party secretary of Half Moon Brigade.[1] Although a lifelong resident of the area, he was quite new to the position, having been recently

---

[1]Half Moon is a natural village with a distinct history. In 1979, it was also a "brigade," that is, an administrative unit responsible for coordinating agricultural and sideline production and managing local educational and social service agencies, such as primary schools and day-care nurseries. The next highest administrative unit was the district, one of 10 within Red Flag Commune.

Removing kernels of corn by hand in a family courtyard.

appointed to it by the district party committee, the supervisory unit responsible for Half Moon and 14 adjacent villages. So the meeting would likely offer some insight into Jiang's leadership abilities.

From the point of view of the Wang family, there was added interest in the fact that Jiang belonged to a different lineage than the previous party leader—one without any links at all to the many Wang relatives in the village. In old China, whatever security peasants could command was intimately connected to their placement within a given lineage or clan. When someone was in need of assistance, other clan members were expected to help in whatever way they could.

By the time I had arrived in the village, the expanded cooperative economic relations linking villagers together had provided the basis for a shift in the locus of economic security from the extended family and clan to the collective. However, the extent to which this shift actually occurred was mediated by many complex factors, not the least of which was the way the leaders related to the people they served. Such relations included the possibility of continuing the age-old custom of giving preferential treatment to their own relatives.

Since significant leadership at any level was closely linked to membership in the powerful Chinese Communist Party, using one's position for unfair privilege was a constant problem for both the party and the people. Mother Wang knew that, and so did the village leader Jiang. I too had become increasingly interested in the issue, since it appeared to be a serious point of conflict in the village. Perhaps the appointment of Jiang to the local party leadership represented an effort by the district leaders to weaken an old lineage power base. I hoped that the late-afternoon meeting would shed some light on the problem. At least I would find out shortly.

THE NEW BRIGADE LEADER

On the other side of the village plaza, near the main road, someone else was also thinking of the afternoon meeting. Jiang Lijiang, the newly installed party secretary of Half Moon Village, was a big-boned man in his mid-30s. Tall, well-proportioned, and bearing a decidedly large, broad face, he easily stood out in any small group. "Big Face" had been his nickname since early childhood. Neither positive nor negative associations were conjured up by its use, but everyone in the village knew the man to whom the name referred.

Jiang's day had begun even earlier than usual, since he had been awakened early in the morning by the insistent knocking of Du Yulin, an elderly peasant woman who wanted his help in finding her chickens, which had "escaped" from an unbolted courtyard gate during the night. After downing an all-too-quick breakfast of rice porridge mixed with strips of salted turnip and not-so-fresh steamed bread, he assisted Old Du in getting back her hens.

Then, at eight o'clock, he headed over to the brigade clinic just off the plaza to meet with the three paraprofessional clinic workers—"barefoot doctors"—and two of the Women's Federation members concerning how best to implement locally the new nationwide family-planning program. Recently put into effect, the program gave incentives for limiting family births to one child and imposed financial penalties for having more than two. After that long discussion, Jiang hiked over to the edge of the village to see how much manure had been spread on the brigade fields. Not satisfied with the result, he urged the team leader to have his men work harder. Then, returning to the village, he dropped in on the day-care nursery, the director of which had been out ill for a week. The two older women "grannies" taking over responsibility for the sick director wanted some additional help. He told them he thought he could find someone and would let them know soon.

Now, standing by his doorway, Jiang looked at his watch and swore softly. Then, scattering chickens in his wake, he strode out his courtyard gate, turned left on the gravel roadway, and with great strides, headed toward the brigade office 50 yards away. He knew he was slightly late for an appointment with Ma Haimen, the vice brigade leader in charge of grain production. They had earlier agreed to go over the agenda for the afternoon meeting. Approaching the office, he saw a group of dark-jacketed women leaving the fields and heading toward the village, a reminder that it was already lunchtime.

Cui Huifang, the team leader, briefly nodded to him as she passed. Cui, skilled in her knowledge of plants, soil, and people, was among the very best of the village field workers. Such attributes had insured her election as the leader of the older women's agricultural work team for as many years as anyone could remember. Jiang knew he could count on her to urge her teammates to arrive promptly for the 4:30 meeting—not that such effort would have much impact, however. Why was it, he reflected, that people never came to meetings on time? If they had to go to as many meetings as he did, maybe they would change. But he wouldn't wish that hardship on anyone. Of course, there was one obvious answer: they didn't want to attend. But he chose not to dwell on that possibility.

He soon reached the brigade office. Located at the northeast corner of the village, next to the bathhouse, the simple 10-by-12-foot room gave little indication of being an important communication link between the village and the outside world—or, at least, not until the incessant ringing of the phone reminded one that this was the only telephone for the whole community. Jiang's eye immediately focused on a piece of scrap paper attached to a nail on the door. Penned in rough characters was a note from Ma Haimen saying that he couldn't wait; if needed, he could be found at the grain-storage shed.

Crumpling the paper in his large hand, Jiang unlocked the door and went in. Before him stood two familiar old desks held up by crooked legs, two benches, and one *kang,* the top covered by a tattered green sheet. Leaning over his desk, he took a deep breath, puffed up his lips, and let out a blast of air, sending dust from the table to the floor beyond. This daily ritual stemmed from the high accumulation of powdery earth that regularly blows across China's Northern Plain.

Pulling up one of the old benches, he then sat down and stared at the phone in front of him. It was black and very ancient. There was no dial or cranking mechanism, so all one could do was pick up the receiver and wait for the operator. If there was no response—an all-too-common occurrence—the caller could at least flick the receiver lever up and down a couple of times, thereby expressing his or her frustration. When the operator, based at the district headquarters three miles away, came back from having tea, or whatever, she would politely inquire as to the nature of the call. This time, however, she responded immediately.

"Yao nar? Where are you calling?"

A village leader on his way to the brigade office.

"Uh. This is Jiang Lijiang at Half Moon Village. We're low on diesel fuel. Will you tell the district supplier to bring over a full barrel? We need it by two this afternoon, if possible."

"Secretary Jiang. I can't hear you."

This time, Jiang shouted his message into the phone.

"You got that?"

"Yes."

"Now. Get me the commune headquarters?"

"I'm sorry. I can't. Something's wrong with the line. I'll let you know when it's back in service."

"Very well."

Hanging up the receiver, Jiang opened the desk drawer and took out a sheaf of papers held together by a black clip. These reports, from the leaders of different production units, were on efforts to meet the appropriate quotas and were, for the most part, quite encouraging. Even given the wet fall, the various teams had all surpassed their agreed-upon goals. Given the minimal increase in production costs, it meant more income for the brigade members and more money for the village accumulation and welfare funds. In his meeting this afternoon, he would wait until the end of his talk to report on this favorable outcome. That way, he could more easily hold the people's attention. Everyone was anxious to learn whether they would receive more or less income than last year, when the harvest had been particularly good.

The immediate issue, however, was that of moving large piles of manure from the brigade pig farm to the fields. The work was going much too slowly; team leaders reported that many peasants were coming to work late and going home early. Jiang knew why they were spending less time in the fields. In every peasant household, courtyard gardens were fast being replaced by large, five-feet-deep earthen cellars, hollowed out of the ground by family members actively preparing for winter. Their purpose was to store brigade-grown cabbages recently distributed to all villagers as part of their collective "in kind" income.

This activity too had to be finished before the winter freeze settled in. But, thought Jiang, if the same freeze turned the pig manure into the consistency of hard rock, the spring crops would be seriously damaged. Which should come first—storing household cabbages or protecting the brigade-owned crops? As far as he was concerned, the brigade responsibility came first, especially during work hours. He would have to speak sharply about it at the afternoon meeting. Those villagers who refused to take the work seriously now would receive fewer work points when decisions on such matters were made later in the month.

Such reflections were cut short by someone opening the door and walking in. It was the caretaker, Wang. An older man in his 60s, Wang Baoshun had been permanently assigned the responsibility for the brigade office some time ago. Like workers in the fields and sideline industries, Wang received eight work points a day from the brigade for his job in the office, points that twice a year were added up and then translated into his share of the collective brigade income. On many days, he also took care of his grandson while his daughter worked in the fields. But mostly he sorted out and delivered papers and mail, watched over the public bathhouse next door, answered the phone, and delivered messages—especially he delivered messages. Much of his day was often spent tracking down one of the brigade leaders, a clinic "barefoot doctor," schoolteacher, or another village cadre with one communication or another.

Jiang, looking up from the desk, spoke first.

"Lao Wang, I'm going home for a quick bite to eat and a little work around the house. If Ma Haimen shows up, tell him all the brigade leaders are to come here at four o'clock. Then we can go to the meeting together. I'm also expecting some diesel oil around two o'clock. Zhang Yanzi may need it before plowing the southwest field."

"All right. I'll be here all afternoon. If I see Ma, I'll tell him."

As Jiang went out the door, he turned to Wang and added, "Is it true that the women's bathhouse key is lost again?"

Wang, appearing not to hear Jiang's question, stared intently at a crack in the floor.

"Well, they will want the key to the men's shower room. But you remind them about the meeting right after work. If they start showering after the men are finished, we'll never begin the meeting. So tell them to bathe later."

Wang acknowledged the instruction with a brief nod, knowing full well that if the women wanted a bath after coming in from the field, they were going to get it. Nor would he refuse them access to the men's shower room—especially since he had again misplaced the key to the women's side of the bathhouse.

A little later, after cleaning up the room, Wang Baoshun beard the sound of a diesel engine. Stepping out the door, he looked down the main roadway. Far away, a large red tractor appeared, moving slowly toward the turnoff to Half Moon.

Zhang Yanzi, a sturdy woman in her late 20s, hunched her shoulder forward and, after reaching for a firm grip on the steering wheel, pulled sharply to the right, sending the tractor in the direction of the village. Zhang was proud of being a tractor driver, and for good reason—her skills in driving and mechanical repair were known throughout the whole district.

She was one of millions of urban educated youth who had left the city for the much harder life of the countryside. Serving first as an agricultural worker on a state farm, she had soon been offered a job teaching primary school. Aware of the serious difficulties teachers and other intellectuals, including her educated father, had encountered in 1966, the first year of the Cultural Revolution, Zhang had not wanted the assignment, but she had had to accept it for a while. Only after many requests for transfer had she finally been relocated to a production unit, first feeding pigs, then serving as a cook, and finally being trained as a tractor driver. In the mid-1970s, her health had deteriorated, causing her to return to the Beijing area. She was then posted to this suburban village. Given the easing of government restrictions, enabling many Beijing youth to return to the city, Zhang could probably go back too if she applied. But she enjoyed being a tractor driver and so decided to remain.

Arriving at the brigade office, she switched off the diesel engine, stepped down from the tractor, and, seeing Wang in the doorway, waved hello.

Wang Baoshun spoke first.

"Secretary Jiang left just a little while ago. He said you might need some fuel before going down to the southwest field. Only it hasn't arrived."

Zhang responded, "I've got enough for this afternoon, so don't worry."

"I'll tell Jiang. By the way, if you haven't heard, there's a village meeting at 4:30 this afternoon after work. Most field workers will be there."

"O.K."

Wang watched as the newly painted diesel tractor again sprang to life and moved toward the southwest corner of the village. Being a tractor driver is an important job, thought Wang. He remembered a recent discussion with the district purchasing agent, who had said that in some parts of China, tractor operators wouldn't drive unless they were given a good-tasting, high-quality cigarette. And if they were contracted out to drive for another brigade or commune, they expected a delicious meal in payment. Without it, the agent had commented, they would plow only the middle of the fields and leave the edges untouched. Caretaker Wang knew that was not a common practice in the Beijing area, and he hoped it wasn't elsewhere either.

A CRITICISM OFFERED

Around 4:30 in the afternoon I walked over to the village plaza and waited for Zhou Xing. Jiang Lijiang was already there, as were the other village leaders, having just concluded a brief meeting in the brigade office down the road. Except for a few children playing cards on the corner, no other villagers were in sight, a fact that reminded me of Mother Wang's morning comment that meetings like these were always late.

I waited on one side of the plaza, and Jiang and the others stood opposite me, looking down the roadway. After a while, Zhou arrived, followed by several peasants carrying small wooden stools. Chatting with Zhou, I watched as the plaza slowly filled with men and women. Some stood talking together in small groups of three or four. Others came and stood along a plaza wall that offered some protection from the chill of a late afternoon wind. Once satisfied that all had arrived, Jiang Lijiang went over to a door of a large rectangular building, pushed it open, and stepped inside.

Soon the room was fully occupied by peasant villagers. When it looked like the meeting was about to begin, Zhou and I also stepped inside and looked around. The structure was completely barren, from packed earth floor to unpainted walls and ceiling. At one end, a boarded-up interior window frame with a metal hasp and lock gave little indication of protecting the village television set enclosed in the closet behind. On warm summer evenings, as many as 200 or more local residents could be found outside the building. Lined up 8 to 10 feet deep, they watched the latest offerings from Beijing and elsewhere through another window facing the main road. Now, in winter, few individuals were sufficiently interested in the evening fare to brave the chill air. However, the community building was an obvious meeting place for events such as this.

Big Face Jiang watched carefully as we came in and sat down, our backs resting against the cold adobe wall. He observed me even more closely when I brought out a small portable tape recorder, propped it upright on the earthen floor, and pushed the appropriate switch. I offered in response my most disarming smile. Other villagers either nodded in recognition or disregarded us completely. There were quite a few children in the room. Some stayed close to a parent, while others ran around with little or no supervision. What particularly struck me was the spatial division by sex: men at one end of the room, women and children at the other. Clearing his throat, Jiang Lijiang began.

"I announced on the loudspeaker that we would get together at 4:30, but as you came here later, we have had to start after 5:00. Now, we should pay attention to this and not be late the next time.

"The main purpose of today's meeting is to ask you to make good use of your time. Don't waste time in production work. This afternoon all the brigade leaders came to my office and talked. We discussed the situation over the past few months and at present. All the leaders said we have a big problem. Too many people are going out to work late and coming back early. That won't do. It won't do any good for all of you."

At that point a child burst out crying, and most of the peasants in the room began to laugh. Turning toward a woman who appeared to be the child's mother, Jiang Lijiang spoke sternly.

"Don't let the child cry. If it cries, take it outside."

I watched as the woman drew the crying child to her.

Jiang continued.

"This sort of thing happens every year. It's because we don't have a lot of work to do in the fields and because it's cold outside. On the one hand, the leaders don't pay enough attention to the situation. They are just interested in keeping track of their accounts and similar problems. This is a natural tendency. On the other hand,

An old man and a boy at the village plaza.

you brigade members don't pay attention to your work either. You come out late and go back early. Today, at our brigade leader's meeting, we all agreed that something must be done. If the situation goes on like this, it will be bad for you."

A few peasants listened carefully, while others appeared largely uninterested, watching children play or whispering among themselves.

"Tomorrow, the weather is expected to be good, quite warm. Not as cold as today. So we must seize this good opportunity to finish all kinds of work. Don't let this chance get away."

Across the room, two young men began talking quietly. Jiang stopped his remarks and stared at them. Not realizing they were the object of his attention, they went right on with their conversation. Angrily, Jiang responded.

"If you two want to talk, go ahead. I have no objection. You talk to the other brigade members."

The two men, realizing that they were the focus of Jiang's remarks, stopped speaking and turned attentively toward him.

"We should finish our work now in warm weather, so when it becomes cold we can have some holidays, have some meetings, or something like that. If you don't work now, you will have to do it later when it's much colder, and that's not good. We have 200 piles of manure, and we have to plant some vegetables. First, we have to get the manure to the fields. We also have to put rice stalks in the pigsties along with ashes and dirt to make more fertilizer. This is also the advice from the district."

By this time, several other of the younger men were talking among themselves. A few children had also begun to run around the room. Jiang became frustrated.

"What is wrong with you?" he demanded, turning toward the men. "Don't you realize what you are doing is against what I am saying?"

The young men stopped talking.

"Some people think there isn't much to do and therefore don't work hard. But this won't do. Others may have heard that the total income of our brigade has decreased from last year and are therefore in low spirits. You think you work hard all year but achieve less than before. Still others of you want to go out to make some money on your own, and because you can't you are upset. Therefore, you slow down, get mixed up, or do nothing. But that won't help. Remember, the state won't give us money to support ourselves. It depends on us. We can't count on state support or a state loan. Most people work hard. Only a few are lazy. But the effect is quite strong. It undermines the people's spirit.

"Do not think we cadres are unaware of what you are doing, even though we can't go to the fields and work with you. Of course, it is not good to criticize you in this room by name, but we know those who work hard and those who do not. In a few weeks we are going to evaluate your work points, and at that time you will realize the consequences. That's why we think it is important to have a meeting here and tell you beforehand—so you will repent by the time we evaluate the work points. And remember, if you come out to the fields late you will waste a steambread."

Jiang's effort at introducing a little humor largely went unheeded, although a few smiles greeted his remark. Zhou whispered in my ear that most peasants like to eat three steambreads before going to work in the fields, although they need only two if they are not working. So, if they eat three and go out late, they are wasting one.

Jiang went on.

"We must complete our work before the cold sets in. If the manure becomes frozen it will be hard to spread. In this way we waste our labor. Two years ago we had 270 field workers. Last year it dropped to 240. This year there are only 190 people working in the fields. This is because some of us have become contract workers, working in the chemical plant and elsewhere. Remember, the profit you make is less than those who are employed under contract in the factories. So they are making more money for you, and you have to work harder also.[2]

"On the whole, the total income this year is very good. Today, we checked both income and expenses. We found that, overall, we will perhaps reach 240,000 dollars [1 Chinese dollar, or *yuan,* is equivalent to 65 American cents] for the whole brigade. The total expense is 130,000 dollars, so we will still have 110,000 left. This is our net profit. This income is even a little better than last year. So don't think our overall income has decreased.[3] Don't be in low spirits. Our living standard is slowly improving. Remember, it is the economic base that determines the super-structure. This is the same in the family. If the family is rich, or has no economic problems, then the family members will be in high spirits. If you have money, your life will be easy. So if you work hard in the fields, it will be good for you. But if you come out late, the team leader should see to it that your work points are cut. Even if the team leader doesn't do that, many brigade members will criticize you. That is all I want to say. Are there any announcements?"

The vice brigade leader, Ma Haimen, spoke first.

"This year each person will have 135 *jin* [one *jin* equals 1.1 pounds] of rice, so please get your sacks ready. The brigade will bring the grain to your family so you won't have to come to the threshing ground to get it."

Another young man stood up.

"All Communist Youth League members meet at the nursery at seven this evening."

By this time, most peasants were pouring through the doorway into the rapidly darkening evening. A few carried their young children. Others walked together with stools under their arms. As Zhou and I got up to leave, no one paid us any attention. All appeared eager to get home and begin the evening meal.

Following dinner, Zhou and I went to my room to transcribe the tape into the field notes. After a while, I realized that Mother Wang, in the adjoining room, was listening intently to the tape. I was curious why she appeared so interested. I invited her into the room, but she declined. She did offer one comment, however. When Jiang warned those field workers who had been coming to work late and going home early, "In a few weeks we are going to evaluate your work points, and at that

---

[2]Contract workers were temporarily employed outside the village by the commune or the state, usually in construction or factory jobs. Though they received a higher income, the excess was allocated to the brigade accumulation fund rather than the individual.

[3]Although the total income was higher than that in 1978, a more detailed study of brigade income suggests that net income was slightly less (see Chapter 3).

time you will realize the consequences," Mother Wang spoke out sharply. "Who does he mean by *we?* All the peasants in the brigade evaluate. Then the leaders check it."

"Could a leader change an evaluation without talking with the peasants about it?" I queried.

"No. They have to ask the opinion of the brigade members."

"What if all leaders agree?"

"One leader can't change an evaluation. But if they all agree, then they don't have to discuss it any more."

"How do the villagers feel about that?" I then asked.

She looked at me briefly, then turned away and headed toward the door. Just before going outside, she paused, turned again, and said quietly: *"Zhong kou nan tiao. Na neng renren chengxin.* People have different opinions. Some are satisfied and some are not."

At that moment, I didn't feel it would be appropriate to inquire further. It was clear how she felt. After she left, Zhou Xing and I turned back to the transcription, finishing about an hour later. Thanking Zhou and saying good-night, I took a brief stroll through the now silent village. It was quite cold, and the winds were picking up. Quite possibly the 200 manure piles would freeze overnight. But if others were concerned, I would never know—except perhaps Jiang Lijiang. Looking down the main roadway, I saw the soft light of the brigade office shining through the window. Inside, Jiang was sitting at his desk, writing. Slowly, I turned away and headed back toward the warmth of my own room.

2/Half Moon Village

THE SETTING

In 1979, China's capital city of Beijing had myriad government offices, tall apartment buildings, paved streets, crowded buses, historical sites, lovely parks, and almost six million residents—all of whom were far removed in sight, sound, and smell from the quieter, slower-paced, agriculturally based community of Half Moon. Situated on the city's outskirts, the village was located over 25 miles from the urban center—almost two hours by bicycle, a common form of transportation to and from the city at that time. Although contained within the municipal boundary, the community was surprisingly rural in character, as were most other villages that composed Red Flag Commune and State Farm. It was also fairly small, with a total population of 543.[1]

In summer and early fall, bright rays of the morning sun warmed the ten-feet-high courtyard walls that defined both the outer perimeter of the village proper and the family residences within. In winter, these same walls deflected occasional snow and more frequent wind that swept across China's Northern Plain. Winter mornings brought another feature unique to that season—a soft blanket of smoky haze from 100 cooking fires, a haze that hung over the village until dissipated by the thermal-producing heat of a bright sun or a light gust of wind. With the arrival of spring in April and May, courtyards were bathed in profusions of white lilac blossoms and the pale red flowering plum. Nearby, looking almost like a huge abstract painting, crisscrossed mosaics of sparkling green edged in brown defined the village's irrigation ditches, freshly lined with new grass. Each square marked one border of the six collectively owned fields.

Several features distinguished Half Moon's rural character. Most obvious were the flat agricultural fields bounding the living area. Depending on the season of the year, these fields produced rice, wheat, and corn as well as many varieties of vegetables. Rice was the major crop, closely followed by wheat and vegetables. A little over 50 percent of the village holdings of 800 *mu* (1 *mu* = ⅙ acre) was used to grow rice, at an average yield of 1000 *jin* per *mu*.

---

[1]Beijing Municipality contains nine districts and nine counties. Four districts are urban, four are "near urban" *(jin jiaoqa),* and one is a special mining area. Red Flag Commune was located in a more "remote-suburban" *(yuan jiaoqu)* area of Daxing County. Although the commune was decollectivized in the early 1980s, the state farm remains in existence today.

For many years, the poor quality of the soil seriously limited the peasants' ability to produce adequate crops. Situated on an alluvial plain near a meandering river, the land was low-lying, with a high water table and a high alkaline content. As such, until communewide efforts were made to control the water through better drainage and irrigation, the land suffered from waterlogging and was therefore quite barren and only minimally productive for farming.

The ruralism of the community was also emphasized by the nature of its housing: peasant dwellings of adobe and brick whose joined outer courtyard walls abutted the agricultural fields. Within, well-worn dirt lanes defined the routes used by residents to visit and carry on their daily village activities. At regular intervals along these roadways, tile-roofed arches sheltered swinging doors that opened into each family courtyard. Looking inside, one could see small gardens planted with Chinese cabbages, onions, string beans, and other vegetables for winter consumption. Date trees provided fresh, delicious fruit. Persimmons too were grown, though less satisfactorily. And always, special fenced-in areas were set aside for raising chickens and fattening pigs.

Stacked piles of twigs next to every courtyard wall served as kindling for household fires. Once trees had been the main source of peasant fuel, but by 1979 timber had become a scarce item throughout China's deforested Northern Plain. In Half Moon and similar villages of Red Flag Commune, wood chips and compressed coal had become the common cooking and heating fuel. Those few households that were fortunate enough to have obtained a sizable pile of cut wood or sawdust were likely to have a resident carpenter as well.

Finally, water was a precious commodity. In Half Moon, water was pumped from a well into family courtyards, where a single spigot controlled the access. In poorer villages like Little River, a half mile away, the peasants carried water to their homes from a common well. But all used it sparingly. Whatever was left after cooking, washing, and laundering was drained into the garden to nourish growing produce and flowers. Only in late fall, when the family garden had been trans-

Early morning at Half Moon Village.

formed into a root cellar for the winter storage of vegetables, did the remaining water trickle through a small hole in the bottom of the courtyard wall to the lane outside.

Although visitors were occasionally entertained in family courtyards, more informal socializing occurred in the small plaza located in the village center. Here, during the day, children and youth came to play. In summer evenings after work, as many as 100 villagers of all ages joined together to watch the news, opera, and other programs from Beijing on the large black-and-white, brigade-owned television set purchased in 1978.

Through this same plaza passed the main gravel road linking Half Moon with nearby villages and with such institutions as the district administrative office, the food and general store, the primary and middle schools, the hospital, and a small jade-carving factory. Bordering both sides of this roadway, tall young trees planted two decades ago during a major reforestation program offered valuable shade from the heat of the summer or needed protection from the biting cold of a winter wind. A 20-minute bicycle ride down this road, past numerous other small villages and

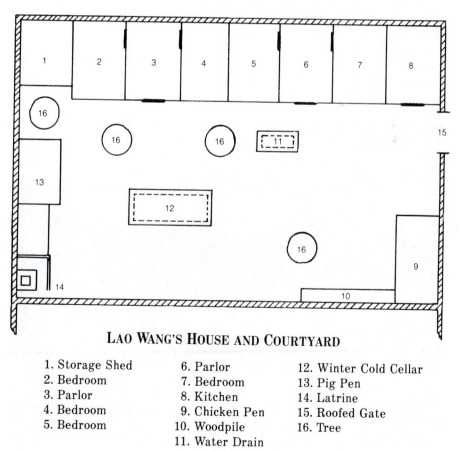

LAO WANG'S HOUSE AND COURTYARD

1. Storage Shed
2. Bedroom
3. Parlor
4. Bedroom
5. Bedroom
6. Parlor
7. Bedroom
8. Kitchen
9. Chicken Pen
10. Woodpile
11. Water Drain
12. Winter Cold Cellar
13. Pig Pen
14. Latrine
15. Roofed Gate
16. Tree

The Wang family house and courtyard.

fields, brought the local traveler to the headquarters of Red Flag People's Commune and the old market town that lay adjacent to it. From there, buses left regularly for Beijing and the outside world.

At the edge of the village, near the brigade office, stood a very modern-looking structure: the local bathhouse. Its completion a year earlier was quite an event in Half Moon. Not only was it contemporary in design and large in size, providing showers for over 20 people at a time in both the men's and women's sections, but it was solar heated! Hearing from some factory workers about a passive solar bathhouse that had been built in Beijing, several village leaders went to the city to learn more about it. Reporting back home, they concluded that with money from the brigade accumulation fund and bricks from an old building, along with some financial and skilled help from the commune, they could construct their own solar bathhouse. After several years of discussion by the villagers and commune leadership, the brigade received approval and decided to go ahead. Since then, everyone had become quite proud of it—except perhaps when the sun went behind the clouds for several days at a time.

Although Half Moon had a rural character, its location near the nation's capital set it dramatically apart from tens of thousands of communities situated in more isolated areas of North China. For example, its close proximity to Beijing greatly increased its economic potential, particularly in vegetable production. In addition to growing vegetables for city dwellers, an immediate and constant market for the villagers' produce, residents were employed in nonagricultural pursuits as well.

The author bicycling on the main road between the village and the commune headquarters.

Such employment included work in sideline industries, small factories and service agencies that composed a rising secondary layer of the economy characteristic of suburban communes located near cities. Many villages within Red Flag Commune had developed small local enterprises producing consumer goods ranging from light bulbs and parts for electronic switches to machine nuts and rice planters.[2]

One might suppose that the more-developed transportation and communication technology associated with urban life had an important impact on the adjacent rural sector. And indeed, it did. But this impact was still far less significant than that found in the industrialized West, where advanced transportation and communication facilities immediately involved city and countryside in an extensive network of social and cultural linkages.

At this time Half Moon had no direct access to any bus service or other scheduled means of transportation. When needing to travel somewhere nearby, a resident would commonly use a bicycle or simply walk. Shortly after my arrival in the village, a peasant commented that unless I could get a bicycle, I would have to rely on the number 11 bus. After several days of keeping an eye out for a passing bus, I asked a neighbor when it came to the village.

"The number 11 bus?" he repeated, a big grin spreading across his face. Then, bursting with laughter and slapping his thigh, he pointed toward my legs. "That's the number 11 bus. Your own two feet!"

There was one other form of transportation well recognized throughout rural China: catching a ride on the back of a wagon. In Half Moon and similar, more prosperous villages surrounding Beijing, the old horse-drawn wagons were being replaced with large two-wheeled hand-held "walking tractors." Although originally designed for agricultural purposes, these machines were easily converted into motorized four-wheeled vehicles by attaching a cart or wagon to the frame. Since residents had no access to cars, and very limited use of trucks and motorcycles, the noisy but adaptable two-cycle minitractor served admirably.

For communicating news to the village, Half Moon relied heavily on its six conveniently placed loudspeakers. Direct contact outside the village was limited to the single telephone in the brigade office. However, the quality of this line was so poor that its effective range extended only to the commune perimeter. Anyone wishing to place a call to Beijing or elsewhere usually went to commune headquarters. Actually, peasants oriented around agricultural production had few reasons to either call or visit the city except on rare occasions such as attending the funeral of a close relative, a special holiday, or some other similarly important event. So the direct cultural influence of the city on this segment of the village was more limited than one might imagine.

Still, economically speaking, some residents of Half Moon and other nearby communities were not really peasants at all. Some were employed in small industries and factories located close by. Others worked in commune- and state-owned suburban factories. One man even worked at a large auto-assembly plant in an urban

---

[2]However, as will be seen shortly, Half Moon participated only minimally in these economic endeavors.

A brigade tractor with the solar bathhouse in the background.

district of Beijing. Living in a factory dormitory during the week, he returned home to his family on weekends or whenever he had time off from his workplace.

More important, two very modern state-controlled industries also provided jobs for local villagers, including quite a few from Half Moon.[3] One plant produced chemicals, including fertilizer, and the other processed grain for animal fodder. Since both were partially automated, they offered rural-based workers their first glimpse of a technological future unheard of in their own communities. As employees in these plants, such individuals brought back to their villages important knowledge about advanced production techniques and methods. As they formed friendships with city workers, they brought news of urban lifeways and culture as well.

One other group contributed significantly to bringing urban knowledge and experience to Half Moon: the "sent-down educated youth." Beginning in the mid-1950s and dramatically expanding during the Cultural Revolution, the *shangshan xiaxiang* ("Up to the Mountains and Down to the Countryside") campaign assigned millions of young urban middle-school students to work in villages and towns throughout rural China. Urged to learn from the peasants the values of frugality, hard work, and self-reliance, these young people were assigned to the fields. Occasionally, when feelings of trust had developed between them and the

---

[3] A household census taken by the author and others in 1979 showed that over one-third of Half Moon villagers were state employees—a much higher than usual percentage, which helps account for the village's affluence vis-à-vis most commune villages. Red Flag itself was atypical in having state-owned enterprises of both an agricultural and industrial nature within its borders. These included dairy and duck farms providing milk and meat to the city, a tractor-repair facility, a machine-nut shop, and two modern chemical and grain-processing factories.

rural populace, relocated youth were also asked by village leaders to teach primary school, become production team accountants, or serve as "barefoot doctors."

Although this nationwide relocation movement did much to minimize urban unemployment, it presented the government with a great many political problems, not the least of which concerned the severe social and psychological disruption experienced by many of the youths and their families—particularly those who were separated from family and friends for long periods. However, it was not until the late 1970s, several years after Mao's death, that the new leadership brought the movement to a close.[4]

At Half Moon, except for the few young men and women who married into the community, the one physical reminder of this dramatic social experiment was a vacant brick building located near the far corner of the village. Its construction was initially paid for with state funds, the eight rooms serving as dormitory quarters, lounge, library, and kitchen for the 20 or more educated youth from the Beijing area who were regularly assigned to work in the village. In 1979, an outsider walking past the abandoned structure could not help but be struck by the almost ghost-town quality of the place. An impressive solid-cement ping-pong table, not used for years and surrounded by weeds, stood in the center of the courtyard under a large, lifeless tree. Locked dormitory doors and torn or broken paper and glass windows added to the forlorn atmosphere of the place.

Curious about such an unused facility in an otherwise lively village, I decided to explore the area more fully. Late one fall afternoon, after walking around the courtyard, I looked in the window of what was once a library. On the other side of the glass I saw row upon row of paperback books resting on four home-built bookcases. Close by were two well-made straight-backed chairs, one lying on its side and the other standing next to a dusty wooden table. On the wall were tacked several brightly colored pictures of highly-motivated-looking youth in various work settings, obviously taken from a popular magazine of the day. And next to one of the pictures, written in bold letters with a dark, thick-lead pencil on the faded plaster, was a long poem. From my angle of view outside the window, it was almost impossible to read. Still, I took out pen and paper and began writing down some of the words. Then, hearing a sound behind me, I turned around to face a handsome man in his mid-30s, standing in the middle of the roadway 40 feet away.

Frowning and looking firm, he said nothing. But with a series of brusque movements of his arm he made it clear that I was not wanted there. I quickly moved away from the building and the strange man, who was unknown to me. Neither of us spoke. For my part, I was still very caught up in what I had seen on the wall. Unable to clearly read the poem because of the angle of the window and the locked door, I could only barely determine its general content As best I could tell, it was a pessimistic commentary on the future Chinese youth. But what fascinated me the most was the language in which it was written: English!

In summary, any outsider looking at Half Moon and other villages of Red Flag

---

[4]Seven thousand came to Red Flag Commune alone, most to work in the state sector. Others served in large state-owned farms, particularly in China's isolated border areas. A brief life history of one such educated youth is described in Chapter 5.

Commune could easily see that they had advantages not characteristic of communities located in more remote settings of northern China.[5] Economically, the opportunity to produce vegetables for the urban market offered a steady source of income. Electrification, introduced in the 1950s, brought important benefits to local agriculture, industries, and homes. Improved means of transportation continuing to expand out from the center city enabled a few villagers to work in and around Beijing and to return home on weekends. Soon, daily commuting was expected to become feasible, with all the economic and cultural benefits and problems that entailed.

Half Moon also had two distinct qualities that set it off from surrounding communities. One was the newness of its buildings, the majority of which had been constructed within the past two decades. Equally eye-catching was the way in which the village was laid out—to resemlbe a half-moon. Why the recent construction and unique shape? The reason was interesting.

LOCAL HISTORY

In the early twentieth century, the place that became Half Moon was part of the Emperor's private hunting grounds. To keep the game in and unwanted people out, the Emperor protected the land by large adobe walls. Access was by means of one of four large red gates located to the east, west, north, and south. After the collapse of the imperial dynasty in 1911, a few government officials and private entrepreneurs sought and eventually obtained control over the area. At the same time, squatters from the famine-stricken regions of Hebei and other nearby provinces began moving in.

Carrying their few possessions on baskets strung between shoulder poles, these landless peasants and beggars came to build small mud houses and make arrangements with the newly installed but largely absentee landowners to raise grain, cotton, and other crops. Additional work opportunities included the extraction of saltpeter from the alkaline soil in spring for the making of gunpowder. In winter, most peasants moved outside the old walls, since there was nothing available to live on at that season of the year and the earlier harvest was too small to tide them over. Hardships also came in the form of bandits who continually preyed on the vast countryside of North China. Beholden to landlords for their livelihood, continually threatened by the ragtag bands of robbers that surrounded them, and attempting to eke out an existence from the unforgiving soil, these poor peasants become the pool from which Half Moon Village was eventually formed.

It should be noted that under these circumstances, the more common type of rural Chinese residence pattern, which utilized extended clan networks within and between villages, was difficult if not impossible to establish. The new settlers came from different provinces, some having no relatives at all and others very few. The tendency was for individuals and small nuclear or at most three-generational

---

[5]Of Red Flag's many villages, Half Moon was particularly clean and attractive—no doubt a major reason it was chosen by the commune leadership as the site for the research. It was not, however, the most affluent village in the commune.

families from a given area to join together as best they could, often without more extended kin. During the war with Japan, a more structured and integrated form of village organization *(baojia)* was encouraged by the military occupation forces in order to exert civil control more effectively. Nevertheless, most of the low mud houses remained scattered across the landscape, thus limiting any efforts to instill greater social cohesion. Intervillage clan ties were correspondingly weak or nonexistent.

The area was declared liberated in 1948, after the fall of Japan and somewhat before the complete victory of the Communist forces over Chiang Kai-shek's Kuomintang government. Soon the peasants, with the help of several young party members assigned to the area, organized a new village government. The next ten years brought significant economic and social changes, beginning with the implementation of land reform and concluding with the emergence of Red Flag Commune in 1958.

The stated purpose of land reform was first to break the back of the traditional elite by redistributing the land more equitably—though not equally—among the large number of peasants who had little or none and, through this initial change in the social relations of production, to encourage greater cooperation that could substantially increase agricultural productivity. Underlying this goal was a second: by actively participating in the redistribution process whereby landlord holdings (and to a lesser extent those of rich peasants) were divided among the poorer peasantry, the latter could gain an understanding of themselves as a force for change. This effort to create a new class consciousness through active struggle against the powerful landlords, and the social and economic responsibilities that emerged from it, came to be known as *fanshen,* or literally the process of "turning the body over."[6]

Wanting to know more precisely how this process was implemented in Half Moon, early in my stay I asked several villagers who could give me that information. Their response was almost universal. "You want to know about the old days? Go see Old Li. He's retired and has plenty of time. But watch out, he'll talk your head off." And they were right.

After meeting Li Haiping several times, I knew more than I needed about his early childhood in Hebei Province and what he had done after moving to Half Moon in the early 1940s. He had first worked as a laborer for an absentee landowner; then he had found a job with the Japanese—"under duress," he assured me—and finally had become active in the peasant movement. By 1950, he was a leader of the local peasant association and shortly thereafter joined the party. Now retired because of a heart problem, he continued to assume small duties around the village. I often saw him running errands or shopping for someone at the district food store.

One afternoon, we talked specifically about the land reform movement in the village. It was obvious Old Li was looking forward to sharing his story by the lively way in which he greeted me. Others said he knew it well, having talked before

---

[6]A detailed ethnographic portrayal of how this process was carried out in the North China village of Long Bow is contained in a book by William Hinton (1966). A follow-up study by the same author (1983) is also well worth pursuing.

middle school students as part of a general series on the political history of the commune. We were joined by Li Haiping's friend Yu Futian, who had lived in the area even longer. Sitting under a small shade tree along the roadside near the edge of the village, Li began by pointing to the fields and waving his arm in a half circle. I immediately turned on my small tape recorder.

"This whole area was liberated in 1948, and land reform began a year later. Before that I worked at almost every kind of job—like making gunpowder and growing wheat as a farmhand. I even rented some land once, one dozen *mu* from a small landlord. At that time life was very hard."

"How did land reform begin?" I inquired, hoping to focus the questioning on several key points.

"First we had to decide who to include and who to work with. There were no

An old village leader.

party members in our village, so we asked two nearby cadres to come over and help. They suggested that we get the peasants together and have a big meeting and they would come too. At that meeting, they told us the party's basic policy for land reform was 'to rely on the poor peasants, unite with the middle peasants, isolate the rich peasants, and overthrow the landlords and wipe out feudalism.' Well, it took us some time to figure out what they meant by that statement. It wasn't until much later that we really began to understand."

"When it came to actually dividing the land, how was it done?"

"At that time, about 90 percent was under control of middle or rich peasants and landlords. When it was finally divided, the poor peasants received their share according to the number of persons in the family and the quality of the soil. If there were four or five persons in a family they got about 20 *mu*. But it could have been more or less according to the quality."

"And the landlords?" As I asked the question, Yu Futian took a worn leather pouch out of his pocket, opened it, and shook some tobacco into the bowl of his long-stemmed pipe. After watching Yu light it, Li continued.

"The landlords were given a share of the land according to their family size, just like the others. Their houses, animals, and tools were divided up among all the people, and they were given their share too. But with the rich peasants, we did not take all their lands. We only took the part that they had rented out to others. We let them keep the land they worked themselves. For the next few years, all the families did their own individual farming. Of course, some made out better than others. But by 1952, several had become bankrupt, due partly to poor management of their land. They even received a little state aid, but it didn't help enough."

"How did you distinguish between well-to-do, middle, and poor? There must have been a lot of disagreements among the peasants?"

"It was easy to determine who the landlords were. They didn't work the land at all. Rich peasants did some work in the fields, but they made more of their income renting land to others. In this area, if a family got 30 percent of its income from the work of others, it was defined as a rich peasant family. In some other places not far from here, it was 25 percent. As for the middle peasants, they worked in the fields, but not for landlords. Only the poor worked for them. Most poor peasants rented land, and a few owned a small amount. And, of course, the tenant peasants were the worst off—they owned nothing."

"What about the mutual aid teams?" I asked. "Were they very helpful?"

I knew that after land redistribution, voluntary cooperative work groups had been formed, which pooled labor in a manner not dissimilar from earlier forms of cooperation common in the past. However, newly distributed land and peasant tools remained under the ownership of individual households.

"Yes, although there was opposition from the landlords and rich peasants, naturally, and also from some of the middle peasants. They had a better situation— more land and more tools and animals. For that reason, they had no interest in joining the rest of us. But they did spread rumors that the KMT government would return and take the land back. They also kept their old deeds carefully hidden in jars underground, hoping they would become usable again sometime in the future. And later, when we built several irrigation ditches, one household head tried to sabotage us by not allowing a right-of-way access through his land."

"What did you do?"

"We built them anyway. By this time the mutual aid teams had become pretty successful. That is, production increased. Even some of the poor peasants who at first were afraid to join began to participate. Also, there was a lot of talk in the area about starting a cooperative farm. Not too far from here, near East Gate Village, 60 households organized themselves into such a farm. It became quite well known. Yu Futian knows all about that."

Yu had been listening attentively, though somewhat restlessly. I could see that Haiping was not the only one who liked to talk about the early days of the cooperatives. I turned and watched as Yu relit his pipe. As he began talking, I again turned on my recorder.

"I am uneducated. I've never been to school. I first came here with my parents when I was six. I've been here now for 60 years. When I was eleven I began working for a landlord and received food in return. Nothing else. Later, I was a tenant farmer. During land reform, I lived a little north of here, in a village that had less land than most places. We received just three *mu* of land per peasant. We grew crops, but the harvest was not good. Only those who had better land could get a yield of 100 *jin* or more per *mu*. The rest of us got around 80. Then, in 1954, we organized our first agricultural cooperative. That's when things really began to improve. Harvests increased, and our living standard went up. In the following year, every member of the cooperative received 100 *jin* per *mu* or corn and wheat. Ten percent was wheat and the rest corn. With poor land and no irrigation, we couldn't improve much more. Still, just about everybody supported the cooperative."

"How many?"

"Around 80 percent. Some were excluded, like landlords. Others simply didn't want to get involved. But most did."

Old Li had told me earlier how his village had moved from the mutual aid teams to the elementary APCs. It had apparently begun with 15 families volunteering to form a work team. Ownership of the land remained in the household, but payment for work completed was calculated on a dual basis: combining the size of landholding contributed and animals donated with the amount of labor performed. Then, in 1956, several lower-level cooperatives in the area were consolidated into a larger one. This advanced cooperative was organized into "production teams" of about 20 households each, then further subdivided into work groups of 5 to 10 households. But what made the higher-level cooperative qualitatively different from the earlier ones was that the contribution of land, animals, and tools no longer influenced the income received. Rather, income was determined solely by one's own labor, measured in number of "work points."

Needless to say, not all the area residents were pleased by this plan, a point Li Haiping readily acknowledged. But was coercive pressure placed on the more reluctant villagers to join the advanced APCs? I was not able to obtain from Li, Yu, or anyone else I spoke with any specific illustration that collectivization had been forced on anyone. Of course, fear of being called a "bad class element," accompanied with appropriate reprisals, may have led some of the more well-to-do peasants to keep any complaints to themselves. But in this area there were very few well-off peasants (and few absentee landlords remained in the area). In other North China villages, with a larger number of well-to-do peasants, coercive pressure was certainly applied, particularly when economic advantages were not forthcoming.

Of course, the government did not limit its support of these developments to verbal encouragement or persuasive pressure. It regularly provided direct incentives, such as the opportunity for cooperative members to borrow money from government-backed loan funds. If Half Moon villagers had not perceived it to be in their own interests, they would not have participated so actively. Still, I wanted to know exactly how much of an economic advantage resulted from this cooperation. Li answered my question.

"From the beginning of the cooperative movement in 1952 to the time the communes were formed in 1958, our average corn and wheat harvest production grew from slightly less than 100 *jin* to 500 *jin* per *mu*. In 1957, we even began to grow rice—a little over 500 *mu* of it. The yield was between 400 and 500 *jin* of rice per *mu*, and believe me, the peasants were very happy to eat more rice and less corn."

Li Haiping and Yu also stressed that after land reform and the establishment of the mutual aid teams, the one other factor enhancing the cooperative's productivity was a revision of old land-use patterns. Traditional inheritance customs required that sons share in a father's estate, often resulting in noncontiguous minuscule plots of "patchwork" land being farmed in a highly irrational manner. Tiny scattered hamlets, such as were found at Half Moon, were equally inefficient as economic units. It was thought that if such land could be combined into larger productive parcels, it not only would enable the peasants to increase their productivity, but in addition would set the stage for an even more significant increase in production through the development of mechanized agriculture. Finally, larger economic units like the newly emerging agricultural producers' cooperatives could also help the peasants undertake community-wide tasks of benefit to all the members, such as extending irrigation ditches and encouraging local reforestation.

In early 1955, members of the Rural Works Department of the Beijing Municipal Party Committee, in conjunction with the Agriculture, Forestry, and Water Conservancy Bureau of Beijing's People's Council, undertook a detailed investigation of an area surrounding Half Moon to determine what factors were limiting the economic growth of the region and what steps might be taken to develop it. The results of their study, published in the October 10, 1955, issue of the *Peking Daily* newspaper, reaffirm the experience of Li Haiping and Yu Futian.

> The dwelling places of farm families are widely scattered because the villages and homes were built in a planless and arbitrary way near the peasant's own plot of land. As a result, small hamlets of two or three household dot the fields, hampering mechanized farming and increasing costs for such construction work as building roads, installing electric power lines and setting up cultural and recreational facilities. . . . [The report concluded with a plan that was carried out several years later.] Villages which are small and scattered will be gradually evacuated . . . with farm members moving in

from other places if their old houses have become ramshackle, and if they themselves are willing and able to do so.

A short time later, Li, Yu, and the other ex-squatters from Hebei Province decided to relocate their scattered homes into a more homogeneous settlement nearby. However, in contrast to similar poor peasants elsewhere who decided to move, this group proceeded to design the plan of their relocated village in such a manner that it took on a crescent-like form similar to the geographic shape of the province from which so many of them had come. Thus was the new beginning of Half Moon Village.

RELATIONS WITH THE COMMUNE

Red Flag Commune was formed in 1958. The poor nature of the marshy and alkaline soil and the accompanying low population density had earlier drawn the active attention of the Beijing Municipal authorities. A state-owned and -managed tractor station had been set up earlier to assist in upgrading the land and improving agricultural production. Other state-owned agricultural and industrial enterprises followed. In the spring of 1958, when the commune movement began, the area had seven large advanced cooperatives and an even larger state farm, the latter employing nearby peasants in agricultural activities, some of which were experimental in nature.[7] In late summer of that year, these different enterprises joined together to form Red Flag People's Commune.

By 1979, Red Flag has become one of the largest communes in the country, comprising nearly 62 square kilometers in area and 85,000 residents in population. It had over 17,000 households, grouped into 10 administrative districts and 116 production brigades, most of the latter equivalent to the older natural villages. The agriculturally based brigades used much of the commune's 160,000 *mu* of cultivated land for growing rice, wheat, vegetables, and other produce, mainly for the city. The remainder of the land was used for dairy, pig, and duck farms run by the commune and the state. Additional commune enterprises included fishponds, orchards, grain- and wood-processing shops, an agricultural machine repair plant, and many small factories, which made such products as fertilizer, bricks, and powdered milk.

Of the total commune work force comprising 40,306 people, 61 percent were employed at the village-brigade level, mostly in agricultural field labor. Another 15 percent worked at one of the ten district-level enterprises, such as the jade-carving factory located close to Half Moon. Three percent were employed at the commune level itself. These were commune members who worked in the state sector. The remaining 21 percent were regular state workers in enterprises located on or close to the commune.

Clearly, Red Flag Commune served as a highly interesting case study of a unique experiment in human history. Economically, it had survived several rather

---

[7]Two American scientist-technicians, commune residents for over a decade, were until the mid-1980s among its active advisors.

outlandish policies that threatened basically sound efforts to increase agricultural production through the cooperative interchange of different sectors of the work force. Socially, it had provided an enlarged structure for the development of a broad range of human services, including clinics and hospitals, day-care centers, and primary and middle schools. Organizationally, it had established an administrative structure that included a director and several vice directors, an administrative committee, and other groups such as the Women's Federation and the militia that dealt with various matters of concern to the commune and the municipality.

Parallel party committees formed at each of these levels of organization determined basic policies, which were then put into effect by the appropriate administrative committees. Similar forms of decision making were maintained at the brigade level. To effectively manage a commune the size of Red Flag, the administration decided to establish ten separate districts, eight of which were in the collective sector and two in the state. The eight districts served as intermediate agencies linking the commune headquarters with the 116 village brigades.[8]

Of the greatest significance in all this activity was the role of the Chinese Communist Party. Who was involved? Through what organizations did the party function? What were its relations with the people? And what were its goals and its methods of attaining them?

THE PARTY AND THE PEOPLE

In Half Moon, the village leadership consisted of a formally defined brigade committee composed of the party secretary, an administrative head (a separate position from that of the party secretary), three vice directors in charge of grain, vegetable, and sideline production, and one of the work-team leaders.

In principle, the party elected its members of the committee, and nonparty villagers did the same, the specific number of representatives of each group being left undecided. In fact, the party had always selected all the committee members—after seeking advice from the villagers on the proposed candidates. Given continuing complaints about the lack of democratic input by nonparty members, various ways to deal with this criticism were discussed. The most significant was a proposal to establish electoral procedures in which villagers could vote for both party and nonparty candidates on the same ballot, with the number of candidates exceeding the number of openings on the committee.

The party secretary always served as the chair of the brigade committee. In Half Moon, the administrative head of the brigade and the vice director in charge of vegetable production were also party members. The vice director for grain production, Ma Haimen, was a probationary party member. Assuming he received a positive evaluation at the end of his probationary period, he would then become a full member. In other words, four out of six members of the most important local administrative committee in 1979 were directly affiliated with the party. As such,

---

[8]Red Flag Commune never had the formally designated village-level production teams characteristic of most communes in China. In Half Moon and other commune villages, the brigade was the unit of accounting for purposes of distribution of income, goods, and services obtained through collective work.

the party had significant control over the decision-making process for day-to-day affairs in the village.

Anyone wishing to join the party could apply to the brigade party branch, which represented the leadership locally. Of the twelve party members then in Half Moon, six belonged to the local branch. All applications were reviewed by this group, which then offered its recommendation to the next highest body, which made the final decision on the applicant. At Half Moon, that higher body was the district party branch.

Cui Huifang, the older-women's work-team leader in the village, had applied several times for party membership, but by 1979 she had yet to be approved by the district. In 1977, there had been six women party members, out of a village total of fifteen members, of whom one had been the party secretary. This much higher than usual proportion of women members reflected a policy undertaken during the later years of the Cultural Revolution to bring more women into positions of leadership. All had since been transferred outside the area, leaving the brigade without any female members at all. Cui thought this imbalance would benefit her application.

Criteria for belonging to the party involved a commitment to build socialism, an ability to work hard and selflessly, and a willingness to support the policies of the organization even if the individual member was in disagreement. This latter feature of party discipline, known as "democratic centralism," was integral to the unity that the party tried to achieve. Members were encouraged to fully express their views on any proposed policy for as long as it was under active discussion; this was the democratic aspect.[9] However, once a course of action had been determined by the leadership at a given level, party members were expected to support that policy irrespective of their own position on the matter; this was the centralist aspect.

The village also had three other formal organizations: the Communist Youth League (CYL), the Women's Federation, and the militia.[10]

Membership in the CYL was drawn from politically active middle school students and other youths in field and factory who wished to work with the party in the workplace, in sports and other recreational activities, and in political study groups. The political socialization of many party members began with their membership in the CYL.

The Women's Federation, like the CYL, was really a party-led organization, in the sense that while taking up issues of direct concern to women, such as improving opportunities for educational and technical training, it explicitly represented the party's views on these issues. By 1979, in keeping with the national emphasis on the "Four Modernizations" and a corresponding need to limit population growth, the chief task of the Women's Federation was to popularize family planning to reduce

---

[9]The open manner in which so many party informants addressed the issues I raised in my research and the varying answers they gave to my questions were no doubt partly due to the active debate and reevaluation of basic party policy occurring throughout much of 1978 and 1979, following the death of Mao and the removal of the "Gang of Four."

[10]There was once a fifth: the Poor and Lower Middle Peasant's Association. It was organized in 1964 as part of a nationwide "Four Clean-up" (siqing) campaign to deal with problems of theft, corruption, profiteering, and other illegal activities of local cadres (see Baum and Teiwes 1968). A party work team from the city was sent to the village to investigate (i.e., "clean up") possible corruption. Since no major problems emerged, the work team moved on, and the association disbanded shortly thereafter.

A probationary party member being interviewed at the clinic.

the number of births per family to one. The group also took part in sanitation and other public health programs.

Though the party defined the federation as a mass organization involving all village women, the actual participating membership was considerably smaller. In a household survey taken in the fall of 1979, less than 10 percent of the women interviewed said they belonged to the federation. Such lack of identification seems clearly associated with the village's limited support for the new birth-control policy.

Finally, the active militia consisted of all brigade members from 18 to 25 years of age. Men 25 to 45 and women 25 to 40 were inactive members. Annually, during winter when agricultural responsibilities were at a minimum, PLA representatives came to an area just outside the village and offered a short refresher course on firearms, including rifle practice. Except for a brief period in 1972, all arms and ammunition had been kept at the district headquarters rather than in the village. The villagers were taught that the purpose of the militia was primarily to protect the country from foreign invasion—an experience vividly etched in the memories of many residents—and secondarily to prevent sabotage at home.

The village leaders of these three organizations were usually active party members. In Half Moon, the one exception was the Women's Federation: the local person in charge was then being considered for membership. It is significant that she was highly respected not only by the relatively few federation women who had elected her, but by the other women in the village as well. However, what might be surprising to those unfamiliar with political life in rural China was that, with the exception of the party, these three groups and the administrative brigade committee were the only organizations in the village. There were no others—no informal voluntary organizations such as are found throughout small-town America. Under such circumstances, the party was not just the ultimate village authority; in many respects it was the only one. The brigade committee, for example, though a distinct entity in its own right, never took an administrative action opposing party guide-lines.

What happened when a villager was caught stealing? When a husband beat his wife? When a local party cadre was accused of embezzling? Actually, crimes such as these were very rare. When they occurred, they were investigated by the Public Security Bureau attached to the district headquarters and run by a party-led district committee. In the mid-1970s, a young couple had taken home vegetables from the collective field for their own use. Shortly thereafter, they were caught stealing a few boards of wood. Brought before a mass public meeting of the village, they were forced to offer a thorough self-criticism of their wrongdoing. Here, the usual custom of separating public and private was purposefully reversed. However, if the offender was a party member, the party rather than the brigade committee de-termined the individual's fate. Such was the case in Half Moon in the fall of 1979, when a district leader was accused of misusing public funds. Significantly, that same fall, China introduced for the first time a legal criminal code, enabling the people to deal with issues of crime and punishment in a formal prescribed manner, separate from the actions of a local party branch or brigade committee.

Given the extent of authority and power held by the party, its responsibilities were awesome. There was a distinct nationwide governmental structure operating at the municipal, county, prefectural, provincial, and national levels. But such agen-cies still functioned in concert with the party, largely as an administrative arm rather than as a separate policy-generating body—similar to the way in which the Half Moon brigade committee operated in concert with the local party branch.

We can see from these examples how the interrelated economies of Half Moon Village and Red Flag Commune were intimately linked to the political structure. There were many ecological, technological, and cultural factors limiting the area's economic development. These constraints required difficult decisions in allocating human and material resources, in establishing an effective economic infrastructure that could raise the productivity of the people, and in providing for the education, health, and general welfare of the populace. The party, drawing on the theories of Marx and on its own experience and that of the people, was the political instrument that made these decisions.

With the above remarks in mind, it would be easy to see the party as monolithic. But it was not. In Half Moon, members regularly disagreed with one another. This shouldn't be surprising, since their ideas were based on the same diverse experi-ences as those found outside the party. Members also found themselves in disagree-ment with their own leadership. This could be due to simple differences of opinion or to conflicts generated by party policies that clashed with the views of family and friends.

Several years ago, the Beijing party leadership in charge of agricultural produc-tion for the municipality urged that villages within its jurisdiction change from a two-crop to a three-crop system, stating that recent research on experimental plots elsewhere had demonstrated the feasibility for the area. Asked to carry out the policy in Half Moon, party leaders soon found themselves at odds with just about all the field workers, who said the plan wouldn't work, that the soil simply wasn't adequate to the task. The leaders, largely agreeing with the field workers, were caught in a classic dilemma. Eventually, the villagers did agree to try the three-crop plan. They understood very well the pressure that their local leaders were under. But as it turned out, their initial evaluation was correct. Crop production temporarily decreased, city officials admitted their error, the peasants went back to their earlier practice, and the local party leaders resolved their dilemma. But the illustration clearly shows the kind of pressure the village cadres were under, located as they were between the higher leadership of the party and the people. The example also suggests that party officials residing in Beijing City had limited experience and understanding of the life and problems of peasant-farmers living within their municipality. And without that knowledge, party officials were severely limited in their ability to offer sound planning strategies.

THE PROBLEM OF BUREAUCRACY

In discussing bureaucracy in Half Moon Village and Red Flag Commune in the 1970s, we should keep in mind two issues: the structure itself, and the way local officials related to the people they served—their "work style." At the core of political power was the party. Like an executive, it generated policies. Like a legislature, it established guidelines, which were equivalent to laws (for example, residency registration). Like an administration, it had various economic, social, and political divisions. And like the judiciary, the party handled wrongdoings of officials and important criminals. Since 1949, some Chinese leaders (such as Mao) had advocated that the party lead all activities within the country. Other leaders encouraged greater separation between the political party structure and the administrative government structure. But no one doubted that the party was the ultimate decision-maker at either the national or the local level.

Within this bureaucratic structure, leaders and followers related to one another in various ways. Decisions could be undertaken in an elitist manner, with little involvement from below. Or they might be undertaken quite democratically, with extensive input by the participants. Half Moon villagers being told by the municipal Department of Agriculture in Beijing to undertake "triple cropping" even though they largely opposed it provides a good example of a bureaucratic work style. In contrast, the establishment of a Worker's Congress at the new state factory near Half Moon, the members of which determined their own criteria for receiving bonuses, is an example of a democratic work style.

China's bureaucratic structure and its accompanying methods have a very long history—dating back 2000 years, when a rising gentry class trained some of its sons to become elite scholar-officials able to amass great power, privilege, and property. However, it was not so much control over property that conferred such long-lasting authority to this elite group as it was their indispensable role as managers—plus a multi-level educational system controlled by examinations at each level. What was the ideological support for this powerful governing structure?

Mencius, a well-known Confucian spokesman of the time, expressed it succinctly: "Great men have their proper business and little men have their proper business. . . . Some labor with their minds and some with their strength. Those who labor with their minds govern others; those who labor with their strength are governed by others" (Balazs 1954:154). Such was the social philosophy that legitimized the great bureaucracy that integrated a diverse population and supported China's many dynasties in the past.[11]

Mencius' view on governance and the distinctions between mental and manual labor were firmly ensconced in Half Moon as well. It was evident in Party Secretary Jiang Lijiang's warning to the village field teams at the December village meeting. He knew the villagers wanted to finish digging their earthen courtyard cellars so that they could store their winter supply of brigade-grown cabbages. He was more concerned that they get the large piles of manure from the collective pig farm to the fields. But instead of raising both of these issues for discussion in a democratic manner, he summarily threatened his listeners with a loss in work-point rating if they persisted in coming out late to or going home early from the fields. In the day-to-day life of the village, he also tended to remain aloof from the people he was expected to serve. Ostentatiously busy, he was always on the move, chasing down a missing chicken, making sure the work teams got to work on time, or checking clinic records. But he never worked side by side with the people he was expected to lead. Jian Lijiang was not considered a bad leader, just one with a bureaucratic work style.

The first time I heard villagers comment on the subject was on a sunny fall afternoon when I was husking corn with the men's work team. We were sitting in a semicircle at the edge of a brigade field with our backs soaking up the warm rays of the sun. That we were barely working was obvious from the almost imperceptible growth of the pile of corn husks before us. The men, talking among themselves, disregarded the slight look of annoyance on the face of the team leader, Chen Defu, until Chu Meiying, the lively village accountant, came up behind us. She had arrived to inform Chen of a meeting to be held shortly at the brigade office.

Seeing Chu, I began husking corn a little more diligently. The others continued talking with one another, paying little regard to Chen, Chu, or the task at hand. Finally, Chen told us we had better work a little harder. Looking up at the team leader from where he was sitting, one of the villagers responded in a semiserious tone of voice, "Chen, why should we have to work when the people at the brigade office just sit around all day knocking heads together doing nothing?"

Following that remark, others quickly joined in the teasing.

"That's right, Chen. Are you going to become one of those bureaucrats with a 'big mouth and lazy hands' *(dong kou bu dong shou),* only talking and not working, or are you going to stay with us and help get the work done?"

"Yes, Defu. Stick around. You're better off with us."

Chu, looking off toward the village, said nothing. But Chen Defu, disregarding the teasing, good-naturedly reminded the men of the need to finish the cornhusking

---

[11]Today, this same ideology continues to be expressed at all levels of the government and in the party itself. Indeed, a major reason Mao Zedong initiated the Cultural Revolution was because he perceived the reemergence of a bureaucratic elite as the chief internal enemy of socialist development. Though the bureaucracy appeared quite able to survive and even grow under socialism, Mao feared that China's socialism wouldn't survive the bureaucracy, hence the need for a cultural (i.e., ideological) revolution in which peasants and workers were to be exalted over bureaucrats and intellectuals.

before the end of the day. Then, turning away, he and Chu both left for the brigade office.

Although team leaders like Chen Defu, Cui Huifang, and Su Xiulan occasionally met with the brigade leaders, they were not regular village-level cadres. Their working day was spent in the fields, and except for carrying out requests in assigning work, they had little to do with making or implementing village policy. The colloquial expression "big mouth and lazy hands" reflected this historic division of labor between worker and manager quite well. The field worker who offered that remark was obviously reminding team leader Chen Defu where his loyalties should lie.

If team leaders were not part of the local bureaucracy, full-time brigade accountants like Chu Meiying definitely were. After finishing school, she spent four years in the fields with Su Xiulan's work team. Then, in 1978, she was chosen by the village leaders to be the accountant. In this position, she was responsible for keeping an accurate record of all financial transactions, as well as recording daily work points. The position was an important one, requiring both thoroughness and honesty. However, since she was not a party member, her status in the decision-making hierarchy was still relatively low.

As described earlier, the key village leaders were members of the party branch, followed by those in the brigade administrative committee, including both party members and nonmembers. All the local CCP members were responsible to the district party committee, which in turn was under the commune committee, and so on up the political ladder to the central leadership in Beijing. Of course, the brigade administrative committee was not bound by the decisions of the district body in the way that the party committee was, since the principle of "democratic centralism" was not directly applicable here. But local administrative committees were expected to follow guidelines laid down by similar governing units at the district and commune levels, thereby insuring the continued maintenance of the bureaucratic structure.

There was another feature of the governing process that enhanced the bureaucratic structure at the expense of democratic input—the lack of a modern legal system. Until 1979, Half Moon villagers had almost no legal protections to call upon when they got into difficulty with the authorities. Given this lack, their only recourse was to appeal to higher official bodies or to mail statements of complaint to the appropriate "Letters to the Editor" column of major newspapers like the *People's Daily*. Courts were available to handle serious crimes and civil disputes, but minor ones were either resolved by a local unit *(danwei)* or simply ignored.

Abuse of power by officials posed a more serious problem, since courts were never established to address this type of issue.[12] This fact was dramatically illustrated during my stay in the commune. Three party officials at the district level—including one living in Half Moon—were removed from their positions because they had used public funds for their own benefit. The whole matter was handled by the party alone, an investigative committee deciding that the individuals concerned should not be prosecuted, though they had to pay back the funds taken.

---

[12]Needless to say, political campaigns did provide a convenient "solution" to such a dilemma.

That same year, China did draw up a formal criminal code offering new legal protection for its citizens. Though the code was still too undeveloped to be effectively used by Half Moon villagers, a process had at least begun whereby individuals could criticize a bureaucratic leader with less fear of being passed over for a factory job or having to wait endlessly for a permit to build a house. Furthermore, when the code was fully implemented, all groups, including the party, would be subject to the legal statutes designed to protect both the individual and the state.

Of course, this lack of a formal civil code in the past did not mean the Chinese were without a sense of justice. Rather, the norms that defined proper conduct continued to remain embedded in Confucian values closely linked to the family. Half Moon villagers, for example, had no concept of civil liberty or individual freedom like that found in the West. But they did have a strong sense of right and wrong. Not based in a transcendental religion like Christianity, their concept of justice was rooted in an existing world that placed greater emphasis on principles of reciprocity and proper interpersonal relations than was characteristic of societies where the value of individualism was primary.

While the centrifugal force of individualism presented its own problems in the West, submissiveness to authority and subordination of the individual to the group provided fertile soil in China for the continuation of a bureaucratic work style. Other Chinese values, such as continuity and inclusiveness in family relations (Hsu 1979:262), had a similar impact. Under these circumstances, local cadres who felt that their positions of authority gave them the right to make decisions with little regard for the views of the governed could quickly become abusive. When such abuses increased in severity, the anger of the villagers grew.

Nepotism and favoritism were the two most common targets of criticism. At first, I didn't appreciate the extent of nepotism in the village and the frustration it caused. Being an outsider largely excluded me from hearing this type of internal criticism. The need for maintaining face with a foreigner and the fear of local criticism usually silenced such expressions. But as my presence was gradually accepted (and sometimes forgotten), I came to learn more of the villagers' disappointments and, on a few occasions, open anger.

While walking to the district store one day with a young field worker, I learned for the first time of the bitterness felt by some villagers over the patronage system, which assured that many factory jobs went to kin and friends of leaders, and relatively few to other village families. The man who first told me of the problem came from a family that had yet to receive a factory assignment. A little later, I heard a similar remark from a local sent-down youth. The village household survey taken in the fall of 1979 illustrated the same pattern even more clearly. When the name of Chu Meiying, the local brigade accountant, appeared on the list drawn from the household sample, I went to see her for an interview. She had talked earlier about her forthcoming marriage to the barefoot doctor, but never about her own life.

During the interview, she spoke of how hard she had worked in the fields before becoming the brigade accountant and how the 9.4 work-point rating she received was one of the highest held by any woman in the village. Then, last year, just before Jiang Lijiang became party secretary, she had been offered the brigade accounting position and had accepted it. The new job entailed a great deal more responsibility than her work in the field, yet her 9.4 work-point income remained the same. Wondering how she felt about that, I decided to ask.

"Chu Meiying, do you like being an accountant?"

Her response was hardly what I expected.

"Well, accounting is all right, but I'm really waiting for a factory job."

Having just completed the survey for her household, I knew that her three older sisters already had permanent positions in nearby factories. As I looked down at my notes to confirm the fact, she must have perceived my thoughts.

"I know that four members of one family having factory jobs is not very common, but you see, my father was head of the brigade for many years, and he was able to help. If people have the opportunity, they always use the back door. It's even getting worse, but what can be done? Nothing. I know it's not fair, but that's the way it is."

Several days later, while weeding with the young field worker who wanted a factory job, I asked whether he thought there was any possibility of his getting one.

"No. There is too much favoritism. If you don't have the right contacts you can do nothing. It's the fault of the leaders, but even they don't know how to change the situation."

The following month, I learned of still another local villager whose brother had found him a job in the state-run chemical factory. His brother had initially arranged it and then had gotten approval from the district leadership. That meant the family would have two members with state-factory jobs. When other villagers without access to factory jobs heard about the arrangement, they complained bitterly to the brigade party secretary. Apparently, they were successful, since when the new worker showed up at the factory gates for his first day on the job, he was told that "he had arrived too late" and that "someone else had been given the position." In this instance, the district leader had saved face, but the villagers had won the day.

Interested in the conflict, I searched through my kinship data, trying to develop a coherent picture of family relations and occupation. Chu Meiying's father's name was Li Yongshan. He had been the party secretary from 1970 until 1976. In that year, he was transferred to the commune electric-power station. The leadership post was then briefly taken over by Li Guiying, the sister of another Li—Li Haiping, the retired party member who was head of the local Poor Peasant's Association and the man I had first interviewed about the early days of the village. Although Li Haiping never held a formal brigade office in Half Moon, his position in the association obviously provided him with considerable influence in the village. Old Li, it turned out, also had ties with the Wang family with whom I was living.

Further study of the household survey showed that the Li family had done very well for itself. In addition to ex-brigade head Li Yongshan's three daughters who had factory jobs, all of Li Haiping's six children were factory workers, as were most of the children of Li Guiying, the party secretary from 1976 to 1978. So too were half the members of the Wang family, in whose household I was living. Then, in 1979, Jiang Lijiang became the party secretary of Half Moon, a man without any kinship ties to either the Li or Wang families. His name was not included on the household sample, and I never did obtain a record of his family's occupational status. But his wife's family was in the sample, and neither she nor any of her relatives living close by had factory jobs.

As far as the villagers were concerned, one back door had been definitely closed. It was not yet clear how wide other doors were going to open. It was obvious, however, that though monopolizing access to scarce social or material resources by taking advantage of one's position might be moderated, this "back-doorism" would not disappear locally as long as similar practices occurred higher up in the bureaucratic structure.

Recognizing this, I decided it was a good time to take up the question with Yu Shanshan, a senior leader of Red Flag Commune. Forty-five years old, he looked far younger. More important, he had the kind of intelligence, openness, quiet energy, and relaxed manner that defined him as highly capable. From our first meeting, which had taken place while he was on an agricultural tour of the United States several months earlier, I liked him immensely. The advice he gave me at the beginning of my research made me realize that anthropological fieldwork had something in common with being a commune leader. "Talk to as many different people as you can. Cross-check what they tell you—and don't let them take you around in circles to avoid answering your questions!"

Now that I was deep into the research, I asked him for a meeting, to which he agreed. We talked of many things: the transition from peasant to worker, the party's summary views of Mao's role in the Cultural Revolution, and finally, the problems of bureaucracy. I laughingly reminded him of his remark about not letting anyone take me "around in circles," and he responded, face wrinkled in an amused smile, "You mean you have a tough question for me?"

"Yu Shanshan, how are new workers selected from the brigades for state-factory jobs?"

"We usually hire new workers once a year. A factory submits its request to the commune, which then passes it on to each division [district] for an equal share of the quota. There is a lot of back-doorism. In any case, a number is given to each division, which then divides the number among the brigades. The brigades then select the individuals. In fact, the children of cadres often get the preference. There were a lot of complaints a few years ago, but the situation is getting better. Now we have introduced a policy that families without workers get the preference. Children of retired, dead, or injured workers also receive preferential treatment."

"Why should a retired worker's child inherit his or her father's job? Is that an example of "back-doorism?"

"Many state enterprises practice this policy. It is not using the back door because it is policy. The main concern is to replace the 30 percent of the wage that the family loses when a worker retires. Hiring another family member will ease the financial burden. Especially when a worker is injured or killed in the factory, the family has a right to the job. Otherwise, people would become demoralized. This way, they remain satisfied."

"What about the criteria for selection?"

"Prospective workers must be junior or senior middle school graduates in good physical condition."

"In Half Moon, there appears to have been a good deal of behind-the-scenes maneuvering to place relatives in factory jobs."

"Back-doorism by brigade cadres cannot be solved just by supervision. It takes a great deal of cadre education. On the other hand, this village may have more people working outside than most because there is less land per capita. Also, the more people go out for jobs, the more contacts they have, and the easier it is for others in the village to find jobs there too."

Then, looking straight at me, his eyes firmly focused on mine and his voice full of feeling, he added: "Back-doorism is a general problem. The solution must start from the top. That's where the roots are. The manifestations are at the bottom."

I responded, "Perhaps the elimination of private plots, peasant markets, and the limited input of villagers into decisions like 'triple-cropping' has strengthened the centralized bureaucracy even more?"

"Perhaps. As for triple-cropping, we learned from the peasants on that one."

"And the problem of bureaucracy?"

With a grin, he concluded, "If there is only one flower blossoming, you get bureaucracy."

At the moment, I didn't fully appreciate the depth of meaning contained in that last statement. Only in the months that followed did its significance become clear.

3/Working

HOUSEHOLD ECONOMY

In Red Flag Commune, most economic activity occurred within five institutions: the family, the work team, the village brigade, the district, and the commune industries. Beyond this outer perimeter lay economic and political structures of larger scale, including the municipality, the county, the province, and the national (state) government, all having less immediate relationship to the daily lives of most residents.

Although the economic role of the family in Half Moon Village had been transformed by collective ownership of land and machines, important continuities with the past remained. Courtyard gardens were still used to grow vegetables and fruits. Chickens continued to be raised, surplus eggs being purchased by neighbors or sold at the local district store. One Half Moon family used their courtyard to produce eggs commercially, earning 400 *yuan* or more a year for their effort.

Almost every courtyard contained a family pigsty, an adobe-walled, lean-to–shaped enclosure that opened into a big pit. Here, one or more porkers savored their daily helping of corn mush mixed with scraps of food left over from the family meal. This low-protein diet extended the pigs' fattening time to a year—four or five months longer than required by the better-fed, collectively owned brigade pigs. Still, a family could add 100 or more *yuan* per pig to its annual private income by selling these animals at the district store or local market. Pigs, of course, produced more than meat, which is why they were once jokingly referred to as "little fertilizer factories," a phrase attributed to Mao. Manure mixed with dirt was periodically removed through a large hole in the exterior courtyard wall and sold to the brigade, increasing family income even more.

In each courtyard, a separate walled enclosure hid a slit trench. Here, human manure—night soil—was occasionally collected by the village "honey man." Sitting next to a holding tank on a mule-drawn cart, he made his regular rounds down Half Moon lanes. Obtaining night soil from each household, he first hauled it to a large earthen pool, where it was mixed with pig manure and allowed to ferment until ready for use as fertilizer in the brigade greenhouse. Sound public health practice precluded human manure from being spread directly on the fields. For its contribution to the collective welfare of the brigade, each household received an additional 12-*jin* ration of grain per person per year.

Of great importance to many household economies in Red Flag Commune was food grown on private plots—the total holdings equaling approximately 5 percent of

A peasant selling small eggplants on the road to the district headquarters.

each brigade's land base.[1] From this private enterprise, families could significantly increase their source of fresh vegetables for home consumption. Or, they could increase their income by selling them to the state or at a nearby peasant market. Thirty-six thousand of these so-called "free" markets were scattered throughout rural China in 1979. None were found within Red Flag Commune itself, but a large one was located along a side street in the old market town that bordered the commune headquarters.

Here, fresh vegetables, chickens, and other meat and produce were sold from the backs of carts and on blankets spread in rows along the ground. Adjacent to the household offerings of these peasant traders were wooden stalls where white-jacketed state workers sold their competing produce. Privately sold vegetables were usually fresher, but also cost more. On the other hand, chickens were looked over very carefully to make sure the buyer hadn't resolved someone else's problem of what to do with a sickly hen.

COLLECTIVE ENTERPRISE

As important as these economic efforts were to the average peasant family, income gained from the collective effort of Red Flag's 116 brigades was much more

[1]In some parts of China at this time, this percentage had grown as high as 15 percent (Domes 1982:261). However, such a great increase did not take place at Red Flag Commune.

important.[2] That is, even though opportunities for expanding privately generated income were increasing, the overall basis for determining the living standard of a given family was still more closely linked to its collective work in brigade, commune, or state-owned field and factory than to its individual entrepreneurial activity.

The most significant collective activity of the 116 brigades within Red Flag Commune was agricultural. Half Moon, for example, had 795 *mu* (130.9 acres) of irrigated fields. Crops planted at different times of the year included rice, wheat, corn, peanuts, rape (for rapeseed oil), and many vegetables, such as string beans, squash, cabbage, spinach, turnip, radish, and fennel. Because of the flatness of the land and the increased availability of large diesel tractors, a great deal of the plowing and planting was mechanized, yet cultivation was done almost entirely by hand. Rice transplanting was accomplished both by hand and by machine, the latter becoming more prevalent as brigades increased their purchasing power (which was channeled through the accumulation fund) and as the technology became more proficient.

Finally, harvesting also utilized machine and human labor. Rice harvesting was particularly difficult to mechanize because of the amount of water that had to be left in the field until just before the rice was cut. The resulting damp earth was too soft for the use of heavy machinery. Therefore, an intensive effort was required of every field worker. Using small scythes, all available villagers, young and old, middle school student and retiree, were asked to come out to the paddies, cut the rice, tie it in small bundles, and then carry the bundles to the edge of the field, where they were stacked before being removed for later threshing. Only in the harvesting of wheat, and to a lesser extent corn, was the use of commune-owned combines possible. Yet even here, there were problems limiting further mechanization.

One had to do with the nature of the two-crop system of wheat and rice under the climatic conditions of the Beijing area. One of the two busiest times of the year for agricultural workers was spring, when winter wheat was harvested and rice, vegetable, and corn crops were planted. The other especially busy season was fall, when the large rice crop was harvested and the wheat planted. Most vegetables were harvested during summer and early fall, although a few grown in greenhouses became available during winter.

The problem for mechanization concerned the speed with which both harvesting and seeding had to be accomplished. If the wheat was not planted by October 10, it would not have adequate time to mature before harvesting. However, early October might be too soon to cut the rice mechanically. Even if the water was drained early, allowing heavier equipment to run on the damp earth, the rice was still too green to

---

[2]Collective income was generated by the shared effort of a particular production unit. In Half Moon and other villages of Red Flag Commune, that unit was the brigade. In most areas of rural China, the accounting unit was the "production team," a working group of smaller size. The collective also referred to a type of ownership of the means of production, the other two types being private and state ownership. A thorough discussion of these differences and their implications is contained in a later chapter.

be accepted by the machinery without becoming snarled. So, it had to be cut by hand. If poor weather slowed down either harvesting or planting, a corresponding loss in productivity occurred.

The mechanization of wheat production was similarly limited by the two-crop system. In contrast to the United States, where harvests could be completed over several weeks, in Red Flag the wheat had to be cut much more quickly in order to plant the rice. For the commune to fully mechanize the wheat harvest required the purchase of several times the number of combines needed to harvest a similar amount of wheat over a longer period of time in the United States. But to obtain this many combines for five to ten days' use, and to have them sit idle for the rest of the year, was financially unfeasible. Therefore, the harvesting of wheat, as well as that of rice and corn, was still done partially by hand.

What happened after the rice, wheat, corn, and vegetables were harvested? Some produce was sold to the state, some distributed to the villagers, and some set aside for seed and as a reserve. The amount allocated to the state was determined by a contract negotiated between the commune and the municipality. The method used to distribute income to the brigade members entailed a choice between two alternatives.

One was the work-point system, used by Half Moon villagers, in which an individual earned up to 10 work points per day. The total number of points earned per year was then used to calculate what portion of the distributable income would be received by that individual. The other alternative was the piece-work system. Under this arrangement, values were assigned to given tasks, and individuals received their share of the income based on the specific work accomplished. In East

Distributing grain at harvest time.

Gate, a large and well-known brigade in Red Flag, the villagers decided several years ago to use the piece-work method of distribution. Once the value of the given task was determined to everyone's satisfaction, the accounting process was direct and simple.

The work-point system was a little more complicated. Once a year in Half Moon, and sometimes twice in other villages that used this system, the brigade held a mass meeting for all field workers. At this meeting, the workers appraised their own worth as defined by the number of work points they thought they should receive, based on a scale from 1 to 10. Other field workers at the meeting then discussed the appraisal, sometimes suggesting that the amount be raised or lowered. It was possible to receive 9 points one year and 7 or 8 the next if the individual was considered to be less productive because of either age or laziness. In most group discussions, however, work point evaluations were increased rather than decreased, since the Chinese value of modesty required a self-appraisal lower than what was generally recognized as the person's true worth. By contrast, those few who tried to overrate themselves were soon informed of their misguided self-perception. Of course, as Mother Wang informed Zhou Xing and me following the December meeting of brigade field workers, the village leaders did review individual work-point ratings and made changes when they thought it necessary.

Why didn't Half Moon villagers use the piece-work method? They found that when distribution was determined by work completed—such as the cutting of a small rice paddy—the field workers were more likely to quit for the day at the conclusion of the particular task. On the other hand, when they were paid according to the number of hours spent in the field, they worked longer. After reflecting on the advantages and disadvantages of the two systems, they decided that the work-point method was best for them. Once that decision was made, they still faced the problem of what to do when brigade members showed up late, especially during the busy harvest season. In an effort to resolve that issue, the villagers decided that anyone not working at harvest time without an acceptable excuse would be penalized three days' work points—one for the specific day missed, plus two additional ones.

In the late 1970s, Half Moon villagers explored several other variations on this theme. Until 1978, they had followed the usual arrangement of receiving up to 10 points a day. But the following year, they experimented with a new policy in which work from December through February was awarded a maximum of 6 points; March through April, 10 points; June through August (the busiest season), 14 points; and the rest of the year, 10 points.

Whatever the specific arrangement used for distribution, all brigade members in each village in the commune met twice a year to divide up the income derived from their collective work. This included a certain amount of cash received from the sale of agricultural and sideline industry products to the state, as well as "in kind" income—including grain, vegetables, and additional foods produced by the peasants themselves. The income was shared with other work-point earners, including health clinic personnel and day-care workers, who provided important human services for the community, and with the temporary contract workers mentioned previously.

A far smaller collective activity of Half Moon Village was the development of its modest sideline industries: a barrel-washing enterprise that cleaned 50-gallon diesel drums for later reuse and a chemical-mixing operation. When fully operative, these utilized the labor of 12 villagers. Between contracts, these sideline workers joined other brigade members in the fields. Additional collective income was generated from two brigade-run farms, which raised 450 pigs and 150 chickens at a time. (The local pig farm was especially popular, since it provided the villagers with healthy piglets at low cost, which were then fattened and sold for additional private household income.) In addition, the brigade had a small reforestation enterprise that brought in a little income, and it rented out the village truck for local transport.

Another collective activity of importance to the village was the contracting of local residents to work on commune construction crews, on water conservation projects, or as temporary factory workers in commune- and state-level enterprises. In 1979, 23 men and women from Half Moon held jobs as contract workers, an arrangement that was particularly beneficial to the brigade. That is, wages earned by these temporary employees came directly to the brigade, which continued to pay the contract worker his or her previous income. Since commune and state wages were always higher, and in the latter case sometimes even double that of local income, the brigade always benefited—a point that Party Secretary Jiang Lijiang reminded the villagers of in his December meeting with them. Of course, the brigade had to continue to provide these temporarily relocated village workers with their share of the collectively owned grain, vegetables, and other homegrown produce. As for the contract workers themselves, they could at least hope that a temporary job might lead to a more permanent one—though the prospects for such a move were minimal.[3]

In Half Moon, the total income from the brigade's collective production for the year 1978 was 226,000 *yuan*. Of this amount, approximately 58 percent came from agriculture—including the sale of grain and vegetables to Beijing Municipality for its urban residents. To encourage higher production, the municipality initially set a low production quota in its contracts with brigades. Agricultural goods sold to the city above that quota brought a 50 percent higher payment, an obvious incentive to produce more. Another 5 percent was earned by the brigade from its sale of pigs and chickens. Nonagricultural collective activities, including sideline production, the loaning out of contract workers to the commune and state, and other miscellaneous efforts, brought in another 37 percent. The year's total income of 226,000 *yuan* was an impressive increase from the 90,000 *yuan* that was their total a decade earlier.

As for the brigade expenses, from their income of 226,000 *yuan* they subtracted approximately 48 percent for production costs (not including payment for labor), almost 11 percent for the accumulation fund, 3 percent for all taxes, and a little over 1 percent for the welfare fund. The accumulation fund was used for capital improvements, such as agricultural machinery and the construction of the new bathhouse. In 1980, the village planned to buy a rice transplanter with its annual earnings. The state agricultural tax was a fixed amount (a specified number of *jin* of

[3]The difficulty in obtaining a permanent state position was greatly magnified by having to change one's category of "residence," a problem with many complexities, as will be seen shortly.

grain) rather than a percentage. Therefore, as the brigade produced more, the proportion of tax paid to the state decreased. In 1978, the tax came to 2.6 percent of the total income.[4] The welfare fund used its annual allotment for programs of community benefit, such as child and health care. If there were childless elderly people in the village with little or no income, this fund was used to assist them as well.

The remaining 85,390 *yuan,* or almost 38 percent of the total income, was then distributed to the brigade members in cash, grain, and vegetables. The grain was allocated so that each member received 450 *jin,* which was more than adequate for an average adult diet. (Some was used for fodder.) Those field workers with a work-point rating of 10 received a little more. In 1978, the value of each 10–work-point day came to 1.3 *yuan,* or about 35 *yuan* per month maximum income from the collective. The following year, when the state increased its purchase price of many agricultural products by 25 percent, the brigade income increased proportionately.

By 1979, the average Half Moon brigade member employed in the collective sphere had an annual income of a little over 400 *yuan,* including that derived from noncollective household enterprises. Although this income was more than adequate to purchase all the necessities of life and some of the luxuries, including the "four jewels"—bicycle, wristwatch, radio, and sewing machine—it was considerably less than the average annual income (720 *yuan*) earned by most state-factory workers of comparable age. To become a factory worker was the goal of almost all village young people at that time. Why this was the case is not difficult to understand.

FROM FIELD TO FACTORY

Most young people began their working lives in the fields, assigned that position by the local brigade production committee. Some preferred to find a job in Beijing but were restricted from doing so by a 1954 government policy that effectively limited anyone from moving away from an established residence and workplace unit *(danwei)* without official approval. By means of this legislation, the Chinese government effectively resolved one of the most pressing problems facing Third World countries—the migration of large numbers of peasants from their own villages into overcrowded urban slums in their search for largely nonexistent jobs. Needless to say, the government did so at the expense of an unprecedented restriction in freedom of movement.

Of course, various efforts could be undertaken to obtain a city job. But such a move seldom brought success. To be an unemployed peasant youth living off one's parents was practically unheard of, and to find work elsewhere was almost impossible. Thus, rural young people accepted the work to which they were assigned. Still, in the back of their minds was the realization that one's first assignment could also be one's last. In the forefront was the commonly accepted belief that "It is far better

---

[4]Except in the case of a few people with very high incomes, there was no individual income tax in China. However, licenses were required to run brigade sideline industries.

to be a worker than a peasant." What were the prospects that a commune youth could get a factory job?

In Half Moon, one of the most likely places to obtain such a position was in the two-year-old jade-carving factory owned by the district. Located a few minutes' bicycle ride from the village, it was housed in the district auditorium, to be vacated when a new factory building was completed a few years later. Inside, row upon row of tables provided work space for many of the 370 employees, 90 percent of whom lived in the villages contained within the district. These workers spent each day grinding and polishing small jade figurines, which when finished were sold to the state export bureau for amounts ranging from several *yuan* to 400 or more.

Several years of negotiation between the district and the Beijing Municipal bureaucracy had eventually led to the formation of this enterprise.[5] Once the district had obtained the necessary used motors, belts, and grinding and polishing machines from the city jade-carving factory, it had hired a retired master craftsman to train the local workers. These new employees were almost all recent junior middle school graduates, recommended to the factory by the teachers from the district middle

Working at the district jade factory.

[5]The effort required to establish this small factory illustrates rather well the immensity of the Chinese bureaucracy. Before setting up the factory, the district leaders had had to obtain formal approval from the following government organizations: the Commune Economic Planning Committee; the County Committee in charge of Commune Affairs; the Beijing Municipal Export Bureau responsible for overseas sales; the Beijing Municipal Planning Committee (the highest authority); and the Industries Bureau. After each had granted its approval of the application, the district was allowed to contact the factory to obtain the needed equipment. Of course, it had already informally contacted the factory long before to make sure that it was willing to lease and later sell its old surplus machinery.

school. Criteria for selection included level of educational competence and ability in drawing, painting, and "completing meticulous tasks with care."

The basic monthly wage of these workers ranged from 33 to 41 *yuan,* with the average just under 40 *yuan.* In addition, all the jade-factory workers were eligible to receive a bonus of up to 10 *yuan* a month if the factory exceeded its state quota. As with the brigade agricultural contract, the initial goal was purposely set at a low figure, enabling factory workers to easily exceed it. Section leaders in charge of particular workshops earned incomes that were little different from those of regular workers, 41 *yuan* a month, plus a bonus that was based on the average output of the workers in their shops. The factory manager received a monthly income of 44 *yuan* and a comparable bonus based on the average output of all 370 workers.

A totally different kind of operation was the Red Flag chemical factory, a large state-owned and commune-run enterprise covering 40 acres and employing 810 workers, slightly less than half of whom were women. Several of these employees came from Half Moon. Originally set up in 1958, at the beginning of the Great Leap Forward, with 10 new workers and one old horse stable, the factory eventually became a highly modern enterprise, turning phosphorus ore into chemicals including formic acid, phosphate fertilizer (which was sold to the commune), and ash for cement. Its annual output of chemicals was valued at over 15 million *yuan,* 3.95 million of which constituted the annual profit for the factory. Before 1980, all profit was turned over to the state treasury. Shortly thereafter, with a change in government policy, the factory kept 30 percent to use for capital improvements, bonuses, and facilities for the general welfare of the factory personnel, including a canteen, dormitories, a nursery, and a clinic staffed with six doctors. Many of the younger unmarried workers, including several from Half Moon, lived in the large men's dormitory during the week, returning home on Sundays or for holidays. Workers' monthly incomes in this state-owned factory ranged from 30 to 80 *yuan,* with an average of approximately 45 *yuan.*

An additional 12 *yuan* in monthly bonuses was earned by most of the work force. Five criteria had been established for these bonuses: individual level of output, quality of work, avoidance of waste, cost efficiency, and attention to safety. In addition, three important attitudes were a part of every worker's evaluation: labor attitude (approach to work), political attitude (political knowledge), and communist spirit (willingness to help others). These "five criteria and three attitudes" were first decided on by the employees at a six-day-long Worker's Congress held at the chemical factory in 1978 and afterward served as the fundamental guidelines for determining bonus eligibility. Such decisions were made collectively in face-to-face work-group meetings, not unlike similar discussions held in village brigades that utilized the work-point system.

Although Half Moon had only a few regular (state) employees in this chemical factory, another 20 had been hired a year earlier as contract workers. Under this arrangement, the brigade received 75 *yuan* a month from the factory for each worker and paid approximately 35 *yuan* of this to the contract worker as a wage. The other 40 *yuan* remained in the brigade's collective treasury. Each year, the brigade committee determined the amount of wage to be given to the contract worker based on the average income of the other brigade members. For the year in question, the brigade average was 35 *yuan*. By such means, the brigade resolved potential conflicts generated by some brigade members receiving much higher wages than others. Furthermore, the brigade benefited financially. All in all, it was quite a successful arrangement for both factory and brigade.

Several other factories in Red Flag Commune also employed Half Moon residents. One, a state-owned grain-processing mill that had recently undergone a large expansion, was situated about ten miles away. Liu Ming, a young villager in his mid-20s, climbed on his bicycle at seven in the morning and arrived 45 minutes later at the factory . While maintaining a room at home, he also had free housing in the factory dormitory. As a permanent state worker receiving a regular wage of 50 *yuan* a month, he had numerous other benefits as well, including free health care, access to technical courses offered by the factory, participation in the local trade union, and a generous pension on retirement. However, he was no longer formally designated a brigade resident, which meant that he no longer received grain or other rations from the village; and if he joined the CYL or the party, his affiliation would be through the factory.

Between the temporary contract worker and the permanent state worker lay one other important category of factory employees—the "commune-member-workers." Half Moon had over 100 such workers. So did many other villages in Red Flag. These men and women were employed by the state sector of the commune rather than the brigade, and received benefits similar to those of other state workers. One such enterprise was a small electrical-parts plant, located at the same district headquarters as the jade factory. It had 465 workers, 80 percent of whom were women. However, these workers, instead of receiving factory coupons enabling them to purchase grain and other commodities from state stores as did other state employees, continued to receive their ration "in kind" from the brigade.

Why this special arrangement? Why not just allow brigade workers to become state workers? Basically, the answer had to do with the question of residency referred to earlier. At birth, one was given a particular residency status *(hukou)*. The designation, urban or rural, followed that of the mother. Rural residents were not usually eligible for employment in the state sector. They could not place their children in the higher-quality urban schools or gain other benefits commonly associated with urban residency, for example, a coupon enabling the individual to purchase a television set. Because of the 1954 residency policy, Half Moon and other peasants were restricted to their present environment, and cities were spared the problem of a massive influx of unemployed rural residents.

To resolve potential conflicts generated by different income levels among brigade, state, and commune workers, the state, through the commune-run factory, paid the brigade 120 *yuan* a year for each commune-member-worker it hired. The brigade then used those funds to provide the grain ration for the worker, who was technically no longer a member of the brigade. By this means, the state was relieved of the responsibility of providing grain coupons (and thereby the guarantee of food grain) to its newly hired workers. Complicated? Yes. But it was also effective in enabling the state sector of the commune to deploy its financial resources in a manner that heightened its industrial development without having to drain off capital to provide a guarantee of grain for its workers.

As noted earlier, with many of its residents working either temporarily or permanently outside the village, Half Moon had done little to develop the nonagricultural potential of the village. In 1979, it did not even have a sideline industry with full-time employees; neither the barrel-washing nor the chemical-mixing sideline enterprise had been able to obtain enough contracts with Beijing factories to keep their minuscule work forces active. Nevertheless, other villages within the commune had a different history, where the working population was not so scattered and where the people had established active local industries with little help from the outside. One such village, Little River, was only a 15-minute walk away from Half Moon.

DIFFERENCES BETWEEN VILLAGES

On arriving at Little River, one immediately noticed its antiquated dwellings, well-worn pockmarked courtyard walls, the poorer dress of the inhabitants, and other attributes that suggested it was considerably less prosperous than Half Moon. An initial exploration of the village also pointed up another difference. Painted on the adobe walls of narrow village lanes were faded but still visible slogans from the Cultural Revolution, such as "Learn from Dazhai," "Politics Is the Life Line of All Work," "Heighten Vigilance, Defend the Motherland," and "Prepare for Wars and for Natural Disasters in the Interests of the People." It did not take long to realize that the village Little River was quite different from the cleaner and more orderly and affluent-looking community of Half Moon. And Little River seldom saw a foreign face.

Yet the village leaders, all of whom were a great deal younger than any I had met elsewhere, were nevertheless pleased to share their experience and knowledge with me. After several meetings with the party secretary, the brigade head, a production vice chairman, and the brigade accountant, a fascinating portrayal of creative local-level planning began to unfold. I soon found that the leaders of Little River were far more ingenious than one might guess from a superficial inquiry.

The village was larger than Half Moon, with a little over 800 residents. More than 75 percent were brigade workers in either agriculture or sideline production. Also, the total amount of cultivated acreage available to the brigade was approximately 20 percent less than that at Half Moon. With less land and more people, the residents of Little River were limited in what they could extract from the soil. Therefore, it was without surprise that I learned their income level was also lower than that of Half Moon. In Little River, the average value of a 10-point day was .77 yuan, a striking difference from Half Moon's 1.3 yuan.

However, on further investigation, it became clear that the initial comparison of differential collective income between the two villages was meaningless, for Little River's figure of .77 yuan was not based on the real level of productivity of the 10-point field worker, as first surmised. Rather, it was a purposely deflated figure reflecting the decision of the village members in 1973 to cut their annual income in order to generate additional capital to develop new sideline industries. Realizing that they had less land than surrounding brigades, they decided to channel their

Two leaders from Little River.

surplus labor into a local sideline industry. Since the government's emphasis on self-reliance precluded any significant state support by either grants or loans, capital to start up the industry had to come from themselves. A decision was then made to reduce the 10-point day from the approximately 1 *yuan* the village had previously received to .77 *yuan*. With this newly generated capital, the brigade established its first sideline industry in 1973—a small jade-carving factory. Employing 33 people, it produced figurines for sale to the state in much the same manner as the larger district-level jade factory located nearby. This effort brought a several-thousand-*yuan* profit each year to the village, but it wasn't enough. So the villagers continued to set aside part of their work-point earnings for capital while their leaders looked for another opportunity.

Although it took several years, the brigade finally negotiated a contract with a Beijing factory in 1978 to make low-wattage fluorescent light bulbs of the kind commonly used in rural homes. The necessary machinery to produce such bulbs required an outlay of 60,000 *yuan*. By continuing their process of reducing individual incomes through lowering the value of the work point, selling their brigade tractor, and bypassing the usual annual contribution to their community welfare fund, the village members amassed sufficient funds to purchase the needed machinery and to start up their second sideline. Thus, Little River peasant-farmers, working collectively in field and sideline, had a lower standard of living than their counterparts in Half Moon Village, but the potential for catching up and perhaps even surpassing their near neighbors was considerable. As the brigade leaders said proudly at our last meeting together, "And we didn't even have to ask for financial assistance from the commune."

Little River, at the lower end of the brigade income scale vis-à-vis Half Moon, could be compared with East Gate Village, at the higher end. East Gate, located 20 miles from Half Moon at the eastern border of the commune, was one of Red Flag's wealthiest villages. For the 873 residents living in 170 households (in 1979), the value of their 10-work-point day was 2.1 *yuan,* much higher than the 1.3 figure for Half Moon. Although East Gate had slightly more land per capita than Half Moon, that was not the chief reason for the difference. Actually, before 1972, East Gate had been poorer than most of the other villages in the commune, including Half Moon. What brought greater wealth to East Gate in such a short number of years? The answer lay with the development of their sideline industries.

In 1972, the brigade had only 120 *yuan* in its welfare fund and three needy families to support. It had sufficient problems in growing grain to feed its population that it was unable to contribute any income to its accumulation fund to be used for capital expenditures. Instead, over the years, the village had amassed a debt to the state of over 70,000 *yuan.* There was inadequate money to regularly insure the purchase of electricity to run the pumps for irrigation and for lighting homes. The houses, made of mud and straw, were poor in quality.

That year, the commune loaned the village 18,000 *yuan* for the development of its sideline industries.[6] The brigade leaders then organized 40 peasants into a construction team, which offered its services in building houses for surrounding villages. This activity brought in 3,000 *yuan* the first year. Shortly thereafter, a contract was obtained to make cardboard. Eventually, the villagers were able to clear their debt to the state and contribute more adequately to their welfare and accumulation funds. With this money, they purchased some agricultural machinery, which enabled them to become self-sufficient in grain production.

Finally, the enterprising leader of East Gate obtained from a Beijing factory an old wire-extruder machine, which reduced the thickness of copper wire to various standard sizes. Through negotiation with the state, the village then arranged a contract that enabled the sideline to significantly increase the collective worth of the village—so much so that the inhabitants began receiving almost half of their income from a sideline industry that employed a very small percentage of its workers.

With this profit, East Gate Village purchased more farm machinery, thereby

---

[6]Throughout the 1970s, the policy at Red Flag Commune was to utilize profits from its successful enterprises to assist in the economic development of its poorer brigades. The commune also had a bureau that assisted these brigades in setting up and finding an outlet for small light-industry sidelines. Of course, brigades with "connections" *(guanxi)* could develop their own sideline industries as well.

freeing additional peasants from work in the fields. By 1979, the brigade had four large tractors of their own, eight walking tractors, three trucks, and a jeep. All rice planting was done by machine. As a result, out of the total of those villagers working in the collective sphere, a little less than a third (between 80 and 100) were still employed in agriculture, whereas the other two-thirds were setting up new sidelines and expanding their educational and social-service programs, including day care, kindergarten, and primary school. Indeed, the recent success of this brigade in raising its standard of living through sideline development was enough to raise a question in the minds of other nearby villagers: Why spend so much time and energy in agricultural field work?

Such questions could send shock waves through the government offices responsible for maintaining and expanding agricultural production. If sideline industries, a vital adjunct to agricultural production in raising the peasant standard of living, replaced food production as the primary economic activity, the resulting loss in available grain and other food staples could create a crisis of massive proportions. It was for this reason that the government set up a minimum production quota that all villages were expected to meet. And as mentioned previously, any sale of grain and vegetables to the state above that quota assured the villagers a large bonus.

In summary, even a brief comparison of these three villages in Red Flag Commune illustrates quite clearly the alternatives available to local leaders as they undertook to develop the economic potential of their brigades. It should also be obvious that such decisions could limit the differing strategies that brigade leaders might wish to utilize in the future. That is, if many villagers were already employed in commune- and state-level enterprises (as was the case in Half Moon), these peasants were no longer available to help in the development of local, collectively organized sideline industries. For Half Moon, the issue was not just that they had practically no sideline industry—a point of self-criticism among the leaders—but also that almost no one was available to develop this aspect of the village economy. At Little River and East Gate, a different situation prevailed. Although Little River was poorer than Half Moon and East Gate was more prosperous, both had derived a greater amount of their annual income from collective sidelines organized by the local brigade.

Evaluations of the merits of these different approaches to raising the standard of living of China's rural villages were a point of active debate throughout the country at this time.[7] Each tried to take into account that different local conditions promoted different solutions and, by implication, that no one strategy should be followed by everyone. This was a significant departure from the days of the Cultural Revolution, when the Dazhai Brigade served as the unitary model of rural development for all of China—emphasizing agricultural grain production over sideline industries and trade.[8] Now that China's approach to economic development was moving in a dif-

[7]Another alternative, the "responsibility system," will be taken up in a later chapter.

[8]The Dazhai Brigade, a small settlement in Shanxi Province, first became a national model in 1964 after it had, through immense effort, transformed the village's badly eroded loess soil into highly productive terraced fields. The brigade was also noted for emphasizing the collective interest over individual self-interest. Chen Yonggui, the brigade party secretary, eventually rose to become a vice premier of the country and a politburo member of the party before losing his position of importance following Mao's death and the change in leadership and political direction.

ferent direction, the Dazhai model was the target of considerable criticism (see Tsou, Blecher, and Meisner 1982). Nevertheless, in economically advanced Red Flag Commune, many leaders continued to advocate the collective approach as the key ingredient in the modernization process.

RESOLVING CONFLICTS

As important as it was to analyze village-level economics, such a study sometimes played down the human element—those who actually did the work. Anthropologists, broadly concerned with the lives of the people they are trying to understand, often spend time in the workplace—whether it be in the agricultural field, the factory, or elsewhere. Immediately on arrival in Half Moon, I made arrangements to spend six or more hours each week working in the fields with the villagers. As the research progressed, however, this plan appeared less and less practical. In some weeks, only two or three hours were devoted to such work. Admittedly, my minimal participation didn't bother the villagers in the slightest. Indeed, on more than one occasion they amusedly suggested that I was spending too much time in the fields.

One day in particular, Ma Haimen, the brigade vice director, strolled over to where I was thinning spinach and, after watching me for a few minutes, offered the comment: "You must be tired. Why don't you stop now." Since Ma knew that I had been there for only a short time, he was clearly aware that I couldn't be tired. Obviously something else was on his mind. Comments offered out of context carry hidden meanings, often of a critical nature. But if that was so, what was he criticizing?

"Ma Haimen. How can I be tired? I just arrived a few minutes ago."

Squatting down beside me, Ma began pulling small green shoots out of the ground, leaving the healthiest-looking spinach to grow.

"Look," he said, answering my question in a highly indirect manner. "See how I do it. It's not hard. But you should be careful not to take too much of the plant out at the same time."

With that remark, several nearby field workers burst out laughing. Ma, now smiling as well, pointed to the extremely sparse row of green shoots behind me and then at the much thicker rows of the other workers. "Look behind you. Most of us are thinning the spinach, but you appear to be harvesting it." At that point, I joined in the laughter, promising to be more careful in the future.

Several weeks later, while I was helping one of the men's work teams harvest corn, another conflict occurred. But this time it was not resolved through the use of humor. Since it was harvest season, everyone was working hard. That morning, over the loudspeaker, Jiang Lijiang had encouraged state workers with the day off, middle school students, and others to spend part of the day helping in the fields. There was no question in my mind that those "others" he was referring to should include me.

Finishing a quick breakfast with the Wang family a little before seven, I headed down the dirt lane toward the main road. At one end of the village, members of the young women's work team were beginning to congregate. A few were bending over, sharpening wooden-handled scythes with a file, while others chatted informally. Su Xiulan, the team leader, was talking with Cui Huifang, the head of the older women's work group, probably coordinating team assignments for the day. Su, a robust and active woman in her late 20s, looked tired this morning, which was not surprising given the long evenings she and her family had spent in the past week laying adobe-and-brick walls for their new house.

At the other end of the village, on the road leading to the district store, the 45 members of the young men's work team had also gathered. Ma Haimen, standing with several of the men, laughed at a joke being told to him by another peasant. Others, dark jackets set off by light blue baggy pants, simply lounged against an adobe wall while watching a "granny" push a tandem baby carriage toward the day-care nursery around the corner.

"Hey, Granny. You have to work today too, huh?" one of them teasingly shouted as she passed by.

"More than you," she responded, drawing an amused grin from the lips of the earlier speaker.

"Ah, old woman, life is hard, all right. But at least you have grandchildren to take care of, and that will keep you out of trouble."

At seven, the tempo quickened. Crossing an irrigation ditch to a nearby field, Su Xiulan's small group moved efficiently down the rows, cutting stalks of corn at their base with long-handled scythes. Cui's larger group followed the same pattern in the next field. I joined the men as they picked up their tools and headed toward the back side of the village, out of sight of the women's teams. Approaching our work site, we saw two peasants from another work team holding metal-tipped wooden poles attached by string, measuring off straight lines as row markers for the next planting. The soil in the field was soft and easy to work, having just been plowed. At our location, several horse-drawn carts had already arrived, drivers dumping their loads of manure into small squares marked with string. As one cart followed another, the men quickly spread the fertilizer in one square, then moved 20 feet down the field and began again. Looking unsuccessfully for a shovel, I soon realized that spreading manure was not to be my task. Instead, I was asked to join a smaller group of older men clearing an adjacent field of precut cornstalks—obviously an assignment the team leader felt I could do fairly well!

But life on the other side of the village was not so harmonious. I learned about it late that afternoon from Zhang Dashen, an older woman field worker and a neighbor of the Wangs. It seemed that Su Xiulan, the young women's work-team leader, had been criticized by Jiang Lijiang for her team's slowness in harvesting a cornfield. Because the stalks had not been promptly cleared after cutting, the young men's team had had to remain idle for an hour before they could begin fertilizing. The party secretary had just happened to pass by at that moment. In his remarks to Su, Jiang referred to Cui Huifang's older women's team and how they had been able to clear the adjoining field, of comparable size, in a shorter time. "Why is it," he had apparently asked, "that an older group of women can accomplish more than a younger group?"

With that remark, Su exploded: "I don't want to be a leader and take all this grief. I try to do my best. If you don't think I'm qualified to be a leader, I'll be glad to quit."

During this exchange, Su continued her work, bending over, cutting the corn-stalks, and then hurling them to the ground. In this manner, she kept from confronting Jiang directly. The other women too went on harvesting the corn, although they listened to every word. Soon, Cui Huifang came over from the adjoining field and, on learning the nature of the argument, turned to the party secretary.

"Secretary Jiang, Su is a good team leader. She is working just as hard, if not harder, than anyone else in the team. And furthermore, there are more women in my team than in hers. How could they finish before my group?"

According to Zhang Dashen, the woman telling the story, Jiang, Su, and Cui continued down the field during the argument, with Su cutting cornstalks and then throwing them down—"getting her anger out," was the way Zhang later described it. Then, Cui turned to Su and spoke very quietly: "Su, we're all here for the same purpose. Let's go back to work." Su didn't say anything at the moment, but soon went over to other members of her team and began helping them. Jiang and Cui also turned away, and the argument was considered over.

In summing up the event, Zhang Dashen said: "Everyone knows that Su is tired. She spends almost every evening with her family working on her new house. But she has energy for the daytime too. She's strong, and the women like her. That's why she was elected to head up the work team. Actually, Ma Haimen was the one who gave out the quota assignment for the two groups. He knew that the younger team had fewer workers and therefore needed more time to complete their share of the work. But he wasn't around when Jiang showed up."

Several important insights were contained in this brief portrayal of a simple village conflict. First, the peasant workers stayed apart from the argument between the leaders—even when it involved their own team representative. Instead of stopping work to observe the conflict, they kept right on cutting corn. Such a response was typical of Red Flag's peasants. It was not primarily because of Jiang's presence, although given the nature of his criticism of Su Xiulan, such a factor had to be taken into account. Rather, the heart of the response was cultural, reflecting an important separation between public and private spheres of activity. Arguments were considered private, even when they occurred in public. Since they were private, the public response was to pretend they didn't happen. So too, Su refrained from confronting Jiang directly, preferring to continue working even though she was very angry. "That is the typical Chinese way," reflected Zhang Dashen in recounting the event.

Still, this cultural pattern was under attack by villagers imbued with the spirit of changing the world rather than adapting to it. Workers, especially, largely freed by new and secure factory jobs from traditional economic and social obligations that linked family and village together, were the ones most likely to challenge these old customs. And such individuals were not necessarily young.

Ke Liming, an older worker in a nearby furniture factory, once became involved in a sharp argument with his team leader over the quality of wood to be used in building wardrobes. He noticed that the leader regularly used high-quality four-by-eight-foot sheets of veneer in the interior construction. Although such use enabled him to work more quickly and easily, it was also highly expensive. From Ke's point of view, it was far better to use smaller, leftover pieces of veneer for the unseen inner portions. One day he took up the issue with the team leader, telling him he thought it was wasteful and wrong. The leader, who was angry and perhaps a little defensive, said to him, "Don't be like a dog trying to catch mice" (that is, stay out of other people's business and mind your own).

Ke shot back, "Cats catch mice, not dogs" (that is, it is my business).

At this moment, a young woman Communist Youth League member came over to where they were standing and defended her friend, the team leader. Ke, his voice rising in anger, shouted back, "How can you be a member of the Communist Youth League when you are so backward?"

Her response was, "Well, you're too old to join."

Following this remark, Ke and the team leader began pushing and punching at one another until they had to be pulled apart by other workers. Finally, the head of the whole workshop came over and asked what was happening. After learning about the argument, he had everyone sit down right on the factory floor and discuss it. Soon, Ke's fellow workers offered their support to him and, by implication, criticized the team leader and the CYL member. Ke's final remark about the episode was: "The team leader was wrong and so was the woman. But she was also selfish."

Selected cases of how particular individuals and small groups approach differences with their leaders help illustrate the nature of conflict and efforts at its resolution. But illustrations of larger scale help even more. One well-known historical example took place in 1958. At the beginning of the Great Leap Forward, differences arose over what strategy to take in developing the countryside. Red Flag Commune, located near the dominant seat of power in Beijing, soon became a testing ground for some of the more radical theories of several national party leaders. Specifically, the commune leadership was asked to eliminate as much private ownership as possible. Banners and slogans proclaiming "Public Ownership for Everyone" were put up. Peasants in Half Moon and nearby villages were urged to turn in their chickens, pigs, grain, vegetables, and other produce to a common pool from which any household could take what it needed. Dining halls were set up in several large villages, and families were encouraged to eat there rather than in their homes.

While receiving initial support from a few of the more romantically inclined, the communist dream of "one for all and all for one" quickly faded. Dining halls were immediately rejected by peasant families as unappealing and impractical. The idea of taking what was needed in the way of food, coal for fuel, and other goods had a certain appeal, but shortages appeared quickly. And finally, tensions began to develop between those who worked hard for the collective welfare and those who either worked hard for themselves or hardly worked at all. Within a few months, the experiment at Red Flag collapsed, those leaders backing the plan were discredited, and the villagers were angered at having been pressured to participate in such a foolish scheme. Old Li Haiping, the Half Moon peasant activist of the early 1950s, put it succinctly: "In those days, we had no experience in dealing with the 'communist wind.' Now we know better."

A second historical example of conflict between the leaders and the people occurred with the collectivization of private plots. Individually farmed plots were first made available to peasant households in Red Flag in 1962, reflecting a shift away from the collective emphasis of the Great Leap. In Half Moon, the size of family plots was calculated at .15 *mu* per person. At that time, the village population was 360, so the total area set aside for these plots was 54 *mu*. This land was cultivated by individual families until the political storm of the mid-1960s swept over the country and villagers were pressured to collectivize their private plots. In 1969, when a new constitution was drafted, Mao insisted on preserving private plots, and they were decollectivized. But in 1972, they were again recollectivized.

From 1972 on, private plots in Half Moon Village remained collectivized. Actually, given the government's reemphasis on expanding private plots, Half Moon's decision to continue its local collectivization was perhaps somewhat surprising. But most significant was not the choice, but the fact that they were able to make it. All previous steps at collectivization of private plots had been taken with little discussion by and participation of the villagers. During the Cultural Revolution particularly, peasants criticizing collectivization were labeled "capitalist-roaders" and threatened with sundry penalties, including economic sanctions and physical punishment. When the government again supported an expansion of private plots, it is noteworthy that villages like Half Moon that wanted to continue collectivizing could do so—even though local party cadres had made it clear publicly that such a decision did not have their active support.

Illustrations such as these provide valuable insights into the relations between local leaders and the people they represented. But the portrayals cover only a very small canvas. The larger picture was considerably more complex. One important point not always given sufficient attention was that most of these leaders had grown up in the immediate area and therefore had close relations with other residents. Emotionally linked to the village through kin and friendship ties, and economically linked through the work-point system, the leaders, through their perceptions and actions, reflected at least in part the needs of those they were trying to serve. And it should be noted in conclusion that some leaders in Half Moon Village and Red Flag Commune were exemplary in this regard.

4/Growing Up

BIRTH

Wang Zhenlan was going to have a baby. After she found out she was pregnant and told her husband, Yu Xiake, a heightened sense of expectation entered the household. She noticed it immediately.

"Are you feeling all right today, Zhenlan?" her mother-in-law frequently asked. Previously, such solicitous concern for her welfare had never been expressed by either her mother-in-law or any other member of the household. Xiao Yu too not only observed her behavior more closely, but also assumed an active role in carrying out various household chores. Of course, Zhenlan continued her daily trek to the brigade fields with the other young women. However, as she grew larger, her work-team leader began assigning her lighter tasks. Although she brushed off such special attention as unnecessary, her teammates regularly took on the heavier work. Some suggested that she remain at home until after the birth of her child, but she preferred to continue as long as possible. Many village women did.

Shortly after learning of her pregnancy, Wang Zhenlan checked in with the village clinic for a prenatal examination. The three barefoot doctors were hardly surprised, since she had not sought any advice about birth control during the first year of her marriage. Once, Ma Xinxian, the older of the two women "doctors," had stopped by Zhenlan's house to inquire whether she might be interested in such information. Zhenlan declined, feeling a little embarrassed to even discuss such matters. Nor did Ma make any attempt to follow up on her original query. But such endeavors commonly were made after the birth of the first child, not before. Concluding the examination, Ma gave her approval, saying that Zhenlan was healthy and that she foresaw no difficulties ahead.

"You should drop in on Dong Shufang sometime, just to let her know," added Ma as Zhenlan stepped out the clinic door.

"I will," responded the quickly receding figure.

Dong Shufang, a fifty-three-year-old widow, had been the brigade midwife for quite a while. She had arrived in Half Moon Village 30 years previously from Jian County in Hebei Province, following an arranged marriage with a local resident. In 1966, at the beginning of the Cultural Revolution, the village women had been asked by the Women's Federation to choose a new brigade midwife. Much to Dong's surprise and pleasure, they had selected her. Qualities that led to her selection included a willingness to help others, a warm personality, cleanliness, few family responsibilities at home, and a mature age—between 40 and 50. After an all-too-brief three-week training internship at the nearby commune hospital, Dong had begun her new practice. She did, however, return to the hospital each year for additional upgrading of her skills.

Since that time, Dong Shufang had delivered almost all the babies in Half Moon. Mostly, she worked in the fields with the other women. Nevertheless, she was on call 24 hours a day and was even available to neighboring villages when needed. For her efforts she received an income based on the brigade's collective work-point system—in Dong's case, a rating of eight points. Parents of a newborn child often gave her a little present, such as a piece of cloth or some food. If she had lived in the city, she might have been offered a small amount of money, but in the village, any money received by the midwife would have to be turned over to the brigade accumulation fund. So at Half Moon, all gifts were nonmonetary in nature.

Young Zhenlan was not the only one preparing for the coming event. As Zhenlan grew in size, her mother-in-law, the expectant grandmother, began making some clothes so small that Zhenlan thought they would never fit her unborn child. Her own mother, who lived in a nearby village, was also busily at work knitting a warm red cotton blanket. As the time for her child's birth came close, she noticed that her sister-in-law stopped taking the family's fresh eggs down to the brigade store for sale. Instead, they were stored in containers of rice in expectation of their future use by the household's new mother-to-be.

One matter of common discussion by both relatives and friends was the possible date of the child's birth. From such a date many in the village believed that the child's fortune could be predicted. If, for example, the child were born on the first or fifteenth day of a given month (according to the lunar calendar), it would have good fortune, whereas if it were born on the eighth day, bad fortune would result. Wang Zhenlan knew several women who had been born on "bad" days, and, indeed, for the most part their lives were not to be envied.

Similar beliefs could be applied to one's *shuxiang,* or horoscope. Zhenlan was born in the year of the rabbit, and that was good. However, her older sister was born in the year of the sheep, and that was not—especially since the birth had occurred in winter. Sheep without grass in winter face a difficult time. So might a child. Zhenlan knew some villagers scoffed at making such associations between infants and animals, considering the ideas old-fashioned and foolish. However, many did not. Actually, it was more often the young who laughed at such ideas. Older people tended to believe in them. She wasn't sure. Perhaps in the old days, when there was much hardship and uncertainty, belief in luck helped to explain one's fortune, good or bad. Today, the village was much better off, and people her age didn't need to worry so much about whether there would be enough food to last the winter. Still, in childbirth something could always happen, so she hoped her child would be born on a good-luck day—just in case.

Shortly thereafter, Wang Zhenlan felt the first contraction. Sitting quietly in the courtyard taking in the warm midday sun, she didn't say anything, waiting to see if it would repeat itself. It did. Following Ma Xinxian's instructions, she tried to estimate the length of time between the contractions. They weren't very uncomfortable and were quite far apart. Still, she thought the time had arrived. She waited a little longer to make sure and then called her mother-in-law, who was washing some corn before taking it to the grinding mill.

"The contractions have begun. Perhaps Dong Shufang should be told."

After a brief discussion, the eldest daughter was dispatched to the Dong home with the request. Within minutes the news spread. A few married women from neighboring households soon appeared outside the courtyard gate to offer help. One woman, a family friend, stepped inside. A simple shake of the head from the mother-in-law was enough to confirm that no assistance was needed. However, a child was dispatched to the neighboring village to tell Zhenlan's mother of the approaching birth.

Shortly thereafter, Dong Shufang arrived. Striding through the courtyard gate, worn dark-brown cloth bag in hand, she immediately went to the room where Zhenlan was now lying down. Satisfied with the answers to her brief questions, she set about the task before her. Taking instruments from her bag, she asked that water be boiled for their sterilization. She also requested a pail of hot water and a brush. When the water was brought in, she added a cup of disinfectant to the liquid. Once satisfied with the mixture, she set out to thoroughly clean the room. She then changed the linen on the *kang,* only minimally disturbing Zhenlan. Glancing round the room, she seemed pleased at its orderliness and neatness. In a covered pan on the dresser, her instruments lay in steaming water. She was ready. Now it was simply a question of waiting. No matter how long it took, she would not leave until the baby had been delivered. Zhenlan's mother-in-law and elder sister were nearby. And, hopefully, her own mother would arrive soon. But that was all. The household had been instructed earlier that no one else was to enter the room until after the birth of the child.

Zhenlan felt the increasing frequency of the contractions and a little pain. Perhaps, she thought, it would be better to deliver the child in a kneeling position instead of lying down. Some of the elderly women in the village had told her that the old way was much easier, even though it was no longer done. As the pain continued, she felt Dong Shufang's hand reach out to hers. She squeezed her hand back in response. And she waited.

Outside in the courtyard, Xiao Yu also waited. A message had been brought to the field where he was working that Zhenlan was in labor and he could return home if he wished. Later in the afternoon, he was joined by his father and then by his younger brother. They talked about unimportant matters, their words occasionally interrupted by little cries from inside the house. Anesthesia was not used in the countryside in either clinic or home. Xiao Yu and his father spoke a little more animatedly in the hope that such effort might lessen the sound within. Unsuccessful, they chose to resolve the problem by walking over to the village plaza and then down to the irrigation ditch, where several dead trees had been set aside for firewood. Together, they hauled some of the larger branches back to the courtyard and began breaking them up for the kitchen stove. Activity in the house increased. Finally, a face appeared at the entryway door. It was Xiao Yu's mother, her face flushed with excitement.

"It's a girl. Everyone is fine." A few moments later, she walked toward the courtyard gate, a small strip of bright-red cloth in her hand.

Lao Yu looked at his eldest son and spoke.

"So, you are now a father and I am a grandfather. It is a good day—a day of double happiness. Look. Your mother is tacking up the cloth. Soon everyone will know you are a father."

Neighbors and other villagers were informed of any local birth when the family took a strip of red cloth and placed it just outside the courtyard gate. Red was a sign of happiness, and in this instance, it meant a new family member has been added to the household. The cloth carried other messages as well. Its presence helped prevent evil spirits who might harm mother and child from entering the home, and it informed other villagers that visitors were not welcome. Such guests were discouraged in the belief that they might carry with them malevolent ethers or wind (xiegi) that could bring sickness or misfortune to the newborn and mother.

Seemingly far from the neighbor's excited discussions over the red ribbon proudly displayed on the courtyard gate, a much quieter scene was being enacted in an inner room of the Yu household. Dong Shufang had finished suturing several minor tears that had occurred during the birth and was putting away her instruments in her old cloth bag. Near the door, the elder sister-in-law waited for her to finish. On the kang lay Zhenlan, and next to her, wrapped in a tiny red-cotton quilt, was her newborn child. Not long ago Zhenlan had thought that the birth would soon be over. Now, she reflected, it was just the beginning.

INFANCY

In Half Moon Village, as elsewhere in rural China, a peasant mother and infant were expected to spend much of the first month indoors. This custom, called zuo yuezi (literally, sitting month), was believed to protect the mother and baby from harmful agents—whether natural or supernatural. For the first few days, the mother remained close to bed, breast-feeding the baby and being taken care of by her own mother. If her mother had died or lived too far away, the woman and child would be assisted by the mother-in-law or sister-in-law. In a few days, relatives and friends began dropping by the house to leave one or two jin of dark brown sugar and a small cloth-covered basket of eggs or perhaps a small helping of chicken. Dark sugar, particularly, was thought to help the body stay warm (whereas white sugar was thought to cool the body down). However, these villagers bringing gifts seldom remained to visit for fear that through their presence they might bring some negative ether that could result in harm to mother or child.

By the end of the first week, the mother had begun to eat regular food and assume minor tasks around the house. Conscious of possible unknown dangers, she was careful to keep her face out of the wind. Further protection was afforded by wearing a square-shaped scarf to cover her hair and forehead. In summer a scarf was commonly worn for at least two months; in winter, even longer. As for the child, the mother of a first-born was frequently reminded not to place her baby on its stomach. "Remember the baby's heart," "Be careful not to let it smother," or "If the baby spends too much time on its stomach it will affect the shape of the head" were common admonitions that had been passed down from one generation to another for centuries.

From the moment of birth, the baby was the recipient of a considerable amount of attention. If it cried, it would very likely be picked up and held, coddled, and played with by the mother or other available member of the family. Milk from the breast was offered whenever the child desired it, although an effort was made to follow a regular schedule. At night the baby slept close to the mother's side. When it awoke, its needs were quickly taken care of, whether it was for feeding, emotional support, or the changing of clothes. The usual dress for a young baby included diapers, made out of old clothing, and an undershirt. The child was then wrapped in a small quilt or blanket tied together by a piece of cloth. In poorer days, when old cloth was valued for making shoes, some babies' diapers even consisted of a kind of sandbag. Instead of changing the diaper, mother, grandmother, or sibling would simply change the sand.

When the child was one month old, a large celebration called *man yue* (full month) was held. All nearby relatives and friends were invited to attend. In preparation for the festivities, tables were set for the guests and stocked with special foods such as cooked pork and eggs mixed with red coloring. Drinks usually included *baigang* (a strong white liquor) or other high-spirited grain alcohol. After all had arrived, the new infant was brought out for everyone to see. Presents from relatives and friends were also admired. Gifts included items such as a simple baby suit, a cotton padded mattress, a swaddling blanket, and a small cap or a pair of shoes and socks. It was at this time that the baby was given a name.

The naming of infants had undergone considerable change in Half Moon Village in recent years. Men and women over 40 years of age usually had three-word names, such as *Zhang Guilin* for a man, which literally means "Zhang precious forest," and *Lu Yulan* for a woman, which means "Lu jade orchid." Not infrequently, old naming practices of this sort called on astrological charts utilizing the Five Elements: water, fire, wood, metal, and earth (see Baker 1979). Men's and women's names were quite distinct, of course, the former commonly associated with money, culture, or something official, and the latter with flowers, chastity, and the like. Given the high infant mortality rate at that time, parents also gave their children informal nicknames such as "ugly boy," "iron egg," "stupid donkey," and "left over by dogs," so that evil spirits or devils would be less likely to take their child away.

Another common naming pattern was to assign the same character to part of the given name in such a way as to indicate one's generation in the family—that is, one's generation name. After moving in with the Wang family, I quickly learned the children's formal names. I soon found they all had one character in common: *Hu.* Old Wang's eldest son was Wang Hulan; the second son was Wang Huhao; his eldest daughter was Wang Huying; the second daughter was Wang Hurong; and the youngest daughter was Wang Huzeng. Needless to say, such a naming pattern was quite helpful in distinguishing the Wang family members from other Wang households in the village. I commented on the fact to Lao Wang.

"Of course," he responded, his face masked in a slight frown.

"But why is it that many babies born today have only two-character names?" And I rattled off several names from my census list of Half Moon—boys living nearby called Mei Jtan (Mei Healthy), Liu Wei (Liu Greatness), and Wu Ming (Wu

Bright); and a baby girl born recently just down the lane called Sun Fang (Sun Fragrant). I knew that such naming practices had become quite common among the more intellectual families of urban Beijing, but was surprised the custom was taking hold in more rural Half Moon.

He responded patiently: "Because we like to give babies modern names. Do names for children not change in America?"

I acknowledged that they did, and for the same reason.

In addition to regular names, which were formally registered in the brigade records, children also had nicknames, as mentioned earlier. A very common nickname was simply the word *xiao,* meaning "little" or "young." Thus, a girl whose formal name was Wu Pingping (Wu Apple) might be called by her close circle of relatives Xiao Ping. When she was older and took a job, her co-workers were likely to call her Xiao Wu, utilizing the Chinese word for "young" and the nickname. (In comparable fashion, when addressing someone more senior, the last name was prefixed with *lao,* meaning "old" or "older," as with Lao Wang, my family host.)

In summary, while naming customs varied from place to place and family to family, some features were quite common in rural areas of China: Men (and, far less frequently, women) often had a character indicating generation as part of their formal name. Everyone had an informal nickname, and formal names usually had no relationship to informal ones. It should also be noted that in the past, peasant women didn't even have formal names. Informal names were only infant names. When such women married, they were still without names of their own and were referred to only by combining the husbands' and fathers' surnames.

After the baby's first-month naming ceremony, the household returned to a more normal routine. In most instances, the mother would begin at least part-time work outside the home, particularly if a mother-in-law or "auntie" was available to care for the child. Women who worked in the fields were given as much as an hour off to feed the baby in addition to their regular morning and afternoon breaks. They also had the opportunity of placing their infants in the brigade nursery. Relatively few women had positions in nearby sideline industries and small factories, but those who did used comparable day-care facilities. Actually, the birth of a first grandchild provided a most convenient reason for a 40-to-50-year-old mother-in-law to retire from the hard life of an agricultural field worker. Who wanted to spend a long day bent over a hoe when one could take care of a first grandchild?

Whether the baby was taken care of mostly by mother or grandmother, its day was largely spent in a supportive environment. In addition to its mother's milk, the infant soon found itself being offered cakes, wheat-flour porridge, and other kinds of soup and perhaps some milk powder mixed with other liquid. Meat, prechewed by mother or grandmother, was also added to the diet, as was salt—the latter perceived as insuring the child's future strength. All this time, the young baby was encouraged to shake its head, clench its fist, clap its hands, smile before friends, and in other ways demonstrate to the family and relatives that it was healthy and happy. By the time the child was a year old, it had become used to being cared for by many relatives other than mother and grandmother. Older sisters and occasionally brothers would feed the child, as would the father. When the weather was fine,

Grannies pushing baby carriages down the main road of the village.

grannies took delight in strolling down the main street of the village, pushing a sturdy handmade pram and conversing animatedly with their counterparts who were pushing similar carriages along the same roadway.

Between the age of one and two, most children were weaned, although those in ill health might be breast-fed a little longer. The task was accomplished rather quickly. If the child complained, the mother might spread a little red pepper on her nipple while offering as a substitute some liquid from warm porridge, an egg and rice cake, or similar nutritious food.

Toilet training, by contrast, was undertaken in a more leisurely manner. By the time an infant was a year old, it would begin wearing trousers and a shirt or jacket. The design of such clothing was the ultimate in preparation for relaxed toilet training—a slit between the trouser legs enabling the child to squat down whenever the need arose. When the mother or grandmother noticed the child about to urinate or defecate, she would bend over and help support it. At the same time she was holding the child, she might make a soft whistling sound. Seldom, if ever, did the mother or other family member bother to take the child to the household or public village toilet. For children, a convenient courtyard or lane was seen as a perfectly adequate location for such activity. Nor was an infant's "night soil" considered as dirty as that of an adult. Once the task was completed, a quick call to a waiting dog or a shovel toss into the courtyard pigsty was all that was needed to clean the area. Obviously, the transition from this pattern to that of actual toilet training occurred very easily. When the child was between the ages of one and two, the mother began to anticipate the bodily functions and at the appropriate time again held the child and whistled softly, waiting for the desired result. For most children, such education was successfully completed by the age of two.

In Half Moon, as in other Chinese villages, responsibility for the upbringing of the infant was not limited to the mother and grandmother, although they did provide much of the day-to-day supervision. In most households, this activity was seen as a mutual responsibility of the extended family and even the larger community. In this socializing group of parents, grandparents, older siblings, and numerous "aunties" and "uncles," only some of which were real kin, the young child had a considerable support network. Indded, some parents, grandparents, and pseudo-kin were often accused of spoiling their children.

Actually, the situation was more complex than this. For example, Half Moon villagers did not in fact recognize fictive kin. All kin were real. Terms like *auntie* and *uncle,* when applied to nonrelatives, were usually modified by adding the prefix *ta,* meaning "not ours." In this way, villagers easily recognized distinctions between kin and nonkin.

So, too, the seemingly abundant expression of affection given to young infants was not so much a traditional socialization practice of the countryside as it was of the city. Not surprisingly, given this difference, city people might even slur their rural counterparts, sometimes going as far as to suggest that peasant parents "treat their children like their pigs and dogs." Rural villagers, on the other hand, felt that many urban parents and grandparents overindulged their children and grandchildren. The fact that infants in Half Moon Village were often coddled, actively indulged, and not infrequently "spoiled"—particularly by grandmothers—may well have reflected some urban influence.

Seldom were village infants punished. If a baby cried incessantly, or engaged in some similar frustrating behavior, a parent might possibly spank it, but even these slaps were more symbolic than real, since they were given so gently. Much more likely, the child would be handed a wooden rattle or other plaything to distract its attention from whatever was bothering it. Or an older sibling might go over to the *kang* and stroke, play, or gently rock the child back and forth until it stopped fussing. In good weather, the baby was taken outside to play or watch some courtyard activity.

If the problem was more persistent, such as the child's developing a habit of throwing food on the floor when no longer hungry, the mother responded first by telling the infant to be sensible and eat properly. If it continued to be "naughty," the mother then spoke more firmly. If it still misbehaved, the mother might then give the infant a brief swat on the buttocks. However, such an effort to teach good behavior was often sidetracked by the ever-attentive mother-in-law who, seeing the baby being reprimanded, would come over to the table or chair, sweep the infant up in her arms, and proceed to coddle it in complete disregard for the educational efforts of her daughter-in-law.

CHILDHOOD

Between the ages of three and six, children began to explore more actively the world outside their courtyard. Some of this time was spent in play with other children in the village. Boys spent a considerable amount of time playing marbles, climbing trees, making kites out of cornstalks and newspapers, or finding old iron hoops to roll along the road with a stick. Outdoor activities for girls included a variety of simple games. Mother and daughter might make a shuttlecock out of cloth and feathers. Taking it outside, the daughter would kick it in the air seeing how many times she could keep it up without letting it touch the ground. Then she might try to find other girls to pair up with in teams to see who could keep the toy in the air the longest. Or a girl might obtain a rubber band and attach it to a paddle and a cloth ball, and then see how many times she could hit the ball.

Very popular group activities among girls were skip-rope and kick-stone. In the former, the girl was expected to sing a song of eight or ten stanzas without tripping on the rope. In the latter game, somewhat like hopscotch, four adjacent squares were drawn in the earth. Then, with one foot off the ground, the child tried to kick a stone from one square to the next without losing balance. One's turn was lost when the second foot touched the ground or the stone remained in the original square.

Other games carried on throughout childhood involved the use of a six-sided ball filled with sand. Two teams of boys or girls were formed, each trying to hit an opposite team member without their catching the ball. When it was caught, the other team gained possession of the ball and attempted a similar process. Another game involved the use of a multicolored pig's or sheep's knucklebone. The participant had to throw the bone in the air, walk across a line drawn in the earth, and then catch it, making sure the surface color differed from toss to catch. Of the relatively few games participated in by both boys and girls, hide-and-seek and card playing were the most popular.

Children playing games in Half Moon Village.

While adults rarely participated in these games, they often served as objects of interest and entertainment for the children. A stranger automatically fit this category, whether the individual was a pottery seller, an egg buyer for the district store, a member of a traveling puppet troupe, or a visiting film projectionist from commune headquarters setting up a movie screen. An American anthropologist was always worth a little observation, especially since his physical features, mannerisms, and expressions were so different. Attention could even become entertainment when such an individual tried to keep a shuttlecock in the air for more than a few seconds.

A time when children and adults did come together for leisure activities was in the evening. In summer particularly, after the close of the meal and cleanup, many family members would take their young children and walk down to the village plaza to visit with friends and neighbors or, very likely, watch a program on the brigade-owned television set. In an average summer evening, 100 or more villagers would spend at least a half hour or more standing, seated on stools, or squatting close to the ground, taking in the latest Beijing opera, drama, or comedy. Always in the front were the young children with their mothers or older siblings, behind them the teenagers, followed by other adults.

Given the newness of television to the village, the first T.V. set having arrived in 1978, almost all programs were acceptable forms of entertainment. Some, of course, utilized more traditional art forms. In comedy, the famous "cross-talk" dialogue, in which two men (never women) shared a fast-paced and often straight-faced, but humorous, commentary on some particular theme, was very popular. One summer evening, I walked over to the village plaza to find more than 50 adults and quite a few teenagers laughing loudly over a particularly funny cross-talk. The butt of the humor was the well-known pattern of Chinese film heroes who "would not die." Many propaganda movies of that time portrayed a courageous leader who, on his deathbed and fatally wounded or ill, continued to expound, in a most lengthy monologue, a rather amazing number of self-effacing pronouncements, such as criticizing himself over not serving the people enough or pledging to give all his money on his death to the party.[1] I was impressed at the government-run television's ability to poke fun at its own officialdom, but I was not prepared for the response of the villagers who thought the cross-talk uproariously funny. Of course, I had not seen these propaganda films anywhere near as many times as they had. Only the young children missed the humor.

The lives of children were not just filled with play, however, After reaching the age of three, youngsters were given responsibilities ranging from sweeping the floor to gathering sticks for fuel, weeding or picking vegetables, and washing rice for cooking. The actual age at which the child was introduced to work varied from family to family, the intervening factor usually being the number of children already available to assist in completing household chores. In the 1950s, when nurseries were nonexistent and families tended to be larger, older children spent considerable time looking after their younger siblings. Girls, particularly, ran errands for parents, helped with the cooking, and cleaned the courtyard. Not infrequently at this time,

---

[1]The humor focused on the length of the hero's monologue, not the political content.

parents would postpone a daughter's going to primary school until after the age of seven because her work at home was seen as being more important.

More recently, as families became smaller (averaging between two and three rather than three and four or more) and as more day-care nurseries were established, there was a reduction in the amount of responsibility given to children, young as well as older. The increase in standard of living had also lessened the family's work load. Higher income shared within a smaller family enabled its members to purchase more goods and services, thereby reducing the household chores.

Young children were also taught to be thrifty. If a child dropped a few pieces of grain or some vegetables on the table, the parents asked that the child pick the food up and eat it. If a larger amount of food was dropped on the floor by the child, a request was made to wash it off before eating it. Not surprisingly, such thrift applied equally to clothing. Without exception, youngsters wore the outgrown clothing of older siblings. In the early years, such sharing caused little problem, since dress seldom distinguished between the sexes. However, as the child grew older, such distinctions gained in importance. By late childhood, a boy asked to wear his older sister's shirt would likely complain to his mother, "I don't want to wear this." To his mother's questioning response, he might then add: "This is for girls. Look at the flower pattern. It's for girls. I'm not wearing this. I'm a boy!"

Parents held different expectations for girls and boys. If the child was a girl, she was held responsible for herself at an earlier age—especially if she was the oldest, since she might soon have to assist in caring for a younger sibling. When younger brothers and sisters were born, she would be asked to help feed them, take them outside, clean them up, and in other ways free the mother or grandmother for other housework tasks like feeding the pigs and washing clothes—tasks considered too heavy for young girls. If, because of death or another cause, the particular household was without a grandmother, the young girl would be given even more responsibilities—sewing clothes, simple cooking, and managing the fire.

A boy was also expected to care for himself at an early age. By the time he reached three or four, he would help his father collect firewood, bring home the tools from the family plot, or even work a little in the garden, weeding or picking vegetables. However, with the trend toward smaller families, young boys found themselves increasingly told to assist in housework and in caring for other siblings, effectively reducing the earlier differential expectations between the sexes. Needless to say, if a family consisted of three boys and one younger sister, the boys carried the major childhood tasks in the home. The girl not only would have considerably less to do but also might become somewhat spoiled. This could also be true for the oldest girl if she was the only one in a large family. So too, a single boy in a family of girls soon found himself being given much more care and special attention than was the case in a more sexually balanced group of siblings. In Half Moon, such a child was always perceived as spoiled.

As children became older, punishments for wrongdoing became more frequent and harsher. A child might be punished for not listening to his or her parents, especially when they had told the child not to do something, like going down to the drainage ditch and becoming dirty. If the child went alone to a ditch or pond that was full of water, the parents were likely to become angry because of the danger involved. Punishment for such an act would most likely be a spanking on the buttocks.

Another form of behavior likely to bring on harsh punishment was serious fighting among children. Such fighting could quickly disrupt the tight web of harmonious relations that were encouraged within the village, thereby causing considerable unease among parents. Thus, when children began to fight, parents quickly stepped in. The immediate point at issue was not who was right or wrong, but that the fighting had to stop.

If fighting between children of different families was considered a serious offense, fighting within the family was condemned even more. Such conflict could assume several different forms. For example, an older sibling might become angry at a younger one. Since anger was not supposed to be expressed directly, the older child might try to frighten the younger. This was most likely to occur when the parents and other adults were temporarily away. During one fall evening in Half Moon Village, Liu Wei, a young boy of seven, was told by his parents that they were going next door to visit briefly with a neighbor. Before they left, Wei was asked to keep a close watch over his younger sister, Fang. When they returned 15 minutes later, they found a worried Wei trying to comfort his little sister, while wiping large tears from her face.

"What happened?" asked his mother.

"Fang is crying."

"That's obvious," said Father Liu, a little suspicious of Wei's remark.

Somewhat defensively, the boy countered with the admission that he had made a tiger face and growled at Fang, who had then burst out crying.

"That's a bad thing to do," Father Liu shouted angrily. Raising his hand, he slapped Wei on the face, at which point Wei joined his sister in tears. The mother stood by the table, looking firm and saying nothing. Eventually, both children settled down, as did the parents, and the incident was laid to rest. But it was not forgotten. Hitting a child on the face was a major form of punishment, reserved for serious offenses. The usual admonition was, "When hitting someone, never use the face; when cursing someone, never expose the defect." That is, never strike someone's face and never speak in anger about someone else's weakness, particularly in front of others.

While such an admonition was not infrequently broken, the lesson for Wei was clear: an older brother must not scare his younger sister. He must care for her, take responsibility for her. When siblings fought, the responsibility rested with the older child. Younger brothers and sisters were less knowledgeable, less understanding, less experienced in how to behave. Also, when a younger brother or sister did misbehave, older siblings were expected to report the event to the parents, rather than punish the child themselves.

Differences in the parents' approaches to childhood discipline began to appear fairly quickly. As the child grew up, the father's manner became more aloof and his role in discipline more important. Children, in turn, were more afraid of their fathers. Such fear was not only due to the greater strictness and more severe administration of punishment—including caning as well as spanking. It was also grounded in the social distance that characterized the father-child relationship. At the time, fathers were more likely to joke or play with their children than in the past, but they were still firm. They said little and seldom lost their tempers. Having less interpersonal contact, of course, made them more venerable. Although this too was changing, the father was still the dominant authority figure.

Mothers, on the other hand, were more sympathetic. They might be equally angry over a child's transgression; they might also slap or curse a child. But most often, their anger expressed itself in words: "There is no supper for you. You get enough from fighting." Or, "You must be too full to stay idle; so you go out and fight with other children. Since you are so full, you won't have any supper tonight." However, the child knew these were often empty words. Mothers were too kind to let a child go hungry, especially if it was a girl. Boys normally received stricter punishment.

Children were also punished for damage they inflicted upon themselves while playing. If a boy fell down and injured an arm or leg, or if a girl cut herself with a knife, the parent would punish the child first and take care of the hurt second. The message was that children must be careful about their bodies, take care of them. If children hurt themselves, they might not be able to carry out their responsibilities in the household, and others would have to do more.

In summary, Half Moon Village provided a secure environment for its children. Dangers were few and the social conditioning precise. Children growing up in the household knew from an early age their responsibilities and their freedoms, their obligations and their leisure. Even though firmness was the rule from age three on, and punishment for wrongdoing could be swift and direct, the security provided by this family patterning was substantial. It was little wonder that the children of Half Moon Village, like children throughout China, so often appeared to outsiders as shy but friendly in manner and exemplary in behavior. Such "presentation of self" to strangers was exactly what they had been taught by their families, and usually they did it well.[2]

However, such expression should not be seen as the norm of early childhood life. The picture was much more complex, as has been illustrated. Although there was emotional support as well as firmness, the links were stronger between mothers and sons, with fathers remaining more in the background. Daughters too knew that when they married, they had to leave their family for that of the groom, frequently in another village. The old adage that "a daughter who has married out is like spilled water that cannot be replaced" still lingered in the minds of some parents, who knew that eventually they had to replace their daughters with one or more daughters-in-law.

Half Moon had one additional institution with some responsibility for the care and upbringing of young children—the brigade day-care nursery. Located in a renovated house and courtyard near the brigade office, this facility regularly accepted the preschool children of parents who worked in the nearby fields. However, most families preferred looking after the young infant at home, at least

---

[2]Urban Beijing newspapers, commenting on the success of the one-child family-planning campaign, regularly received many letters to the editor complaining about one serious side effect of "having only one"—a large increase in spoiled children!

until it could speak and assume some responsibility itself. For them, the day-care nursery was viewed as a very poor substitute for the much more personal attention given by mother and grandmother. Therefore, the majority of infants whose households included a grandmother or nonworking mother, remained at home for a year or longer. Still, for a variety of reasons, including limited availability of family members, economic need, and other personal factors, babies could be enrolled as early as one to six months.

For much of the year, the nursery opened at seven in the morning, just before the village work-team members headed out to the fields; it closed temporarily for the noon break around 11:30 and opened again for the afternoon work period from 2:00 to 4:30, or for however long the villagers spent in the fields. At harvest time, when all worked a 12- to 14-hour day, the nursery stayed open for a correspondingly longer time.

The nursery had one large room providing space for the 25 or more children that usually attended each day. At one end, a large *kang* stretching from wall to wall enabled infants to take regular naps. At the other end, a few chairs and a table were used by slightly older children, who could draw on slate boards or play games together. The oldest children were occasionally encouraged to use their boards to learn numbers and simple Chinese characters. Outside, courtyard facilities were equally spartan. Except for a sliding board and roundabout, large toys were nonexistent. Children did have access to smaller items such as rubber balls, beanbags, skip ropes, and picture books.

The nursery school staff included two or more older women, the actual number depending on how many children were present, and two younger women who carried out more specific educational responsibilities. Staff income was based on the brigade work-point system, although sometimes older women served as volunteer assistants. All looked after the children in a general way, organizing simple games, telling stories, and making sure occasional disagreements and fights were resolved with minimum difficulty. The younger women, who had received some training in childhood education, were expected to provide older infants with a little practical knowledge, as well as lead them in singing group songs and learning simple dance steps.

In all these activities, there was considerable continuity between what was learned at home and in school. Young children were held often and were well cared for. But they and their older playmates were seldom played with. In the adult-centered world of Half Moon Village, parents and nursery school staff were expected to teach their children, not play with them. Nor was much attention given to reasoning before the age of six or seven. That effort was generally reserved for a later period, when the child entered primary school.

5/Schooling

A VISIT FROM THE TEACHER

Su Shitou, 10 years old, attended third grade in a nearby primary school. Though bright and full of wit, he didn't like to study. For him, working with figures and characters was boring, especially when he could spend time with his dad in the fields or collecting different kinds of insects by the irrigation ditch at the edge of the village.

In class, Su didn't listen to his teacher either, preferring to talk with his nearby schoolmates. For this reason, the teacher recently reassigned him to share a desk with a girl in the hope that his classroom behavior might improve. Yet he continued to get into trouble. One day he put a broom on top of the half-open classroom door, expecting it to fall on a student walking into the room. Only this time it fell on the teacher. There were a few giggles from his friends, but that was all. Every set of eyes focused on the tall man standing, broom in hand, at the front of the room. In a calm but firm voice, Teacher Wang addressed the class.

"Students, who is responsible for this?" he asked, gently waving the broom before him.

The room was still. Then, as Su Shitou rose from behind his desk, the other students turned in his direction.

"I'm sorry, teacher. I did not expect the broom to fall on you. I was playing a joke."

"Su Shitou, you and I will have a little talk after school." With that remark, the teacher turned, walked toward a small platform at the front of the room, and sat down behind his desk. Reaching into a drawer, he pulled out a black notebook. As the students watched, he wrote a few comments on a back page under the name *Su*. Then, looking at Shitou once again, he closed the book, returned it to his desk, and addressed the class, informing them that it was time to begin the day's language lesson.

In midafternoon, at the close of school, Shitou stood before his teacher, waiting for the pronouncement.

"Xiao Su, I want you to inform your parents I am coming by the village this evening before dark to talk to them."

It was the answer Shitou expected. He had been forewarned the last time he got into trouble. There were two reasons why a teacher might come to a student's home. One was simply to inform the parents how the child was progressing and answer any questions they might have about the school. The other was the more dreaded *gaozhuang*, in which a complaint was lodged about bad behavior. Unfortunately for Shitou, this definitely appeared to be a *gaozhuang* type of visit. Since teachers were highly respected in Half Moon, as in other villages of Red Flag Commune, a complaint expressed by them about a student was taken seriously. But that was not all. Such a criticism also cast shame on the whole family. As a result, Shitou knew that, at the very least, he would get a good dressing down. More likely, it would be a good beating.

That evening, shortly before sunset, Teacher Wang arrived at the Su courtyard gate.

"Hello. May I come in?"

"Oh yes, Teacher Wang," responded Mother Su. "Come in and have a seat. Have you had your dinner? Please, let me give you some here."

Father Su added: "You must be tired, I'm sure. Have a seat. Shitou, make some hot water for your teacher." As a solemn-looking Shitou turned toward the kitchen, his father admonished him, "Shitou, say hello first."

"Hello, Xiao Shitou," the teacher said. "I've already had my dinner, so just some water will be fine. I simply dropped by to visit a little with your parents."

"Thank you, Teacher Wang," responded Mother Su. "You are always so busy attending to the students. Sometimes they don't understand very well. And other times, they are naughty. How is our Shitou doing in school? Does he cause any trouble in class?"

"Oh, no. He is a good boy. He had made real progress recently."

"Around here, he likes to play and run around. Can't sit still even for five minutes. He must give you a lot of headaches, I suppose?" inquired the father.

"Boys get restless easily. Shitou used to talk with other students in class, but he doesn't do that anymore. Is he reading at home and doing schoolwork by himself?"

"He reads picture books quite a bit. Stories about various heroes. But he doesn't like homework. When we force him, he does it with friends."

During this whole exchange, Xiao Shitou was sitting quietly on a *kang* in the back of the room, observing everything and saying nothing.

"I see. He likes to read storybooks. Good. What we have to do now is show him that he can't just learn from pictures. He must do well in schoolwork too."

"You're right. Mother Su and I are sorry we don't pay enough attention to his schoolwork. It's important to learn things. Children don't know that. Whenever I get angry with Shitou, I give him a good slapping."

"That's no use. It's not the way to put him on the right track. Remember, he is still young. Teachers and parents need to cooperate to train the younger generation to be useful to the country."

While addressing the teacher, Father Su kept glancing at his son. "Teacher Wang, what you say is correct. Whenever Shitou does anything wrong in school, tell him I support whatever punishment you give him."

"Punishment is not the best way to educate students. We do reasoning. The result is better. That way he will understand. Actually, Shitou is making progress. That's all that counts. Of course, sometimes he forgets. It is best if he listens to the teacher. Children are like small trees. It takes careful nurturing for them to grow straight and tall."

"You are right again, Teacher Wang. We should do more with Shitou. We don't pay enough attention to his schoolwork."

"I should do more too. But he is making some headway. Don't worry about him too much. Well, it's getting late. I must be going. Thanks for the water."

"Good-bye, Teacher Wang. Thank you for coming, and for all the work you are doing with Shitou. We appreciate it."

This portrayal of the teacher Wang's visit to the Su family, described in detail by a perceptive key informant, illustrates both the continuity and the change in the education of village children like Su Shitou. Wang, aware of the impact that his high status had in the village, chose to underplay his problems with Shitou. He knew that his presence in the Su household was indication enough that the son was in difficulty at school. Such a visit was usually followed by punishment handed out by the father: a slap or beating if the child was in primary school, and at least a severe verbal reprimand if the student was older. In this case, the father not only indicated that he supported that course of action but went even further, giving blanket approval to the teacher to impose any punishment he deemed advisable while Shitou was at school. At this time, that type of parental response was more likely to be challenged by modern teachers like Wang. That is, the family was encouraged to become involved in the child's education, instead of simply treating the offending son (almost never a daughter) as an object bringing shame to the household.[1]

From the beginning of primary schools in the 1950s until the early 1970s, enrollment in the area around Half Moon was fairly small; many peasants questioned the importance of all but the first few years of schooling. At that time, knowledge gained in the classroom was seen to have little bearing on knowing how to plant, weed, and harvest crops. For young girls who cared for younger brothers and sisters at home, there was even more reason to either delay entrance into primary school or drop out early. Boys, on the other hand, not only had fewer tasks to complete in the home but also were not expected to begin work in the fields until their early or mid-teens. Relatively free of daily work responsibilities, they were better able to take advantage of what school had to offer. Furthermore, peasant parents, many of whom were illiterate, wanted their sons at least to be able to read newspapers and perhaps even simple books. By 1979, over 90 percent of the children, girls and boys, had completed their five-year primary school education—a substantial achievement in two decades. Exactly what did that education entail?

---

[1]This belief that the shame (and also the honor) of an individual is shared by the family and lineage has a long history in China. Under the emperors, a well-known principle in the penal system, called *lianzou,* stated that the whole family was to be held responsible for serious political crimes committed by any one member. Even close relatives of the given family, such as the wife's patrilineal kin, could be executed along with the criminal—all pointing to the fact that within the traditional Chinese cultural framework, individuals were not seen as independent beings but as members of the larger kinship network. This relationship between the individual and the group is discussed more fully in a later chapter.

PRIMARY EDUCATION

Children began their formal education at age seven. Half Moon didn't have its own primary school. So, depending on the students' ages, they attended one of two schools shared by several nearby villages. The total population of the two institutions was 416, less than 3 percent of Red Flag Commune's overall primary school enrollment of 14,000. Each of the five grades contained approximately 40 students. There were 10 teachers, one for each classroom. Other members of the staff included a director and a physical education instructor, who shared their time between the two facilities.

Although school began at 7:30, children usually arrived 15 to 20 minutes early. Chatting in small groups on the playground, they waited until a bell informed them of the approaching class time. At its sound, they jogged twice around the yard and then split up, heading for their own homerooms. At the second bell, the teachers entered the rooms and classes began.

Classrooms were arranged quite simply. In some, each student had his or her own table or desk, while in others the tables were shared. The much larger, flat-topped desk at the front of the room was reserved for the teacher. On the wall behind the teacher's desk hung a large blackboard and above that, painted in bold red colors, were eight large Chinese characters: *tuanjie, jinzhang, yan su, huopo,* meaning "Be united, alert, earnest, and lively." For the class, it was a reminder that all students should work together as one, not be lazy, be serious in study, and be energetic. By carefully looking high on the wall between the two sets of characters, one could also see a large, relatively clean rectangular space—the one remaining physical reminder of an earlier time in school history when a picture of Mao Zedong hung in every classroom.

At the back of each room were "study gardens" (bulletin boards), where students posted their better compositions. Other spaces were reserved for the names of students who had been helpful cleaning up or assisting others. Still another location in the "garden" contained a list of all the students and their success in recent personal hygiene inspections, in which hands, front and back, neck, and ears were checked. Those who did well received a small red flag beside their names. Those who did not, received nothing. For this age group, negative evaluations were not considered helpful, especially when they were made public. Advanced primary grades also had "paper-clip gardens" (wall newspapers), where brief articles on current issues or new information of interest to students was posted. These wall gardens were organized by teachers and student members of a homeroom class committee.

The primary school curriculum began with a concentrated focus on Chinese language and arithmetic, followed by courses in music, physical education, drawing, and calligraphy. From grade three on, depending on the availability and skill level of the teachers, courses were offered in common knowledge (elementary science), geography, history, and painting. Most classes met for 40 minutes. Lunch break was from 11:30 to 2:00, followed by two more class periods. Though school was over at 3:30, students were encouraged to remain longer to complete their homework or receive additional help from a teacher. Physical education was also included in the daily curriculum. In addition to the early-morning jog around the school yard, students participated in regular exercises during 10-minute intervals between class periods throughout the day.

What was sometimes referred to as "moral education" was a vital part of learning in both primary and middle school. Although the subject was not formally taught, it pervaded school activity both in and outside the classroom. In meetings with teachers, in summaries of the semester's work, and in various outdoor activities, actions of students were utilized to illustrate important moral precepts such as "being responsible to others." Common illustrations included children who found an object such as a pen or a workbook on the school playground and returned it to the teacher, or children who found pieces of scrap metal and turned them in at the local state-run recycling center. Praise for such action was not given immediately but was reserved for a class meeting, where other children could learn what was good and proper behavior.[2]

Training in social responsibility was further developed through student committees. In the lower primary grades, such committees relied heavily on the teacher's guidance, although even here, children elected a monitor to organize simple group tasks. Classes in advanced primary grades elected committees that assumed responsibility for leading morning exercises, supervising study periods, collecting homework assignments, and preparing class performances for holiday occasions.

Similar moral education occurred outside the classroom. In harvest season, children from primary school were taken out to the fields to watch their parents and neighbors working. Older brothers and sisters from middle school also helped with the harvest, as did retired peasant men and women, the latter organized through the Women's Federation. While there, the children husked small ears of corn left behind by their parents or, if taken to the threshing ground, they swept up gleanings of wheat for later storage. Such activity not only instilled in the student the value of work but also emphasized the importance of being thrifty with what one produced. In all these efforts, the child was reminded to cooperate with teachers, parents, and "grannies," to follow instructions, and to share with others. The values conveyed in such an environment—respect for age, cooperation in work, and generosity—were obvious extensions of similar themes inculcated at home.

Of course, moral education was sometimes overdone, as the parents of one young student found, to their chagrin. In the early 1970s, during the Cultural Revolution, the son learned at school about a selfless hero named Lei Feng, who spent his whole life helping others rather than concentrating on his own interests and those of his family. The eager pupil, deciding to follow the hero's example of "devoting his life to the collective effort," proceeded to take some manure set aside for his family's courtyard plot and spread it over the adjacent, collectively owned brigade land. His family was not impressed.

For the most part, this kind of education was not only pervasive but also effective. Students continually learned proper behavior from teachers, parents, textbooks, radio, newspapers, and television. In all these instances, they were

---

[2]In this instance, face was "given" rather than "lost" (see Hu 1944:56; Stover and Stover 1976:206).

encouraged to help each other, care for each other, learn from each other, and "take each others' happiness as their own." In contrast, activities that caused embarrassment or remarks that emphasized a negative attribute were discouraged. Envision, for example, a Chinese child's participation in a game like musical chairs. In an American school, such a game encourages children to be competitive and to look out for themselves. But to young Chinese, the negative aspect was much more noticeable. That is, losers became objects of attention because they had lost their space—and therefore "face." In China, winning was fun too. But it should not be achieved at the expense of causing someone else embarrassment. In all kinds of daily activity, including study as well as games, Chinese children were regularly reminded that they must work hard and be sensitive to the needs of others, for only through such effort would their own lives become truly meaningful. Of course, Shitou's classroom behavior was a reminder of the distance that separated reality from the ideal.

Self-discipline, encouraged through moral education, was also applied to "the three Rs." For example, in a second-grade classroom, a great deal of effort was spent learning to read Chinese. American children had only 26 letters to memorize and a system of phonetics to assist in recognizing new words. Chinese students had no comparable system to assist them in learning an immensely larger set of characters that were needed to transcribe the Chinese language. Memorization, and its application through intensive reading, was the only way to master the many hundreds of ideographs that children had to know in order to read and write effectively. And that took considerable self-control.

On a typical day, the teacher entered the classroom and put on the blackboard four words written in *pinyin,* the romanized form of standard Chinese. In primary school, this system was used to help children learn how to pronounce characters, a practice similar to the way in which phonetic systems have been used in the United States to assist in learning English pronunciation. Next to each word was placed the corresponding ideograph. The teacher pointed to the written word and the ideograph, pronouncing it each time. Then, the character was broken down into its subparts and interpretations made.

Finally, using a pointer, the teacher demonstrated the correct steps for writing the ideograph—the stroke order—naming each part at the appropriate moment. After this demonstration, a volunteer was asked to repeat the process. After being selected, the child stood straight up beside his or her desk and responded by drawing the Chinese character in the air with a finger. Next, the teacher asked the whole class to go through the same procedure. If a volunteer made an error in answering, the teacher usually did not comment negatively, since any possible embarrassment to the student was to be avoided. Instead, another volunteer was quickly selected. Finally, the class used flash cards with *pinyin* on one side and the Chinese character on the other. In sequence, the teacher and a volunteer, followed by the rest of the class recited what was inscribed on the card held in the air. Blackboard and cards were then used to reinforce each other. The quick pace of the lesson easily held the attention of most children as they repeated over and over again the drill necessary to retain the new words.

This type of rote learning, though most pronounced in language classes, was not limited to such subject matter. In early primary grades the child was regularly expected to follow the instructions of the teacher. The idea for the child to develop individual initiative or creative expression on his or her own or in "free" classroom periods was not a part of the educational process. Art classes, for example, were common in primary school, but the usual tasks were paper cutting or copying drawings made on the blackboard by the teacher. They did not tap the possible artistic talent of the student. So too, in Chinese literature classes, students were expected to respond briefly to precise questions posed by the teacher or to partici-pate in group recitation of selected passages of text, rather than to discuss or debate possible interpretations of the author's meaning in the selected passage. Again, this cultural patterning in the classroom was consistent with similar learning in the home. Teachers, parents, and other authority figures were knowledgeable. Students and children were not. Therefore, they were to listen, study hard, and emulate their elders, so that they too would have that knowledge in the future.

Such an approach to education instilled a feeling of group solidarity among students. However, it did little to develop in the child a sense of inquiry, creative challenge, or deductive reasoning. Wanting to explore more deeply the relationship between the group-oriented, rote-focused learning so common in the primary school and the more individual-oriented, problem-focused approach characteristic of mid-dle-class America, I asked the director of the school near Half Moon Village if I could attend a class and then meet with him afterward. He expressed his pleasure at my interest and welcomed me to attend any class I wished.

A primary school classroom near Half Moon Village.

A few minutes before seven on a chilly morning in early December, I left my room and walked down to the end of the lane, where another member of the Wang lineage lived. Wang Yingying, a fifth-grade student, had agreed, somewhat hesitantly, that I could accompany her and her friends to school on this day. Outside her courtyard gate, Jia, another student, was already waiting.

"Yingying, it's time to go to school. Are you ready?" little Jia called through the open gate.

"Almost. I'll be there in a minute," Yingying responded.

Joining Jia, I listened as Yingying's mother spoke: "Take your younger brother down to Granny's room. I have to go to the fields."

"But Mum, Jia is waiting for me. I'll be late for school."

"O.K. Give the baby to me. You go ahead, but come back right after class. Don't fool around, do you hear?"

Yingying headed toward the door.

"And listen to the teacher. . . ."

"I know, I know," responded Yingying, rapidly approaching the gate. Seeing both of us, she smiled, and with a quick tilt of her head suggested that we head on down the lane toward the main road beyond.

Ten minutes later, we arrived at the low one-story adobe-and-brick buildings that housed the school. Young people from other villages stood around in small groups waiting for the bell to ring. Two primary students had already entered a nearby classroom. One was sweeping the floor, and the other was cleaning the blackboard. At the bell, the rest made their usual jog around the outer perimeter of the playground and then headed toward their homerooms.

The school director, who had been waiting for my arrival, greeted me warmly and then introduced the fourth-grade teacher who was to be my host for the morning. Together, we entered his classroom, and I sat down in the back, trying unsuccessfully to be inconspicuous. Still, after a few brief stares and whispers, the class began to settle down. The 42 students were about evenly divided between boys and girls. Remembering the story of Su Shitou, I wasn't surprised to see several couples sharing small desks and benches. Young girls, who rarely misbehaved in school, were used to help the teacher keep order in this classroom too.

Of the 42 students in the room, 12 wore red scarves, indicating their participation in the Young Pioneers, a loosely organized group of children (somewhat similar to the Scout movement in the United States) whose activities included cleaning streets, assisting the elderly, and aiding teachers. Since most children between eight or nine and fourteen belonged, it was obvious many hadn't bothered to wear their scarves on that day. Only a few children defined as "bad" or "consistently naughty" were excluded from the organization.[3] Needless to say, such naughty children were urged to improve their ways so that they too could become Young Pioneers.

As the teacher began the lessons—first in math, then in language—I watched

---

[3]Until 1980, children from landlord, rich peasant, or "class enemy" households could also be excluded.

the children's responses. It was difficult, of course, to determine the extent to which my being in the room influenced their behavior. Most were attentive, sitting straight and fairly still unless they were writing, drawing, holding a notebook, or reciting. As the morning progressed, and one set of lessons and exercises followed another, some children began using their pencils and paper for play. A few others simply stared out the window. All sat quietly, however, and only infrequently did anyone disturb the tenor of the class by whispering loudly or getting up and walking around. On such occasions, the teacher first looked sternly at the child and asked that the whispering stop. If that tactic was unsuccessful, he then walked down the aisle and firmly tapped his pencil on the student's desk, at which time all inappropriate activity at the desk quickly ceased.

By midmorning, the old pot-bellied coal stove was laboring rather un-successfully to heat the drafty and still cold classroom. Most students wore padded jackets and a few wore mittens or gloves, the latter being removed only when the student wrote in a notebook or on the blackboard. When the next bell rang, indicating an outdoor exercise break, all filed out the door quickly, seeking to throw off the chill brought on by sitting so long in the drafty room. After thanking the fourth-grade teacher, I too walked briskly around the school yard and then headed for the director's office at the end of the long building. I stepped into his consider-ably warmer room, and we chatted informally for a short while. Then he offered his view of the present educational system. It was one I had heard on several occasions that year while interviewing officials from the Ministry of Education in Beijing.

"Education is improving now," commented the middle-aged director, speaking in a friendly but slightly bored manner. "Before [meaning during the decade of the Cultural Revolution], the children had no discipline. They didn't behave properly and couldn't learn anything. Now that is all changed. We have ten rules and regulations for behavior, and they have settled down. Now they are learning very well."

I remembered the large poster I had seen on the classroom wall showing several students happily reading their textbooks. Below the picture was a statement urging everyone to study hard, work diligently, and help the teacher and others when needed.

"What changes do you envision for the future?"

"We want to help the teachers improve their skills. This coming year the commune will hold special enrichment classes for fifth-grade teachers under the direction of the Ministry of Education. Unfortunately, our level of teacher training is quite low. Even in communes like this one, close to the city, funds for advanced training of our staff are very limited."

I was reminded of a discussion with the Deputy Vice Minister of Education for Beijing Municipality, who had emphasized that education could not be dis-connected from the development of the region as a whole. Given the overall limitations of the country's economy, funds to upgrade educational quality had to be weighted against other modernizing efforts. Because rural students were still the vast majority of the total student population—over 100 million—the costs were immense. To spend one more dollar per student, the government official reminded me, would cost an additional 100 million dollars! My thoughts returned to the more manageable Half Moon Village.

The primary school director continued: "The Ministry of Education plans to improve rural education in two ways in the next two or three years. First, we must raise the level of training of those teachers presently in the classroom. This will be done by setting up training centers. Teachers who pass examinations after taking the new courses will be given a more senior status. Second, we want to establish more 'spare-time schools' so that the new illiteracy that has reemerged over the past ten years can be eliminated. Finally, I hope we will be able to reinstate the six years of primary school education that we had before the Cultural Revolution. But, unfortunately, that will not be soon, given the cost involved."

Both primary and secondary education had expanded significantly throughout the commune by the early 1970s. Much of this activity, closely linked to the educational policies of the Cultural Revolution, emphasized the importance of utilizing local initiative. And indeed, many villages had established new primary (and junior middle) schools by using local people and urban-trained "educated youth" to staff them. Wages for these new teachers were largely paid by the villagers themselves, through brigade-based work points. To obtain additional teachers for the new facilities, villages had reduced the earlier system of six-year primary schools to five years—justification for the step being summed up in the slogan "less but better."

This dramatic educational effort put forward during the Cultural Revolution brought the benefits of expanded primary and secondary education to many commune youth—a real achievement, given the large increase in population between 1950 and the 1970s. Yet it did so at the expense of improving educational quality. The local primary school director was obviously identifying with the quality side of this equation. After obtaining some data on the history and size of the school, I expressed my appreciation for his efforts and took my leave. Walking home, I thought about how far the primary schools serving Half Moon and other nearby villages had come from their small beginnings in the early 1950s. Given that progress, it wasn't surprising that attention had now shifted to the junior and senior middle school, which still had considerably fewer graduates.

MIDDLE SCHOOL

Of Red Flag Commune's 22,200 students, approximately 8,200 were in secondary, or middle, school. Of the latter, the large majority were enrolled in three-year junior middle schools, which were organized at the district level. The commune also had a few two-year senior middle schools, whose total enrollment was about 2,000. However, only one, located near the commune headquarters, offered courses (including English) of sufficiently high level that it could even consider preparing its students to take the nationwide examinations for advanced technical school or university. Not surprisingly, most of these students were sons and daughters of middle-level commune officials or senior-level state workers who lived nearby. The highest-level commune officials (whose income was received from the state sector) usually maintained their residence in Beijing City, thereby enabling their children to have an even better, urban education.

About 80 percent of all primary school graduates in the commune began middle school, although less than 30 percent finished. Of those who did, almost none entered higher education. In 1979, for example, of the commune's senior secondary school students who chose to take the nationwide examination for entrance to a technical school or a university, only 18 passed.[4] A few went on to university, but most were admitted to a less competitive, lower-level technical school. Educational quality at even the best commune school was simply not adequate to meet the highly competitive standards set by the Ministry of Education for entrance to higher education. This was true even though nonurban students were allowed a lower passing score on the entrance examination than were their city counterparts. As a result, the gap between educational opportunities for urban and rural (or, in this case, suburban) students was still very much an issue.

Why did so many middle school students drop out before finishing? There were several reasons, most pertaining in one way or another to economic problems. From the point of view of the commune, secondary education cost more to support and required more highly trained instructors. Furthermore, such teachers usually lived in urban areas and had little or no interest in moving to more rural locations. Second, education was not compulsory. Many families felt they could not spare their sons' and daughters' potential income after age 14, 15, or 16. This was particularly true in the poorer villages of the commune. Third, middle schools, and especially the very few senior middle schools, were located quite some distance from those aspiring to attend. With poor roads and a lack of bus transportation, some students wanting to participate were unable to attend on a daily basis and unable to pay the cost of having someone house them away from home.

Given the unlikelihood of receiving a passing examination grade for university or technical school entrance, most students and their parents saw little reason to spend more than a year or two furthering their education. Some acknowledged that 14 might be a little early to begin work in the fields or a factory. But if the children continued in school, their parents had to pay for notebooks, clothing, and other related costs. Poorer peasant families found this difficult. Furthermore, such expenses were always weighed against the gains. Not uncommon was the question: Why waste time in school if the training won't help in the future? Especially so when the time could be better spent bringing more income into the household.[5] And finally, some young people did not have either the interest or the ability to complete five additional years of school. In 1979, students had to receive a passing grade of at least 60 to enter both junior and senior middle school. Failures always occurred, whether through lack of commitment or ability.

The junior middle school that Half Moon students attended was located near district headquarters, not far from the village. As a district school, it offered a large range of courses, including Chinese language and literature, algebra, chemistry, biology, physics, agricultural machinery, politics, and Chinese and Western his-

[4]Unfortunately, the number of students taking the examination could not be obtained.
[5]As will be seen shortly, this perception was most often applied to male students.

tory. In 1979, a young teacher from the school was sent to Beijing Normal College to learn English; on her return, that subject was to be added to the curriculum.

The school had one other distinguishing feature: a two-story-high classroom, library, and office building—a feature that set it apart from all other structures for miles around. The 600 district young people who attended this school had use of the enlarged facility because of the efforts of earlier students and staff. In 1971, as part of the "self-reliance in education" phase of the Cultural Revolution, the district government, with the active assistance of students and their parents, had built a small pharmaceutical factory and printshop, which was then partially integrated into the school. Throughout China at this time, all students were expected to "combine mental and manual labor," spending at least part of each school week in constructive work.

Once construction was completed, Half Moon and other village students from the district worked part-time in the factory or the printshop for the 42 weeks of the school year. Eventually they, together with newly hired district workers, produced enough chemical products for sale to the state that the district was able to pay off its loan for building materials and purchase much-needed school equipment and supplies. By 1978, the factory's annual profits, all of which were allocated to the school, had reached 100,000 *yuan*. The total income earned in this educational sideline industry since 1971 was a substantial 530,000 *yuan*.

For peasants in the area, their junior middle school was a source of pride. Furthermore, they perceived the effort to provide a middle school education for all eligible students, rather than a selected few, as basically sound. As several parents put it: Fifteen years ago, who would have thought our children could attend middle school? Now, anyone can go. When local people were asked what positive gains were made in the commune during the Cultural Revolution, this school was frequently given as an illustration.

With educational policy strongly emphasizing the latter side of the quantity-quality equation, one might assume that the earlier Cultural Revolution focus would have been completely rejected. But such an assumption would not be quite accurate. For example, in the academic year 1978–79, students in the district middle school were divided into two groups, rapid and slow learners, and then placed in different classrooms according to their designation. Within a short period of time, serious problems began to emerge, leading eventually to a discontinuation of the tracking scheme. What happened? Evaluating the change at the end of the year, the principal reported: "It didn't work. It undermined the students' spirit and stereotyped their behavior. Therefore, we have gone back to the earlier system of mixing fast and slow learners in the same classes. Now, the faster ones are given more work and the slower ones more help. The result appears to be much better for everyone."

Most of the revised policies were supported by middle school teachers. Those almost universally acclaimed were regulations for proper behavior, stricter academic standards with a corresponding emphasis on grades, and the removal of "revolutionary" (that is, rhetorical) content from the subject matter. Student responses to these changes are also significant. Academic study was now taken much more seriously than when I had first visited middle schools in the area in 1972. At that time, political study and manual labor accounted for a much larger portion of the student's time. Academic study, as such, had less appeal.

By 1979, the greater commitment to study was seen everywhere. Younger siblings regularly asked older ones for help in solving basic mathematical problems, writing a short essay, or classifying plants. Students spoke positively of their elderly literature teacher, who joyfully used old Chinese classics as basic reading material—now that they were no longer branded as unacceptable because of a lack of revolutionary content. And students worried about their examinations. Gone was Mao's famous quotation, once used to challenge the educational bureaucracy: "To take an examination is to participate in one's own ambush!" For those seeking positions requiring educational knowledge, examinations were vital. For the rest, simply necessary.

Did education have much influence on one's later employment? The question was an important one in Red Flag Commune. Interestingly, in at least one instance, the answer appeared to be negative for young men and affirmative for young women. Commune statistics for the year 1978 revealed that there were 3,202 male junior middle school students and 3,037 female. However, the senior middle school had only 859 young men, whereas 1,035 were young women. Given the approximately equal balance between the sexes in the commune and the equal access to school facilities, what was the reason for the difference?

Unfortunately, data were unavailable from the commune for further study. However, in Half Moon, information from a village-level census showed that although there was a strong relationship between some junior middle school education and occupation for young men, its effect on income was not a positive factor. For young women, the correlation between education and income was pronounced. It seemed, therefore, that young men could enter the work force early without financial penalty, whereas young women benefited financially only by remaining in school.

PORTRAIT OF AN "EDUCATED YOUTH"

Not all the young people living in Half Moon and surrounding villages were educated in local schools. A few had received their middle school education in Beijing City or another urban location, after which they had been assigned to Red Flag Commune as "sent-down educated youth." This movement, most closely associated with the Cultural Revolution, actually had a longer history—beginning on a small scale in the mid-1950s, increasing gradually from 1962 to 1966, and then expanding dramatically from 1968 to 1976 before finally being concluded in late 1979. Although difficult to estimate, it was probable that between 18 and 20 million urban middle school graduates were sent to the countryside from 1956 to 1979. In this time period, over 7,000 were assigned to Red Flag Commune alone, most to work in the state sector.

The goal underlying this effort was threefold: first, to alleviate urban unemployment, which by 1957 had become a problem, particularly in the placement of recently graduated middle school students; second, to enable city youth to bring to the countryside their recently acquired modernizing skills and, in so doing, reduce the gap between urban and rural populations; and finally, to enable urban youth to live with, contribute to, and learn from the peasants in such a manner as to become ideologically "remolded" in order to assume the role of China's revolutionary successors.

The first aim was largely accomplished. Large-scale unemployment of urban youth did not become a serious problem in China until the late 1970s. The other two aims were successful only in particular instances in which sent-down youth were able to integrate themselves economically and socially into the life of the country-side. For the most part, even though the experience of living in villages deepened the urban youths' understanding of the economic poverty and social problems of rural life, it did little to help alleviate that condition for the villagers. At least, that latter point was the characteristic response of Half Moon villagers asked to comment on this massive experiment. In the peasants' view, urban youth lacked the experience, physical stamina, and commitment to be able to work effectively in the fields.

However, this appraisal hid an important fact. The young people of Red Flag Commune, living as they did near Beijing City, had many advantages over those more isolated rural youths located at a greater distance from China's urban centers. Although commune young people were not comparable to urban youth in their level of education, sophistication, and life experience, neither were they comparable to those in much of North China's vast hinterland. As a result, when Beijing youths were assigned to Half Moon and other Red Flag villages, they were immediately placed in competition with local young people for the few semiskilled or skilled positions requiring at least a partial middle school education.

Not surprisingly, local youths usually received better placements, such as that of accountant, while youths from Beijing found themselves relegated to the life of a relatively unskilled field worker. The latter's limited success in this endeavor was reflected in their work-point average: in 1978, the last full year in which "sent-down educated youth" were assigned to Half Moon Village, the average was a very low six points. The one real financial contribution received by the village came not from the educated youth themselves, but from a block grant of several hundred *yuan* that the central government had given the village for the settling-in costs of each arriving youth. In other words, Half Moon didn't really need city youth, though it could always use them as field hands, especially if the government helped support them.

In the state-controlled sector of the country, the situation was different. Indeed, many thousands of urban youths had been initially assigned to state farms through-out China's countryside, especially in its remote border areas. So too, various state-run enterprises of Red Flag Commune received large numbers of urban youths, who were immediately put to work in tractor stations, machinery-repair shops, dairy farms, experimental agricultural plots, and other locations where their knowledge and experience could be put to more constructive use.

Interested in the innovative nature of the movement to send urban youth "Up to the Mountains and Down to the Villages," and at the same time wanting to learn more of the problems that had seriously weakened its effectiveness, I sought out several relocated youth who still lived in the commune. Of those interviewed, one individual stood out as having the special kind of maturity, objectivity, and sensitivity that an anthropological fieldworker always seeks in a key informant. In this case, that person was Zhang Yanzi, the local tractor driver.

Actually, most of her life as a sent-down youth had not been spent in the commune. Rather, she had originally volunteered to go to a state farm in Northeast China. However, the fact that she had discussed her Northeast experiences with Half Moon Village and other commune members was important, for only by such means were local residents able to deepen their knowledge of the sent-down youth movement elsewhere in China. Wanting to learn what other villagers already knew, I asked if she would be willing to share that part of her life history. After some initial hesitation, she agreed.

It wasn't until late October that she was able to arrange some time in her busy schedule for our get-together. We met at the home of some common friends, who, after offering us some hot water in the courtyard, excused themselves to clean up and prepare for the evening meal. Sitting on two straight-backed wooden chairs, facing the warm rays of the late afternoon sun, we chatted for a few minutes, sipping our water and commenting on Half Moon's efforts to obtain a new tractor. It wasn't easy for her, having to exchange her role as tractor driver for that of social historian and analyst. I watched carefully as she tried to relax, leaning forward in her chair and blowing gently into a metal teacup held in both hands. A smudge of grease on her strong angular face helped communicate her occupation as mechanical worker, just as her muscular body spoke of a decade of outdoor work in the countryside. Only one incongruous feature gave any evidence of her earlier life as an urban youth: the slightly waved set of her dark hair. I switched on the tape recorder and began the interview with a question.

"Zhang Yanzi, when did you decide to join the movement to the countryside?"

"I first heard about the 'Going to the Countryside and Settling Down with the Peasants' campaign when I was in middle school and decided to apply. After graduation, I was assigned to a state farm in the Northeast and left Beijing on December 5, 1967. Really, it was run as an army production unit, but it was no different from a state farm except for the army. When I arrived, there were only 200 students, but in the following year, 3,000 more arrived. They came from all over, including Beijing, Shanghai, and Hangzhou. Many educated youth went to the Northeast—in all about 300,000. Some of the farms had as many as 70, or even 90 percent, youths in each unit. Before we came, there were only a few older cadre and workers. Some had been reassigned in 1955–56, after the Korean War, and others had come from Shandong Province in 1958. They were the only older people in the area. Having been in the army, they had a good work history and tradition.

"When I arrived at the farm, my first job was as an agricultural worker. Then I was a primary school teacher for a while. I was only 16 then, and some of my students were older than me. I didn't feel much like teaching them because my parents were intellectuals. During the Cultural Revolution, my father was badly treated by his students, so I didn't want to be a teacher in the school. I complained a lot and finally got transferred to a production unit. The conditions were pretty bad. I fed pigs for a while and then worked as a cook. Finally I became a tractor driver. Then, for health reasons, I went back to teaching in 1976 and was finally transferred here in 1977."

"Were you under any pressure to go to the Northeast?" I asked Zhang.

"In the beginning, no pressure was put on anyone to go. It was all on a volunteer basis. Each individual had to pass the 'Three O.K.'s.' One was from the actual student, one from the family, and one from the school. If there was any disagreement, then the person wouldn't go. Even if you hesitated just before climbing on the train you could stay. But we didn't do that. We were all very enthusiastic.

"Only later was the policy changed. Then, instead of volunteering, every urban family with three educated children had to send two of them to the countryside. Only one could stay behind. If you didn't go, your parents would be organized into a study group. Before my brother went, they had my parents in a study group. Once the parents agreed that the children could leave, then they stopped. Otherwise, they had to continue."

"Were other means also used?"

"If a family still didn't agree, neighborhood committees would come out to the street and beat big gongs, hang up 'big character posters,' and use other kinds of propaganda to persuade you to let your children go. They would just keep on coming back, trying to talk to you over and over again until you finally agreed.

"But in the beginning it wasn't like that. It was different. We went because we were filled with the spirit of conquering difficulties. We knew the countryside was backward and life would be hard. Actually, except for the weather, it wasn't as bad as we thought it was going to be. We had good preparation, and we wanted to make a contribution. But it was cold. We were told that if you went outside in winter without a hat, your ears would fall off. Nobody lost their ears, but a few lost some fingers and toes.

"We all ate together in the public dining halls with some of the older workers. Even though conditions were bad, they took pretty good care of us, giving us easier jobs and better housing. There were a few peasants at the farm, and they too were helpful. But not long afterward, the political factionalism began. It started among some of the older workers and soon spread throughout the farm. We got involved, and the younger workers did too. Because we dared to speak up, we were sometimes used as a tool by one faction against another. And more and more students arrived. After a while, all you could see on the farm were educated youth. We were supposed to learn from the peasants, but the only ones around were the storekeeper and a few others. Pretty soon the young people began talking down to the peasants, saying they were dirty and uncultured. They called them 'countrymen.' It sounded good but it was really sarcastic, sort of like 'country bumpkin.' In units where there were few educated youth, the work was done better, but where they were the majority, the problems became severe."

"What were some examples?"

"There were all sorts of problems. One was not enough concern being given to our political development. Another was the factionalism. Some of our leaders were not very healthy in their minds either. A few senior cadres, even those wearing army uniforms, began abusing the educated youth, molesting them. These included a few pretty high officials. One, in particular, molested many young girls, raped them and made them afraid to talk to anyone else. If they spoke out, he asked their units to accuse them, criticize them, and put a lot of 'labels' on them. If they wanted to go home for a vacation, he wouldn't let them go. It was like house arrest. At other times he would try to soften them up by giving them a better job.

"After a while, these corrupt officials became a network of people molesting and covering up for their activity. Once, an educated youth's parents who were working in a central government office in Beijing started an investigation through the Ministry of Agriculture. It took a long time for the investigators to find out anything, mostly because people were afraid to tell the truth. Then, the PLA headquarters in Beijing also began investigating. Eventually, they came to the unit leader and asked him to admit his crime and rectify his ways. But he refused to admit it. He was then arrested and later executed. That shocked a lot of people, especially because he was so well known. Afterward, the situation got a little better."

"Looking back on the overall policy, what is your evaluation of it?"

"I think educated youth going to the countryside was sound. It enabled them to learn more about the good qualities of the peasants and also some production skills. The problem was in the method used during the Cultural Revolution. Some locations didn't really need any more workers. In those places, instead of helping the local cadre to do their jobs better, it actually caused a lot of trouble. On the surface, people supported it because Chairman Mao said it was a good thing to do. People agreed publicly, but not privately. That was especially true in the army units. There were few organized plans to open up new areas for agriculture, light industry, or sideline production. In many areas, this lack of planning meant that more labor power had to be used to solve problems, rather than mechanization. This is not really the way out for agriculture. It is very tiring and low in efficiency. After a while, a lot of young people began to feel discouraged.

"In all those years, no machines were brought in to improve mechanization or open up new lands. Everyone looked to industry because it was developing faster. Eventually, the educated young people felt that anything was better than working in agriculture. Lots of empty slogans but no increase in production. So they began to talk about returning home. They said, 'If so little can be done here, we should be allowed to return to the city.' I too thought about returning. It wasn't an easy decision, and after I came to it, I found it was very hard to accomplish."

"What made you decide to go home?"

"I have two younger brothers. Both of my parents went to a May Seventh Cadre School early in the Cultural Revolution for political reeducation. One younger brother was still in primary school, and the other had just begun middle school. The whole city was pretty much in chaos, and no one was really able to care for them. My parents were quite concerned about having to leave the two children in the city by themselves, but there was nothing they could do about it except come back from the cadre school and visit them once a month.

"Soon my 11-year-old brother began running around with some bad kids. He learned to smoke and pretty much stopped going to school. The neighbors tried to help, but he wouldn't listen. My father still calls him illiterate. He thinks London is the capital of the United States and Spartacus is French. He is always confused about these things. Now, he is supposed to be a middle school graduate, but he sure didn't learn much of anything in all those years of school. That's what they got in the way of education during the Cultural Revolution. Anyway, when my older brother graduated and went to the countryside, that left my younger one home alone. So my parents thought I should return. Also, my health wasn't very good. So I applied to go home."

"Was it approved?"

"Going through the 'front door' is very difficult."[6] There are many procedures at different levels of government. And no one cares about you. First, they tell you to wait. Then you have to have a physical examination at the local hospital, followed by a check-up at the higher hospital. They just keep on delaying. They delayed my request for a year and a half, and still nothing happened.

"Some had their requests for going back to the city approved really fast. That raised many questions with the others. How did they do it? What did they depend on? Well, they depended on the 'back door.' At that time, the only way to get anything done was through the back door. My parents were once opposed to going through the back door. They didn't like that style of work. They told me that before the Cultural Revolution, back-doorism wasn't so common. So they asked themselves, if the Cultural Revolution is so good, why are there so many back doors now?"

"What happened then?"

"They didn't understand the change. They tried all the approved ways to get me back to the city, and nothing worked. They finally realized that if they didn't use the back door, nothing would happen. That had become my decision too. Others had submitted requests to return later than me, but all were approved except for me. They said my method was no good, that what was needed were cigarettes and wine to send to the right places. 'Go through the back door or it won't work,' they told me.

"I was hesitant. In some ways I wanted to stay in the Northeast. I had already been there almost 10 years. I saw all the changes. On my arrival, there were only 9 units. By the time I left, there were over 40. I was personally involved in the construction of several new units. It was just grassland before we started. We built a lot of houses, a storage barn, and a day-care center. We also reclaimed some land. There is a lot of my work and sweat in that place. So I really loved it.

"Most of the educated youth didn't think about how the peasants had to work that hard all their life. They didn't compare themselves with the peasants at all. They just thought that if they had a way to return to the city, why should they suffer there? Finally, in our company, there were only two educated youth left. All the others had fathers who were able to get them out. Then I began to think, 'How come my parents can't get me back to Beijing? I must not have a good father or I would be back there now.' That was my thought at the time. But still, I hadn't really made up my mind. Other things finally helped me to decide."

"What were they?"

"There were two reasons actually. On four different occasions, I applied to go to a university, once to Beijing and three other times in other parts of the country.

---

[6]In China, a commonly heard expression is *zou houmen*, which means "going through the back door." The history of this custom is as old as China's bureaucracy. It enables leaders, civil servant cadres, and others to benefit themselves, their kin, and groups they represent through personal ties, contacts, and behind-the-scenes dealings, often to the detriment of the larger population of which they are a part. Going through the "front door" is to follow proper procedures.

There were tests then, but it was just a formality. The results didn't make any difference. Who went to school was still based on political requirements and one's class background. Whether one was qualified academically didn't make any difference. When I applied, each time I was approved by my local leadership. On three occasions I was almost admitted, but it fell through because of the political department. I was not a party member. Second, my parents were not workers or peasants or cadres. For these reasons, I was seen as politically inferior, and therefore never was admitted to college. I wanted to learn mechanization, machine building, things like that, or go to agricultural school. I did a lot of self-study, and I wanted a university education. But it wasn't going to happen. So I felt very pained, very disappointed.

"The other reason why I finally decided to leave was that the party branch was trying to train me and educate me. I was hard-working, sincere, and very active. I never complained about the work or that it was difficult and tiring. Also, I felt free to express my ideas. Two times I filled out an application form for party membership at the local party branch. Each time, they discussed it with me and then reported to the higher leadership. Neither time did they get approval. The higher leaders told them I was not determined to stay in the countryside. My boyfriend had joined the PLA for five years. He was in radar. After his service, he went back home. Because he returned to Beijing, I was in trouble. If my boyfriend is there, people will think I'll want to return also. A person without the determination to remain in the countryside cannot join the party.

"Then my boyfriend asked his unit if he could be transferred to the Northeast, but it wasn't approved. His family opposed it strongly. So did his friends. The reputation about Heilongjiang [Province] was really pretty bad, especially among Beijing people. Since his family and friends were opposed to his coming, it made me think about why everyone hated the Northeast and the army production unit. Finally, I decided I didn't want to stay there any longer. It was not for me any more.

"It was under these circumstances that I wrote my parents. Before I first left Beijing, my father told me something that made a deep impression on me. In his heart he didn't want me to leave home, but because he was a teacher, a 'bourgeois' intellectual, he couldn't say anything. If he opposed my going, a bad label would be put on him for trying to stop the revolutionary action of youth. So he could only support it. What he said was, 'We are not afraid to have you go now, but we are afraid you won't come back later.' He meant, if I was to go he still wanted me to come back. I have remembered his words all these years.

"After receiving my letter asking if he could get me home, my father wrote back and criticized me, saying I shouldn't think in such terms. I should not go through the back door. I should believe the party's policy would solve my problems. Of course, I knew these were empty phrases. So I waited. A little later, a close friend of my parents who worked in the Education Ministry visited their home and told them they shouldn't be so honest. 'It won't work,' he said. Then he went on: 'Listen to me. I won't ask you for money. I won't ask you for anything else, not for cigarettes or liquor. Just find a good teacher for my children so they can be well tutored. If you do that, I will make a recommendation for your daughter to be transferred to the countryside near Beijing in Hebei Province. From there it is not difficult to transfer to the city. You can even help me write the recommendation letter.' My parents finally agreed.

"For me, that was great news. In the past, my parents had always helped other people but never asked for help in return. Now they were going to help me. During Spring Festival, my father asked me to come home. He then told me the whole story. Either I could be assigned to the countryside in nearby Hebei or I could come home and wait for an assignment there. But I did have to return to the Northeast until the formal transfer and teaching certificate had been approved. It wasn't very long before I was home.

"While at home, I met my uncle who lives in Shijiazhuang. He is also an intellectual, an engineer in the city fire department. Because of his educated background and being a leader in the city, he too was hit during the Cultural Revolution. He was beaten up, and one of his legs was broken. He had three children, just like our family. Two went to the countryside. They both married local people and never came back again. My uncle once praised my father, saying that as a result of the Cultural Revolution, he had become an 'enlightened' intellectual. His remark actually had several meanings. On the one hand, he was telling my father that he was smart to have learned these tricks. Of course, he also knew that it could be dangerous if an intellectual was caught using the back door. But mostly, he was criticizing the Cultural Revolution for corrupting people. My uncle had been a party member in Shijiazhuang and had had his membership taken away from him. Now, of course, it has been restored. But all during the Cultural Revolution, he never did use the back or side door for his kids. His wife cursed him, saying he was dumb, that he was a stubborn intellectual while my father was the enlightened one. But he never changed. Now he is doing research at an institute in Hebei."

"And you?"

"As for me, after staying home for a while, I had an opportunity to come here, not as a teacher but a tractor driver. After two years I could have gone back to Beijing. Still, if I accepted a transfer then I could receive only 18 *yuan* a month, whereas if I decided to remain I could get 30 *yuan* or more. So, I decided to stay. I like it here driving a tractor. It is a good life."

I looked up from my note-taking. Having been immersed in her story, I was not quite prepared for its abrupt conclusion. And yet, as the cold chill of the late afternoon air replaced the fading rays of the sun, I knew we should stop. So did our friends, who called from inside the house to their two young children who were playing on the other side of the courtyard. It was time for their dinner and that of the rest of the family. I expressed my appreciation to Zhang for her assistance, said good-bye to our hosts, and took my leave.

Walking down the long lane to the other side of the village, I thought about the interview and how illuminating it was. In one sense, it was simply Zhang Yanzi's story told in her own words. But in another, her life experience and the insights she brought to it had a larger proprietorship, because of the many who could learn from it.

Zhang had committed herself to the same political ideal that guided the self-reliant construction and funding of the middle school near Half Moon. But the material success of this effort was not equaled in the movement of sent-down youth to the Northeast. Poor planning, increasing political factionalism, and corrupt management eventually led her to question the implementation of the whole project and, therefore, her contribution to it. Like many Chinese youth with similar experiences (see Siu and Stern 1983; Liang and Shapiro 1982), she became disillusioned. Deciding to return to Beijing, she finally accepted help through the back door earlier rejected. However, what struck me most in listening to the story was not the adversity she had overcome or the clarity she brought to her analysis, though both were considerable. Rather, Zhang Yanzi's ability to cast her experience in the context of the society's larger goals was what gave her commentary such quality—that, and her sense of humanity.

6/Becoming an Adult

RELATIONS BETWEEN THE SEXES

When was a person considered an adult in Half Moon Village? The answer: when one married. A 22-year-old married man or woman was thought to be more adult than an unwed 25-year-old. And this was true regardless of the financial contribution the man or woman might make to the family income—quite a contrast to the United States, where age and economic independence were the key indicators of adult status.

An equally significant cultural difference between China and America was found in relations between the sexes. In both societies, teenage boys and girls became increasingly attentive to one another. But there the similarity ended. In Half Moon Village, relations between young men and women were far more constrained than in a typical rural American community. This was illustrated in patterns of courtship and engagement. In Half Moon, courtship usually began after one's engagement, rather than before. Why not the other way around? Part of the answer was found in the manner in which members of the opposite sex related to one another socially and sexually. More significant was the close relationship maintained within the adult-centered family. And as far as the older generation was concerned, the selection of a marriage partner was far too important to be left to the son or daughter. Let's look at each relationship in turn.

After finishing school, most village youths were assigned by the brigade production committee to work in the fields. Middle school graduates, and those who showed particular promise or had good family "connections" *(guanxi),* hoped for factory placements. Still, wherever they were assigned, young people soon learned that their new status greatly expanded their ability to develop friendships with members of the opposite sex. In contrast to the household and the classroom, where parental constraints discouraged close relations between the sexes, the workplace offered a more open environment. In the fields, young men and women occasionally shared tasks, particularly during planting and harvesting seasons. In the factory, they often worked side by side and in other ways found time to talk and visit freely. Being attracted to each other, late adolescent youths made use of such settings to explore common interests out of which affection could grow.

Still, in Half Moon Village, any expression of serious interest between two young people was hidden from outsiders as much as possible. Indeed, the strictures and pressures were sufficiently strong that even commonplace activities, such as informal conversations between two people of the opposite sex, could lead others in the village to suspect that a "love relationship" was being established. In villages where many peasants belonged to the same lineage, informal social ties between two related members of the opposite sex did not lead to such conclusions. But in Half Moon, with its larger number of nonrelated families, a couple talking in a "natural" way, or conversing regularly, could easily become an object of gossip.

In evenings after work, young people's accessibility to members of the opposite sex was more limited. Sporting events, Communist Youth League meetings, or political study classes could bring young people together. But, for the most part, unmarried women remained indoors helping their mothers make clothes for younger siblings or perhaps sewing their own. If they had nothing else to do, they could always knit! The underlying theme was obvious: women always had work to do. Furthermore, unmarried women should not wander around the village at night. To do so aroused unfavorable comment. Decent, well-behaved girls stayed home and worked.

In contrast, young men rarely remained at home in the evening. They did not have the responsibility of a family. Life was considered boring at home, and if they stayed, they might be asked to do some housework, repair a tool, or take on another task preferably left to a younger sibling. So, after dinner and cleanup, young men regularly headed out the courtyard door for the cooperative store, plaza corner, clinic office, or other center of social activity where they could talk with friends or join one of the seemingly endless card games that formed an important part of adolescent leisure-time activity.

However, one recent village innovation had substantially altered this pattern of youthful socializing: the brigade-owned television set. On any summer evening at the plaza's edge, crowds of people of all ages watched the news, drama, and other programming from Beijing and elsewhere. Young people too were drawn to the evening television fare, though not just for electronic entertainment. If an adolescent male wanted to invite a woman friend to watch the community T.V. after dinner, he did not go to her home and ask directly, for that would draw suspicious remarks from others. Rather, he got his seven-or-eight-year-old brother to propose to the girl's younger sibling that the two of them watch T.V. together—knowing full well that the woman he admired would be asked by her parents to go along too, just to keep an eye on her younger sibling. In that way, the couple could be together without being too obvious.

Finally, various festivals and celebrations offered opportunities for young people to meet and get to know one another. Spring Festival (Chinese New Year), held in late winter, was a particularly important period. With little work to be done in the fields, more time was available to spend visiting friends and relatives.

The Communist Youth League was also quite active at this time, organizing young people to popularize the party's policies, such as "Equal Pay for Equal Work" or "Strive to Implement the Four Modernizations." Such popularization commonly involved group performances, including singing, simple dancing, excerpts from traditional or local opera, and "cross-talks." Performances always involved a rehearsal or two, and sometimes even more. Thus, young people gained another opportunity to become better acquainted.

An evening card game.

As these individuals approached their mid- to late teens, relations between the sexes assumed a more romantic flavor. I once asked several adolescent boys and girls what they looked for in a friend of the opposite sex. Most responded with embarrassed silence followed by nervous laughter. On further probing, they spoke of the importance of sharing common interests and "seeing things in a similar way." But my next question—"Might this individual be seen as a possible marriage partner?"—turned out to be my last. The topic was too uncomfortable for them to discuss with a foreigner in mixed company, or perhaps even separately. Still, older boys and girls were drawn to one another even though physical manifestations of this feeling were actively discouraged by the elder guardians of village norms.

What about the sexual side of adolescent behavior? Was village life as puritan as it appeared on the surface? Not really, although to a Westerner, the atmosphere appeared strikingly asexual. Physical features were deemphasized by loose-fitting clothing. Sexually oriented advertising, whether direct or subliminal, was completely lacking. Touching between members of the opposite sex in public was rare. In this kind of environment, peasant youth simply did not have the problem so often faced by American youth of having to adapt to a multitude of sexual stimuli.

Discussion between youths and adults about human sexuality was also muted. Young girls, for example, received little if any information about menstruation prior to its occurrence. Therefore, on the eventual day, a girl might have to ask her mother what was "wrong." Nor did mothers or grandmothers easily engage in discussions about sex with their unmarried daughters and granddaughters.[1] In

---

[1]Married women had few constraints in their discussions with one another. They joked about their husbands' sexual prowess or lack of it, commented on a rumored village adultery, and in other ways exhibited considerably greater freedom of expression than either unmarried peasant or urban women.

contrast, training in modesty was emphasized over and over again. Girls were taught to sit with their legs close together and to speak in a quiet voice. When resting in the fields, they were expected to lie on their sides rather than face the sky. Natural science teachers or lecturers on family planning from the Women's Federation might refer to the biological aspects of sex, but that was all. For village girls, other knowledge of sexual matters came from talks with older unmarried female youths or from observation of local animals and, occasionally, parents and resident married siblings.

Adolescent boys, on the other hand, were less constrained in discussions of sex. Peasant cursing, a popular pastime, was very detailed in its sexual descriptions. Boys commonly shared sexually stimulating stories and songs, such as the tale "Great Auntie, Listen to Me," which described a girl who traveled to a local fair. On the way she met a soldier, who grabbed her and threw her down in a nearby field. The encounter that followed was highlighted with explicit sexual descriptions. Needless to say, the story also portrayed the repressive side of male-female sexuality, with its accompanying dehumanization of women. Also sexually explicit were stories about the rape of a bride on her wedding night or songs about lovers who met in secret.

Such an approach to this aspect of human relations had its obvious penalty. Expressions of warmth between individuals were viewed positively. Sex, other than for reproductive purposes, was viewed more ambiguously. Boys caught masturbating (literally translated, the word means "hand lewdness") were told that they would suffer from insomnia and impotence. Young unmarried men and women who expressed special friendliness toward one another were gossiped about. By the time a couple married, social and psychological tensions about sexuality were fairly pronounced. Sex and procreation were largely synonymous, but sex and recreation were not.

Problems caused by this ambivalent attitude toward sexuality even had their ramifications in the political sphere. Walking by the plaza one day, I noticed several young men laughing over a newspaper cartoon that had recently been brought to the village by a worker from the city. Joining them, I asked what was so funny. They pointed to the cartoon and then looked at me, waiting for my response. The drawing was of a young man and a young woman talking with one another. However, the man was dressed to look much older, and he wore a fake long white beard, which was attached to the top of his head with a string. In his hand he held a wooden cane. From his lips came the words, "Comrade, the next meeting of the Communist Youth League will be held . . ." The underlying message was that young men and women could have perfectly good reasons to meet together. One shouldn't have to pretend to be old in order to ward off gossip about being seen with a member of the opposite sex.

SELECTING A MATE

When a young man became 19 or 20, and a woman slightly younger, the parents— and particularly the mother—began asking relatives in other villages, friends, and neighbors to look for a possible spouse for their son or daughter. If the parents had a specific person in mind, they asked a relative or friend to inquire of the other family whether they might be interested in such a marriage. The economic and social importance of this process was so significant that, historically, it often required the skills of a go-between or matchmaker to negotiate a fair exchange of goods between the families, taking into account the age, status, and wealth of the two groups. In 1979, except for receiving a small present, the introducer was not directly paid for her services. But she did exist in another form—as a friend who could assist in establishing a new link between two families. Usually, such an individual was a relative from a nearby village.

Regardless of who proposed the candidate, once a suitable prospect was found, the parents discussed it with the son or daughter. Commonly, the mother was in charge of this activity; first she raised it with the father and, if he approved, then with the son or daughter. Throughout the process, the father remained in the background, acting more as a consultant than an initiator. If both parents considered the potential match a good one, they actively encouraged the son or daughter to accept the arrangement. If the son or daughter opposed it, the parents would try to win the individual over. If these efforts were unsuccessful, the parents accepted their child's decision, though not the judgment. If they did otherwise, they could be blamed for a mismatch or, even worse, a divorce.

What criteria did the parents draw on in their selection of a spouse? Obviously, the individual should be able to make a good living. Beyond that, if their child was a daughter, the future husband should come from a family that didn't have too many younger brothers and sisters; that is, it shouldn't be too large. Second, the man should be honest, in good health, and have a good temper. Third, he should be capable. However, the daughter, taking a more romantic view, might well select appearance as the most important criterion, followed by personality, and finally, the size of the future groom's family. On the other hand, if the child was a son, the parents wanted a future wife who was strong and willing to work hard for the family. Second, she should be attractive in appearance and light-skinned in color. Light skin was a positive attribute reflecting a traditional North China peasant view that women should not have to spend as much time out-of-doors as men. But it was not limited to that. Light skin was also valued in its own right, as was softness of texture and quality of complexion. Peasant sons too usually esteemed a woman's attractive features and personality more than her ability to work hard in the fields.

From the parents' point of view, and that of children as well, the relative status of the prospective in-laws was an important aspect of the selection process. The well-known Chinese phrase "matching doors and windows" *(men dang hu dui)* essentially meant that the social standing and the economic and political background of the two families should be similar. During the Cultural Revolution, one's class background (poor or rich peasant, landlord, etc.) was also emphasized. More recently, this political criterion had been played down in favor of emphasizing the individual's or family's overall worth. Indeed, so many families had been looking for future husbands and wives based on their wealth, or whether they had a television set and good connections with powerful people, that the CYL and other party-led organizations began actively campaigning against it. One amusing cartoon, prominently displayed on a bulletin board at the district headquarters near Half Moon, reflected this concern by showing a woman posing with a young man

whose pockets were bulging with dollar bills and written contracts and whose face resembled a television set!

After an initial exchange of views between the two families under the guidance of a relative or matchmaker, a preliminary meeting was arranged between the prospective spouses. This could take place at the home of the future groom or bride, or that of a friend or relative. In those Red Flag villages located near the market town, the gathering might even be held in a restaurant. Wherever the setting, the meeting was likely to involve a considerable element of tension. This was particularly true of situations in which the prospective spouses, living in different villages, had not previously met. One way to reduce this stress was to limit knowledge of the get-together to the families concerned, along with a few close relatives and friends.

For example, if the young man was a field worker, he might choose to say nothing to his team members about the forthcoming meeting. So too, a girl was unlikely to mention it to others if she thought the initial effort might not be successful. Most commonly, the event was planned around a noon meal. If the man came to the woman's home, he ate with the whole family and in so doing had an opportunity to see what his potential wife looked like. But the prospective bride didn't have to be present all the time. The main purpose of the visit was for the parents to get to know the young man, to learn more about his background and his thoughts of family and future. Nevertheless, while he was responding to questions raised by her family, she could be sitting quietly, perhaps in a nearby room, listening most carefully to the conversation.

Obviously, this first meeting had an important bearing on the future. Shy young peasant men and women might say only a few words to each other, whereas more modern ones would take an active role in the discussion. In either case, if the couple decided to go ahead with the arrangement, they informed their mothers, who told the matchmaker, who in turn passed on the information to the members of the opposite family. At this point, the young man was free to go to the woman's village and visit her whenever he wished. The girl was more restricted in her visits to his family home. If, on the other hand, either of the two were adamantly opposed to the proposed marriage, and so informed his or her parents, the matter would be quickly dropped, with little discussion occurring outside the immediate family.

What about the reverse situation, in which peasant youths chose to marry in defiance of their parents' wishes? This was very rare, even under conditions of modern courtship. Such a decision was invariably limited to well-educated youth, particularly cadres such as teachers, accountants, and specially trained workers. These young people, almost all of whom were middle school graduates, had greater exposure to the urban world of Beijing, where it was more acceptable for young people to make the key decision concerning a marriage partner.

This exposure, begun in the senior middle school, brought together students from a larger network of villages and from families with a higher social and political status. Out of this experience, new friendships were formed, expanding further the pool of possible spouses. Later on, when these young people were assigned work in the brigade and factory, they continued their association with one another in political meetings, social gatherings, sport competitions, and similar events. For them, the prospect of parents, relatives, or a matchmaker deciding whom they should marry was old-fashioned and therefore no longer appropriate. Still, even in this circumstance, respect for one's elders led young men to inform their parents of their interest in a particular girl, after which the mother, through a go-between, would take up the question with the woman's family.

These two different courtship patterns, one preceding and the other following the engagement, could occur within the same family. When I first moved to Half Moon Village, I soon learned that Hulan, Father Wang's elder son, was a senior normal school graduate and a physical education teacher at one of the district middle schools. He had married Chao Liling, also a high school graduate and a very capable administrative cadre at a nearby factory. Both were party members. Each had become attracted to the other while they were student activists in the Cultural Revolution. Deciding to marry, they informed their parents. Hulan's mother then sought out an introducer, who went through the ritual of speaking with the bride-to-be's family, even though they were previously aware of their daughter's interest in Hulan. The couple had married several years prior to my arrival in the village.

In contrast, the Wang family's second son, Hubao, began the engagement process shortly after I moved into their house. Hubao was 24 years of age. He had had considerably less schooling than his elder brother, and was both awkward and shy in manner. Several days before the initial meeting between the prospective couple (who had not previously met), the whole family engaged in a massive housecleaning. Noticing the rather unusual collective output of energy, I asked Mother Wang the reason.

"Oh, it's nothing. Just a little cleaning up."

"Can I help too?" I asked, knowing full well that I had yet to bridge the gap between foreign guest and friend.

"No, no. Look, I'm all finished," she responded, putting away the straw broom with which she had been brushing leaves from the overhanging eaves of the roof.

Obviously, my status as guest was still firmly entrenched.

Several days later, on a Saturday morning, an even greater flurry of household activity took place. Though unclear about what was happening, I was fascinated by the family's high state of excitement. Mother Wang first set to work making trays of vegetable-stuffed dumplings, or *jiaozi*. Then she began cleaning and polishing everything in sight. Father Wang, who seldom worked hard around the house, saw fit to straighten the wooden chicken fence and rearrange the stove wood stacked against the courtyard wall. Even to my inexperienced eye, it became increasingly obvious that the family was preparing for an important visitor. And on Sunday morning, when the house was bright and spotless, Mother Wang finally informed me that several friends were arriving around noon and that the family would be quite busy for the remainder of the day—by which she meant, of course, that the gathering was strictly family.

It was not until some time later that I pieced the story together. Visually, it was clear that an important event was taking place. Everyone was carefully dressed in newly washed clothes. Hubao, extremely nervous, hardly talked to anyone, even though everyone else in the household was most attentive to his every movement. At noon, two guests arrived. One was a young, stocky, and quite poised woman of plain features. The other was considerably older. The two were immediately welcomed into the center parlor and offered tea and candy. Soon, a few close relatives dropped by, and their visit was followed by more tea and the serving of a large tray of delicately cooked *jiaozi*. During the whole visit, Hulan, the eldest son, remained with the visitors. However, as soon as the meal was concluded, the second son, Hubao, and his two younger sisters withdrew to the courtyard. An hour or so later, as the invited guests prepared to leave, the family lined up on the dirt lane outside the arched brick gate to say good-bye. The young woman visitor's brother, who had been seeing another friend in the village, briefly appeared, and shortly thereafter, all three departed.

What actually took place? On inquiring, I found that a few months previously, Mother Wang had let it be known to a few close relatives that her younger son was in need of a wife. She consulted as well with an old friend, "quite experienced in matters of this sort." After looking around, the old friend informed Mother Wang that she had found an excellent prospective daughter-in-law, a strong and hard-working young woman of good family. Furthermore, she was a party member. Wang Hubao's mother then informed her son of the matchmaker's efforts, and he agreed to the proposed meeting. However, after the luncheon, Hubao was far less certain about continuing the process. How much his hesitation was due to his own uncomfortableness about marrying and how much due to his initial evaluation of the young woman was difficult to determine. "She is not very pretty" was all he expressed of his feelings, and to that remark, his mother responded with her usual directness: "She's strong, she's capable, she's educated, and she has a good future. That should be enough!" The rest of the family agreed.

At that point, Hubao withdrew completely from the discussion, and there the matter rested for several weeks. I was unable to learn directly what further discussions had taken place within the family. Mother Wang did eventually inform me that, after thinking the matter over carefully, Hubao had decided to go ahead with the engagement. Very likely, the young couple would marry in a year or so. As for Hubao, he never said a word to me about it. Nor did I raise the issue with him. After all, it was strictly a family affair.

BEING ENGAGED

Once both families approved of a marriage, the engagement was formalized. However, the exact timing of the announcement varied from a few weeks to several months or longer after the decision had been made. In the interim, the couple got together occasionally, particularly during traditional festival celebrations. At other times, such as harvest season or if the woman's family was building a new house, the young man might come over and help out. But rarely did the woman appear at the home of her future husband except for a serious crisis, such as the death of a parent or close relative.

The formal engagement party usually took place in the home of the future bride. Present on the occasion were both sets of parents and other family members, plus the matchmaker and the young couple. A large meal was provided, following which the parents of the groom-to-be gave the young woman some new clothes. In addition, her parents received a gift of cash, perhaps 50 to 100 *yuan* or more. Such a gift was called "engagement money" rather than bride price, since it was not seen as a payment to the family for their daughter but rather as a contribution to be used for the purchase of additional clothes, furniture, and other items needed by the bride in setting up the household.

The time between the engagement party and the actual marriage also varied. Both the party and the Women's Federation exerted substantial pressure on families to postpone any planned marriage until the man was at least 25 and the woman 23. If the couple became engaged at an earlier age, they were asked to wait until they had reached the approved age before marrying. Yet, with the exception of a few young villagers either in or close to the party, most youths married between the ages of 19 and 22. Why was this the case?

A major reason was that the groom's parents were eager to obtain the additional labor of the new daughter-in-law, who would move into the household at marriage. Another factor encouraging earlier marriages occurred when the groom had to leave the village for an extended period of time, due perhaps to his being in the army or receiving a work assignment elsewhere. In such instances, the parents not only wanted to help the son obtain a wife but also wanted to be sure they gained a daughter-in-law. Several years ago, a village boy entered the army. On his return home, the parents found that all girls of suitable age were either engaged or married. Unable to find a wife for their son through the usual channels, the family was left with having to select a divorced woman—a highly undesirable prospect chosen only as a last resort.

The few more highly educated engaged couples felt less bound to tradition in contacts with their future spouses. Not only did they meet regularly, but they also socialized together as a couple. Still, whether they came from different villages, which was usually the case, or lived in the same village, they tried not to offend their more conservative older relatives by this behavior. In other words, the couple didn't flaunt the relationship by walking down the road by themselves, talking, smiling, and holding hands. They might do this in private, but in Half Moon and surrounding villages, such privacy was not easy to find.

Although financial considerations were an important part of the proposed marriage contract, they had changed dramatically from years past, when a poor family with three or more daughters dreaded the prospect of marriage because of their limited ability to provide a dowry to the groom's family. The amount of dowry contributed, including furniture, clothes, and daily necessities, as well as money, immediately established the bride's family's status within the village. If they gave very little, they could be ridiculed by both the neighbors and the groom's family. The groom's parents, and most particularly the mother, might even express displeasure directly to the family, causing them even more embarrassment. And needless to say, after the marriage, treatment of the new daughter-in-law was even more exploitative.

In these earlier times, one of the major reasons for the high incidence of female infanticide among Chinese peasants was the high cost of providing for the daughter's marriage. The prospect of having to go into debt or sell land to provide an adequate dowry at the time of marriage was so economically threatening to poor peasant families that they sometimes chose the alternate course of killing their newborn female child by drowning or strangulation.[2]

More recently, although dowries were still given, parents were more reasonable in their expectations, acknowledging that some families might find it difficult to contribute very much. Furthermore, what was contributed, such as clothing and household utensils, was usually given to the bride and groom. It was not the dowry, but the continuing practice of the "bride price" that received critical attention. Excessively demanding parents were criticized for treating their daughters as "money-shaking trees," requiring a large amount of money from the family of a prospective groom as a form of payment for raising their daughter. The parents' argument was that, under present circumstances, when a young woman left the household, it represented a substantial loss of family income, in contrast to earlier years when women were less-active field workers. Since women now earned more at home, the "price" of wives should go up!

Obviously, such an argument received little favor from the Women's Federation and other brigade leaders, who pointed out that such thinking was a carry-over from the past, when daughters were "sold" rather than given away in marriage. But it did occur, particularly in villages that were poorer than Half Moon and where financial need was greater and conservative views more pronounced. Again, the fact that the issue was regularly addressed in local newspaper and magazine articles reflected a continuing need to chastise this type of thinking.

Still, marriage was a costly step for all concerned. The issue was magnified when the groom's family had three or four sons, for along with money and presents, the family had to carry the responsibility for providing furniture and housing as well. This was why families with many sons encouraged one or more of them to try and find work outside the village. In such circumstances, if the son found a wife by himself, the family wouldn't have to spend so much money on his behalf. Or, the parents might allow one son to marry into a family that had only daughters. A family without sons always wanted to have a son-in-law in the house. This, in turn, relieved the family with many sons of having to assist all of them in establishing new homes.

One example of this reverse (uxorilocal) residence pattern occurred in Half Moon about two years before my arrival in the village. In this instance, the bride

---

[2]By the late 1970s, Chinese newspapers were reporting an increase in female infanticide, though for quite different reasons. With family-planning policies trying to limit births to one, married couples wanted to be sure that the "one" was a boy. The issue of family planning is discussed in Chapter 7.

had four sisters and no brothers. It was, in the words of Father Wang, "a very poor family indeed." However, with the arrival of the groom in the household, the family fortune took a decided turn for the better. The young man was welcomed by his new relatives, though he commented that it took quite a while to feel comfortable in his new position as a male in a family of "maternal kin." Some time later, one of the two women barefoot doctors, an educated youth from Beijing known for being more outspoken than was customary in the village, commented on the marriage arrange-ment: "I'm not surprised he found it difficult. Now he knows what we go through all the time."[3]

A second example of a groom moving in with the wife's family had a different cause. It occurred during the height of the Cultural Revolution, when those with a "bad" class background were being attacked by young Red Guards and members of a local radical faction. The young man in question was the grandson of a well-off landlord family. Having been the focus of much verbal abuse and worse, he neatly resolved the problem by moving into his wife's household and assuming her parents lineage, thus improving his political status.

More recently in Half Moon, questions involving courtship and choice of spouse have been given little attention by the local party committee. Only if a villager held an important position in the party or brigade leadership would the committee become involved in the selection process, seeing to it that the person found a spouse who had a good family background and was politically progressive. If a village youth was crippled, disfigured in some way, or partially disabled because of an accident and therefore less desirable as a potential spouse, the local party committee might also assist in finding a mate. If it was successful, the person who married the disabled youth was held up in the local commune newspaper as a model for others to follow.

THE MARRIAGE DAY

The most popular time to hold a wedding was during Spring Festival in either January or February, depending on the lunar calendar. Historically, this has been the slack season for field work, giving peasants more free time for other activities. The old belief system had long supported this custom. If one worked through the new year without taking several days off, bad luck would abound. So Spring Festival was a time for relaxation, visiting relatives and friends, cleaning house, and having a big feast. If a marriage was in the offing, what better time than Spring Festival, when villagers were relieved from work, able to travel, and in a holiday mood? Also, to wait a few months might place a burden on the stored food supply drained by a long winter.

Planning for the event could last anywhere from several days to a year or more. As far as the law was concerned, a wedding was easily accomplished. All the groom

---

[3]Margery Wolf, analyzing this uxorilocal marriage pattern in Taiwan, has pointed out that the wife's relatives, fearful that the husband might take his family and leave the household, may create conflicts between him and his children, in the hope that if he does leave, the children will remain (Wolf 1970:59).

and bride had to do was bicycle over to the commune headquarters with relevant documents showing age, marital status, and occupation. After informing the couple of the legal implications, headquarters staff issued a certificate, and the marriage was completed. Party officials discouraged villagers from having an elaborate wedding, since the considerable cost could easily drain the financial resources of the family.

However, this perspective was not shared by many peasants. Instead, they saw the day as highly important, in that the marriage ceremony defined a new status for the couple—for, as noted earlier, it was not age that defined adulthood in Half Moon Village, but marriage. On such an occasion, a big celebration was called for, with liquor, sweet wine, and special foods. Appropriate rituals were taken seriously as well.

One day, a young, urbane college teacher from Beijing joined me for dinner at the Wang house. Also at the table was Huzeng, the Wang's youngest daughter. During our conversation, I commented on her recent engagement and asked her to describe her forthcoming marriage ceremony. With considerable shyness, Huzeng spoke first of the feast to be prepared by the groom's parents and then of her arrival, on the wedding day, at the groom's house and meeting his many relatives and friends. Village leaders would also attend. After a few speeches were made and acknowledged, she and her husband-to-be would go to the front of the room. Once there, they would bow three times to a picture of Mao—and she turned and pointed to the wall behind our dining room table, on which was tacked a colored poster of the famous leader—three times to the family elders and assembled guests, and three times to each other. Then they would be considered married.

At this point, new and old China came together in a most vivid fashion. The young, sophisticated teacher burst out laughing, slapping his knee and offering an unexpected but joking criticism of Huzeng for her "old-fashioned thinking"— particularly her expression of a feudal-like worship of Mao. Huzeng, red-faced and hurt, looked down at the food before her, embarrassed and angry at the urbanite teacher's response to her simple exposition of what she considered to be proper village behavior. I too was a little distressed at the young teacher's remark, for it was quite clear that it had caused Huzeng real discomfort. It also meant that there would be no further discussion that day of her forthcoming wedding. Still, even her brief description illustrated rather well how the old village rituals associated with marriage continued into the present. Of course, some content had changed, such as the shift in public veneration from heaven and earth and one's deceased ancestors to Mao. But traditional respect for living relatives remained very much intact.

As the time for the wedding approached, family responsibilities increased considerably. New quarters for the bride and groom had to be found, usually a room in the groom's family home. Once selected, it was thoroughly cleaned and the walls either whitewashed or covered with colorful paper. Preparations for the feast were made, including the killing of a pig by father or son. The pig was then sold to the district store in exchange for pork, special vegetables, cigarettes, candy, and cookies. Friends were asked to assume certain responsibilities, such as recording the arrival of guests and keeping a list of presents given. A careful accounting was important so that when the next marriage took place, gifts of equal value could be contributed in return.

Early on the morning of the wedding day, last-minute arrangements were made. A married daughter, returning home for the event, dusted rooms. Younger siblings ran errands. The mother supervised the cooking and similar activities while the groom and his father set up tables and chairs and in other ways made final plans for meeting the guests. Was the couple's new room prepared for their arrival? Were the bed, dresser, table, and chairs properly arranged? Were the presents placed on the table so that the new couple would see them when they first entered the room? Presents included items like a clock, a large thermos bottle, a teapot, and glasses. Tacked on the wall above the table might be several carefully drawn banners wishing the couple a "Happy Marriage" and offering advice to "Work and Study Hard Together Until Your Hair Is White." Clearly displayed at the bottom of each banner would be the signatures of those who had made it. And finally, on the other side of the room, lying on a *kang,* would probably be a new satin-covered quilted blanket, a gift from the groom's family.

Between nine and ten o'clock in the morning, the groom, dressed in his finest new clothes and together with four or five young friends, set out for the bride's home. Often they went on new bicycles borrowed especially for the occasion. When they arrived at the bride's village, her father invited them to enter the house and have some tea. They, in turn, offered the father cigarettes or a similar gift.

Before the groom's arrival, mother and daughter would have spent some emotional moments together, tearfully reflecting on the bride's forthcoming departure from her family. The bride's close friends were there also, helping her dress and comb her hair. An older, experienced woman might be asked to carefully remove the bride's facial hairs by the roots, thereby communicating to others the woman's new married status.

When the bride was ready to depart, the groom brought his new bicycle to the doorway. After saying a final good-bye to her parents (who would not attend the wedding), she climbed on the back of the bike. Several of her close friends, also on bicycles, accompanied the group back to the groom's house, watching all the way to be sure the bride's feet didn't touch the ground—a sure sign of bad luck ahead.

At the groom's home, the couple would find the courtyard filled with relatives, friends, village leaders, and family elders. Passing through the gate, the groom received the congratulations of those present and thanked them in return. The bride, however, stayed in the background, head tilted down, shyly greeting a few guests but saying little until her friends guided her into the house for a brief rest.

The formal ceremony began shortly thereafter, when the party secretary, a work-team leader, or another village authority asked the assembled guests to take their proper places. As voices quieted down, the bride and groom came together either in the courtyard or in the main room of the house, depending on the weather. Behind them was a table, and above that, hanging on a wall, was a picture of Mao or another, more current party leader. Standing at one side of the table were the family elders, at the other, the village leaders. In front were relatives and friends.

The couple was then introduced. This was followed by a short speech in which the village leader in charge extolled the importance of marriage and urged the couple to work hard to improve the economic life of the brigade. Concluding, he might remind them of the importance of carrying out the Four Modernizations and the government's program on birth control. The speech was then followed by another of equal brevity and similar in tone, usually offered by a second local official or a Communist Youth League member.

After these remarks, the groom expressed his thanks to the people present for their support and assured them of his determination to meet their expectations. At that point, the groom and bride turned and bowed to the picture on the wall, to their relatives, and to each other—in each instance acknowledging respect for the appropriate political and family authorities and, importantly, for themselves. A few others might speak briefly about the value of the marriage for the future of the family and the village, at which time the ceremony was completed and the feast began.

During the feast, men and women sat separately. After a while, the bride would excuse herself and to go to her new living quarters, again accompanied by her friends. Sitting on a chair or the *kang,* she would be served tea and special foods prepared for the occasion. The new husband remained in the main room or courtyard, eating and talking with the guests until everyone was finished. By midafternoon the guests would have left, and the couple retired to their room for a period of rest.

At this time, some couples might use the moment to perform certain magical practices, such as placing under their bed various objects symbolizing good fortune and harmony within the family. Dates were one such item. The Chinese word was *zao.* Its pronunciation was the same as that of the word meaning "early." An association was then made that was understood as "get a son early." Another item was peanuts *(huasheng).* The meat was big and white. Hopefully the son would also be fat (meaning strong) and white (meaning handsome).

The last of the day's challenges for the bride and groom was the custom of hazing the couple on the wedding night *(nao dongfang).* Around eight in the evening, young men would begin gathering outside the couple's room. The more popular or important the family, the larger the number of visitors. As the men entered, the bride offered them candies and tea. However, the formality of the greeting soon gave way to a teasing of the bride that steadily increased in its intensity. First, she might be asked to sing. She in turn would decline, head down and eyes averted, feigning total shyness. The young men would then insist. The bride, knowing that as soon as one request was fulfilled another more difficult one would follow, explored every possible strategy to postpone the requested action. But she had to use good judgment, for if she declined too often, the men might leave early, a serious affront to the family.

One common request asked of the bride (and also the groom) was to describe how they had first met, what they thought of each other, and any secret meetings they might have had. To the delight of the guests, the couple might well turn away in confusion, blushing and hanging their heads in embarrassment. For though modesty demanded their restraint, hospitality required a response. Bit by bit, the story would be coaxed out of them, to the immense entertainment of the listeners.

Although sex was seldom alluded to directly, sexual undertones often pervaded the evening's "entertainment." As already described, in the day-to-day lives of Half Moon's young people, touching, holding each other's bodies in an embrace, or kissing in public was definitely considered improper. With that thought in mind, the guests might tie a piece of candy or fruit to a string hung from the ceiling and then ask the couple to each take a bite at the same time, all the while keeping their hands behind their backs. Any attempt to accomplish the task immediately brought the young couple's faces into close contact—again, to the great amusement of the observers.

In another game, a long narrow board would be placed on the floor, and the bride and groom told to stand at each end. Then, both had to walk to the opposite end without falling off. Everyone knew that when the couple met at the middle, they had to hold on to one another to keep their balance. Or, guests might go further and ask the couple to hug or to kiss each other on the lips.[4] To keep the teasing from getting out of hand, the family could invite married couples to join the group. On one such occasion, several married sisters were so successful in protecting their younger sibling from the hazing that she was called on only to hand out candy all evening. Of course, the men also went home early. What was most significant, however, was whether the bride felt secure from the humiliation and loss of face that too much teasing could bring. If she did not have that security, her wedding day would be filled with anxiety.

When the party finally concluded later in the evening, the guests thanked the bride and groom for their hospitality and departed. However, the newly married couple still had to remain alert to possible harassment from young teenagers attempting to look through the window or listen through the wall for whatever might or might not be happening inside.

I once asked an urban educated Chinese woman who had spent several years in a North China village about the custom of *nao dongfang*. Her response was not unexpected.

"During the Cultural Revolution, I was sent down to the countryside like so many other young people. While there, I heard a little about it, but not very much. One evening during Spring Festival, after the wedding of a neighbor, several of my city-bred girlfriends and I decided to go to the groom's home to find out more. On the way, we met the Women's Federation leader, who asked us where we were going. We said, to the new married couple's house. She then laughed heartily and commented: 'I'm glad you saw me when you did. Don't go there.' Of course, we asked why. She said, 'Girls are not supposed to go.' Out of curiosity we asked again. Then she told us a few things that could happen. I learned about even worse things later on. Some of them are unspeakable."

Care must be taken in interpreting this young Chinese woman's remarks. To most Americans, the word *unspeakable* is likely to conjure up images of sexual acts

---

[4]A villager reported that in one instance, male guests had attempted to learn more of the bride's physical anatomy by telling her to bare a breast to show "whether her future children will have enough to eat." In such instances, what initially was a game of mild sensual teasing became a very real sexual humiliation of the woman.

ranging from the bizarre to the brutal. However, in her cultural context, where modesty was expected of all Chinese women and where sex itself carried many negative connotations, the use of such a word could evoke far less dramatic imagery. The subject itself was so taboo that I felt it best not to inquire further as to what she meant by the phrase.

For the first few weeks after the wedding, the couple regularly visited nearby relatives on both sides of the family. Perhaps a month later, the bride might return to her own family for a stay of several weeks, after which she and her husband settled down to a normal household routine. However, if they married during seasons other than winter, or if the groom was a factory worker, he would go back to work shortly after the marriage ceremony. Even in winter, if few relatives were around, the man returned to work quickly. To stay at home with one's wife during the day was not a customary practice.

The wife, on the other hand, knowing that she had to carry increased household responsibilities in her new home, more frequently postponed going back to work. A woman field worker might even wait until summer harvest or another busy season to return. However, such "waste" of field labor was actively criticized on local radio stations and in the press. Short articles tacked on the district office bulletin urged peasant brides to go back to the fields soon after marriage—an effort that appeared to have some effect. Of course, two related factors influenced that decision. First, since the bride had joined the groom's family, their income was increased by the wife's employment. And second, by working during the day, she could escape many of the household chores she would be expected to perform if she remained at home.

Shortly after the couple settled into their new quarters, the husband returned to his earlier practice of spending evenings out. If he spent many evenings at home, he soon found himself the target of his friends' teasing. "Tell us, how is your new wife?" "What do you do together? You must like her a lot, you spend so much time with her," and similar remarks were designed to maintain the male evening recreational pattern.

Within a year or two, the married couple might think about having a home of their own. However, since few could afford one right away, they usually remained with the groom's family for another year or two. The eldest son was always expected to remain at home, and other married sons could stay for as long as there was space. Of course, as children grew up and found work or spouses elsewhere, new rooms became available for those who wished to stay on. Parents, of course, wanted their married sons to remain, since they would bring significant income to the family and were an important form of old-age security. However, if the older generation had many children or a small house, most sons and spouses had to find other quarters.

When a couple had saved enough money, or if they were fortunate enough to have the financial help of their parents, they might decide to build a home. This required applying to the appropriate village leadership for an available piece of land. Since land was collectively owned and could not be bought or sold, it was simply "loaned" without charge. However, land used for housing was no longer available for cultivation. Thus, initial approval had to be sought from the brigade

A young couple building their own home.

production committee. Once approval was granted, construction began. The costs of building materials, ranging from 3,000 to 4,000 *yuan* for a three-room house, were borne by the couple and their parents. Small loans could usually be obtained from friends. Depending on the extent of financial outlay and available resources, the couple might hire a bricklayer or carpenter to help in putting up the shell. But even with such skilled help, most of the work of building a house was carried on by the couple and their nearby relatives.

All married couples electing to remain with the groom's family faced the task of establishing with the older generation a new set of relations based on their recently acquired adult status as husband and wife. Needless to say, such efforts were fraught with difficulty, especially when the conservative views of family elders clashed with the modern ones of their children.

7/Family Relations

KIN TIES

Throughout much of Chinese history, the lineage or clan has been noteworthy as one of the few institutions able to give assistance to individuals and their families in time of need. Unlike in Japan, help provided by the Chinese clan even cut across class lines. But that type of kinship system bore little resemblance to the one utilized by the future residents of Half Moon Village. For them, such extended units were largely an ideal rather than a reality, and the prospect of distant, more well-to-do relatives giving aid was very unlikely. Even the simple "stem," or three-generational family was difficult to hold together under the village's economic conditions.

However, the patriarchal nature of the old Chinese kinship system remained. All family members were taught to observe their "proper place," an arrangement obviously allowing little opportunity for the development of any sense of individuality among children. Instead, they were expected to accept the decisions of their elders without question. If they had any doubts about parental directives, they soon learned to keep them to themselves.

It wasn't until the early 1950s that this kinship system came under strong attack. A marriage law was passed in 1950 giving women new rights, including that of divorce. With land reform and the collectivization movement, the control over fields, animals, and tools shifted from the (stem) family to the cooperative work team and then the village brigade.

The impact of these events on the patriarchal household was considerable.[1] Daughters-in-law were understandably hesitant to leave a household they believed to be oppressive for an unknown future elsewhere, but at least that legal right became available to them. Decisions over land, though still under the control of the male-dominated extended family, were more collectively undertaken. At this same time, new village leaders like Li Haiping and Yu Futian, emerging out of the land-reform movement, began challenging the older established patriarchy. Or, put more precisely, the opportunity to assume a leadership position became increasingly open to capable, revolutionary-minded peasants regardless of their age. Age was no

---

[1]See Parish and Whyte (1978) for a thorough study of family and village life in a South China setting at this time.

longer automatically respected over capability. All these events dealt direct blows to the hierarchical status and privilege of the more senior male members of Half Moon Village. Later on, during the activist years of the Cultural Revolution, the "feudal backward patriarchal thinking" underwent even more criticism.

Although such efforts to change village thinking should not be underestimated, neither should those social forces operating in support of the older family system. For example, despite the improved transportation and communication facilities at Half Moon, its peasant population was relatively immobile—due largely to the strict residency policy enacted in 1954, severely limiting migration to urban areas. So too, the city's concern to obtain an adequate supply of vegetables for urban dwellers insured a certain agricultural stability, which also had its social counterpart. That is, a peasantry working long hours in the fields under a steadily improving economy spent little time questioning traditional ways.

Furthermore, although productivity had increased in the village, there was always the fear that something might happen that could again bring serious economic hardship. In principle, the national government assured any elderly or infirmed Chinese of the "five guarantees" *(wubao)* of food, clothing, medical care, housing, and burial expense. The assumption was that children or other relatives would usually provide such assistance. In situations in which no relatives were available, the question of who was to care for such an individual was less clear. In any case, actual requests for such help were rare. Since the mid-1970s, only four elderly villagers had sought any aid. All had been unable to work, had little income, and most important, had no nearby relatives. One additional partial recipient was mentally ill and barely able to care for herself. When queried, villagers admitted that some sense of shame was associated with receiving such assistance. But they also emphasized that if relatives were unavailable, the brigade or commune should assume responsibility.

In other words, at Half Moon in the late 1970s, kin were still seen as the most essential form of social security for the family. This was why many villagers still wanted three or more children, particularly male children, since they could be counted on to bring more income into the household and, later on, to care for their elderly parents. Obviously, such hopes went directly counter to the government's family-planning policy.

Finally, the traditional kinship system was supported by the custom of using back-door connections. As we have seen, an important example found in Half Moon was when local leaders placed their relatives in state-factory jobs, a decision that generated considerable bitterness among those who either refused to seek individual benefits through such means or, more likely, did not have relatives or friends in leadership positions.

It is against this historical backdrop that existing family relations could best be understood. When a young married couple settled in with the groom's family, they were expected to adjust much of their lives to the needs of the parents and grandparents. This meant, for example, that income received by the couple did not really belong to them. Rather, it became part of the family's overall earnings, and decisions on how it should be spent rested largely with the elders. Family chores were also assigned by the mother, and the daughter-in-law was expected to assume as much, if not more, responsibility than other children in getting them done.

Before the birth of the first child, relations between parents and the young married couple tended to be fairly prescribed in the sense that the latter would follow the guidelines established by the former. However, with the arrival of a baby, new conflicts were likely to arise. The new mother might wish to give most of her attention to the child while the husband worked. Such a decision would both reduce the family income and increase the grandmother's cooking responsibilities. The grandmother might not have complained when the daughter-in-law brought home extra income. But a loss of income and an increase in work load could cause real friction to develop between the two generations of women. How food was distributed at the table could also promote family conflicts. Ordinarily, the best food would be served to the older generation. But following a birth, the needs of the nursing mother and baby were considered primary, in which case they would be given the most nutritious meals. In most instances, such a decision was supported by all. However, if resources were scarce because of a low winter supply of food, problems could emerge quite easily. Finally, as the young mother began to see her child, herself, and her husband as a distinct family unit, she devoted less attention to his family, which further widened the gap between the two generations.

Eventually, the question arose whether the new family should set up a separate household. If the husband was the eldest son, or if there were no younger sons or just a daughter, the two generations might continue to live and eat together. Since the parents knew that at some time they could need the help of their sons and daughters-in-law, they coped with the situation by simply playing down any difficulties that might arise. However, if that strategy wasn't successful, they would actively encourage their son and his wife to move elsewhere, especially if they were assured that at least one other son would be available to care for them later on. Or, the younger couple might themselves come to the conclusion that it was time to leave.

Whatever the reason, after a decision was made to establish separate households (though often within the same compound), new problems emerged. Usually, relations between the son and his parents changed only slightly. In all likelihood, the mother would continue to spoil her son in the hope that he would care for her adequately in her later years, all the while remarking that "marrying a wife makes a son forget his mother." Of course, such a saying was based on a long history of experience. Being involved with his own family did indeed reduce the amount of time a son would spend with his mother and father.

However, more serious conflicts occurred between the young wife and her mother-in-law. Residing in the same household, or at least in the same living area, the two women often spent time together. Though one or both women might work outside the house during the day, they still carried major responsibilities for completing household chores. Naturally, the older woman would have certain established ways of fulfilling these tasks, ways that could easily conflict with those of her daughter-in-law. Or the daughter-in-law might wish to try doing things in new ways that disturbed the existing pattern. Or, quite possibly, the older woman, remembering earlier days when she was required to do most of the household work for her own mother-in-law, felt that she had the right to make similar demands on her new in-law. (Of course, the mother-in-law might try to win her daughter-in-law's support through generosity and kindness as well.)

Obviously, such conflicts were mediated by other factors that worked to bring grandparents, parents, and their children closer together. Young couples, with little experience in raising a family, looked to their older relatives for knowledge and advice. As they became older, grandparents needed the assistance of the younger generation. And as the children grew up, they too had more responsibility, carrying water, chopping wood, and caring for the garden. Essentially, each generation had a vested interest in maintaining relatively harmonious relations with the other. In Half Moon Village, this benefit was still sufficiently pronounced that compromise became the dominant means of conflict resolution within the family.

Nor did the newly established married couple have to face many difficulties with the husband's younger siblings or his grandparents Younger children delighted in having someone new around the house. Later on, the prospect of their becoming an aunt or uncle—a very important increase in family status—would be even more appealing. The kind of conflicts that did occur were caused by brothers and sisters who had too high expectations of the sister-in-law, or she of them. Or the new bride might feel that she was receiving less than equal treatment from her husband's parents in comparison with her sisters- or brothers-in-law, whom she perceived as having less to do around the house. On the other hand, the unmarried sisters, noticing that their mother had additional cooking and housework, might criticize their brother's new wife for not contributing enough labor to the family. Younger brothers, less involved in household chores, hardly ever found themselves in competition with the new sister-in-law and therefore had a more relaxed relationship with her; although, again, she was expected to assist them when the need arose. As for grandparents, they tried to remain aloof from any direct involvement in serious family disputes. If forced to intercede, they would commonly do so in support of their grandson's position.

Most disagreements that did occur between kin were half-buried in subtle nuances not always recognizable to those outside the family. However, within the family, the "message" was clear. For example, in one village home, a daughter-in-law who was often criticized for not carrying out her share of the family housework wanted to go to a nearby movie with her husband. Furthermore, she wanted her mother-in-law to care for her child while she was gone.

"Mother, there is a film being shown tonight in Old Cyprus Village. People say it's very good. Do you want to go?"

"I don't have the time. What are you going to do with the baby?"

"I can take him with me, but if you don't mind . . ."

"I have a *lot* of work to do tonight. Youngest son's shoes need repairing. Food needs preparing for tomorrow."

"Well, in that case, I think husband and I can take him with us."

"Isn't he too young to spend a cold evening outside? If he catches cold, you'll be in trouble."

"Mother, do you mean I had better not go?"

"Suit yourself."

In a somewhat similar incident, a village mother again chastised her daughter-in-law for not helping after the evening meal.

"Come help with the dishes."

"Mother, I can't do the dishes now because the brigade meeting is about to begin. Can I do them when I get back?"

"Well, I hate to see dirty dishes around. Let me do them myself. Next time, I hope you will finish the work first. Then do whatever you want."

These two examples, though somewhat lacking in subtlety for the sake of clarity, reflect the kind of criticism that was regularly shared between kin. Rarely was a negative comment presented directly to the offending individual, for such an act would cause the person to lose face. In the first instance, the woman alluded to her daughter-in-law that work needed to be done at home. In the second, when a direct request for assistance was denied, the mother did not confront the daughter-in-law with the demand that she remain, but she did make her thoughts on the matter clear.

Sometimes, of course, people became so angry that they were unable to control themselves. Yet, even here, face-saving mechanisms were usually respected. Early one Saturday evening, while sitting in the Wang courtyard talking with friends, I heard over the wall the loud shouts of an angry wife speaking to her husband.

"You only come home from the factory one day in seven. Today, I made a really special dinner for you, and you didn't even show up. Where have you been?"

"Now, take it easy. When I got to the village I met some friends in the plaza, and we got to talking about my new bicycle."

"You're always talking with your friends. You don't spend any time at home. The food's cold. Eat by yourself. I'm going out!"

Just at that moment, a visitor walked into the courtyard. The woman immediately stopped shouting, welcomed the guest, and together the three of them went inside the house for a visit.

Of course, most neighbors in the lane heard the argument, but none spoke about it in front of others. Nor did the wife share her frustration with those outside her own family. Angry confrontations of this sort were common in a few families, but they were certainly not a usual occurrence in the village. However, when family problems multiplied, the wife, or more commonly the husband, could become increasingly hostile toward the other spouse. If angry outbursts increased in intensity, or if the husband began to physically abuse his wife, then the neighbors intervened, either by calling for the couple's son if one lived nearby or by taking the woman to her own family home. In such situations, the son faced an obvious dilemma. Although he might be embarrassed by his parents' behavior, and in all likelihood was supportive of his mother's position in the dispute, he was not expected to openly criticize his parents in front of others. Usually he would choose to remain silent in the matter, displeasing both parents in the process, since each wanted his support.

If a couple found that they were totally incompatible, one or both might seek a divorce. But such a step was rare. In Half Moon, there had been only two divorces in over 20 years. Among the 20,000 families in Red Flag Commune, there were less than 30 divorces in the year 1979. Why so few?

Traditionally, divorce represented a break between two families as much as between two people. It was seen as a failure in which both families lost face. Such an event might also carry financial penalties, not the least of which could involve families having to exchange money originally donated as dowry or bride price. At an individual level, the greatest problem was the penalty divorce brought to women. A divorced woman was considered so "stained" that she would be rejected as a possible spouse by all but the poorest of families.

Still, divorce was at least legally possible. A request would be given to the legal affairs office of the commune, which, in turn, established whether the local brigade leaders and Women's Federation had done everything they could to resolve the marital conflict. Reasons given in seeking a divorce included ill-treatment by the husband; adultery, most frequently by the husband (although one husband complained that his wife continued to maintain ties with "an old boyfriend in her native village"); and inability of the wife to become pregnant after several years of marriage. However, in almost every instance, the pressure put on the husband and wife by both family and village leadership was so strong that the couple remained married, coping as best they could, even if that entailed an almost complete refusal to communicate with one another except through others. But this was the exceptional case. In most families, conflicts were common, but so too was their resolution.[2]

In conclusion, the traditional Chinese kinship system placed great emphasis on male heirs—individuals who would care for the parents in their old age, inherit the family property, and most important, carry on the ancestral lineage. With the changing economic, social, and political conditions in the village, including a real increase in the standard of living, this old system had undergone substantial change. No longer was the kinship system an instrument of domination residing in the hands of the elder generation, most particularly the men. Still, because of the village's uneven economic development, which enhanced competition for the limited available resources, and because of the continuation of many traditional beliefs and household practices, a number of these older patterns endured. One of the most entrenched, and therefore most difficult to change, was the economic exploitation of women.

THE CHANGING STATUS OF WOMEN

Before coming to Half Moon Village, I had read much about rural Chinese women and how their existence from birth to death was largely devoted to serving the male side of the family. This custom, summed up in the famous phrase *san cong si de* ("three obediences and four virtues"), required a woman to first follow the lead of her father, then her husband, and on her husband's death, her son, and to be virtuous in morality, proper speech, modesty, and diligent work. Of course, through personal ties with husbands and sons, women could manipulate the situation to gain some measure of control over their own lives. But such efforts were limited to the informal sphere. Women had no legal rights.

---

[2]The fact that the divorce rate was consistently low at Red Flag reflected the low intensity of political campaigns in the commune. Divorce had always been justified during these campaigns as a way of "drawing a line" between a given individual and an accused spouse. In urban Beijing, high divorce rates matched the most intense periods of political movements, such as the Anti-Rightist Campaign and the Cultural Revolution.

Perhaps the most significant event reminding a woman of her powerlessness was the day she left her own home for that of her new husband. Wanting to learn more of these customs of the past, I asked several villagers who might be able to help. As it turned out, Guo Dasao, a hefty, 53-year-old peasant woman who had spent the last 40 years of her life in Half Moon, appeared to be the best candidate. She agreed to the interview as long as two of her friends could attend as well. A week later, after dinner, I went over to her house. In the courtyard, several chairs were arranged in a semicircle. As her friends and I sat down, we were offered the usual hot water and, as a special treat, a bowlful of peanuts. As we slowly sipped our water, Guo Dasao began her story.

"I guess you could say I was a child bride. Or perhaps an un-paid-for daughter-in-law. Usually, the bride's family paid money to the groom's family for taking on the burden of feeding the child. But in my case there was no exchange. My mother felt badly about it, and many years later tried to make up for it by sending me money. Mother always told me that I had bad fortune and that it was in the stars that I would have a poor life. Of course, giving me away was a good example."

In response to my obvious question, she went on to describe life in her new home.

"I was poorly treated in my husband's household. I never had enough to eat and was always being beaten." Reaching behind her neck, she slightly lowered the back of her blouse. Then, turning around, she showed me several scars in verification of her remarks.

"As soon as I arrived here, my mother-in-law told me what to do. She never let up. For four years I did nothing but housework from morning till night . . .

"My wedding day was a very sad one for me. I soon found that my relationship with my husband was not good. I wanted to run away but had no place to go. I lost contact with my parents, and my three sisters had also been given away because there was no money to feed them. I felt very bitter toward my parents, although I knew they had no choice. It was a difficult time."

Then, turning to her friend Zhou, who was busily eating peanuts out of the bowl, she concluded her commentary with the remark: "Your marriage was arranged when you were 16. But your mother-in-law had died earlier, so life wasn't so bad for you!"

From later discussions with Zhou and several other older peasant women about their early lives, I soon came to the conclusion that Guo Dasao's story was not unique. Actually, most older women willing to comment on the matter spoke not only of how they had become quite isolated from their own families after their marriages, but also of how they never really gained a new one. Since women were excluded from the father's descent group because of the patrilineal kinship system and were often betrothed to another family at about the time they could have become economically valuable to their own households, it was hardly surprising that poorer peasant parents came to wonder about the usefulness of their female children. As mentioned previously, it was not uncommon that such "wonder" sometimes resulted in the death of the newborn child either by suffocation or drowning. Such was the intensity of the struggle for life among poorer peasant families. No names were mentioned, but it was clear that such events were not beyond the experience of a few of the older women of Half Moon Village.

A women's work team. Cabbages in the background were used for pig food.

If the marriage of a young peasant woman was the first step in achieving a lineage tie with her husband's family, the second was producing a son. Without such an event, the young woman could not become a part of the lineage genealogy and was effectively removed from having any formal kinship status whatsoever. Her full acceptance into her husband's descent group was not achieved, however, until her death, when a family tablet was made in her honor—thereby permanently placing her in the ancestral registry!

Not surprisingly, folk beliefs gave further support to this low status of women. Ghosts and evil spirits were thought to roam everywhere, often lying in wait for children, on whom they could bring misfortune. To protect a child, the parents might slightly mutilate several fingers, thereby making it less attractive to nearby supernatural beings. But girls, having a status inferior to that of boys, were less likely to be sought by such spirits. Knowing this, parents might place a woman's earring on the head of their baby boy, thereby protecting him from some evil that could otherwise harm their precious male child.

Finally, as long as a woman had produced one or more sons by the time she reached old age, she had gained a significant measure of recognition. Yet, however much that improved status was enjoyed, it was nevertheless frequently marred by her exhibiting over younger women in the household the same authoritarian control that she had once so abhorred herself. This was not to suggest that women never enjoyed the affection of parents or happiness in their daily lives or that they were unable to exert at least some influence on family relations. Indeed, many older studies of Chinese family life illustrate that the opposite was often the case (Wolf 1974). But in utilizing their varied skills to achieve goals large and small, women had to work through the existing kinship network and its spokesmen, sometimes the husband, more commonly the son (Priutt 1979).

This hierarchical pattern was quite effective in enabling the family elders to maintain strict control over the decision-making process. As we know, daughters-in-law had little say in family affairs, and their husbands spent much of their waking hours in the fields. This left the older generation in a position to exert a major influence on the young, thereby reinforcing through the socialization process their own privileged position. However, it should be emphasized again that in the poorer areas of North China, from which most of the older inhabitants of Half Moon Village emigrated, even the three-generation family was not always able to maintain itself as an economically viable unit.

After 1949, the traditional kinship system could hardly serve as a solid base on which to build the socialist society envisioned by China's leaders. Significantly, however, it was not the extended family itself that came under attack, although that proposal had been offered in the early 1900s by Chinese liberal and radical intellectuals, who urged that such families be broken up because they were Confucian and therefore outdated. Rather, it was the issue of women's exploitation that became the focal point of criticism by the new government. In one sense, this new focus simply gave support to a struggle that women had been carrying on for many years. Committing suicide was an active "choice" selected by more than a few women in opposition to the docile acceptance of their plight. Furthermore, for poor peasant families, the rallying cry of equality for women meant that they would no longer have to sell their daughters or give them away. Trying to address such problems, the new government passed the Marriage Law of 1950, which required free choice in marriage by both partners, guaranteed monogamy, and established the right of women to work and to obtain a divorce without necessarily losing their children.

This law, when combined with the Land Reform Act that gave women the right to own land in their own name, did much to challenge the most repressive features of the old family system. Still, much of the land that was redistributed eventually fell under the administrative control of the head of the male-dominated household, even though actual title to part of the land had been turned over to women. At the same time, peasant women, who were increasingly working in the fields—seeding, weeding, and bringing in the harvest—had yet to develop many agricultural skills. This too limited their ability to become involved in more complex economic transactions, to the detriment of their efforts at gaining greater economic equality.

Other difficulties arose over what to do with land treated as household property. When a woman moved to another village and joined her husband's lineage, the best she could do with her own land was to "lease" it to a father or brother (Diamond 1975:377). Only in villages like Half Moon, where there were several lineages (in this case, the result of the immigration of squatters from Hebei and elsewhere), could women sometimes marry within their own village and thereby maintain their personal land holdings intact. Of course, this right to individual land ownership eventually disappeared with the collectivization process.

And, of course, divorce, with its obvious threat to the stability of the kinship network, was viewed negatively. After implementation of the new Marriage Law in 1950, peasant women still found it difficult, if not impossible, to obtain a divorce. Many didn't even try, as Guo Dasao made clear in the conclusion to her story.

"After 1949, a new village government was set up in Half Moon. A little later I heard about the Marriage Law being passed. I thought quite a bit about getting a divorce, but finally decided against it. There were just too many pressures put on me not to. There's an old saying that 'if you marry a shoulder pole you have to carry it around. If you marry a chicken you have to follow it,' and so on. Instead of asking for a divorce, I tried to find my family again. This time I was successful, and shortly afterward, I moved in with them and stayed two years.

"However, the party began to discourage not only divorces but also the breakup of the family. They kept coming to me and emphasizing that my husband and I should try to work it out. He and the others at Half Moon also wanted me to come back. So finally I did. I figured that things in the village were getting better, so maybe our marriage would improve too. At the time there were many meetings organized by the party—a lot of talk about clearing our minds of old ideas. Slowly the situation got better for me, and I stayed."

Guo Dasao's reflections on the past offer important insights into the changing social relations of the time. In Half Moon, the party leaders' efforts to reduce female-male disparities through implementing newly passed laws and holding nightly mass meetings were not simply based on a desire to bring greater equality to women, as important as that was. Very much on their minds was the question of how to increase the economic productivity of the land. One way to do both was to double the size of the work force by bringing village women fully into agricultural labor. The new Marriage Law of 1950, stressing the right of women to work, actively supported this economic effort. Furthermore, such action also had the support of the Marxist principle that only through participation in productive labor could women become fully liberated.

Still, public laws could not reach down into the private world of the household and legislate interactions among husband, wife, and mother-in-law. In addition, efforts to exercise these new rights in selecting a spouse or seeking a divorce often pitted men against women. If such conflicts became too severe, they could jeopardize the success of the land-reform movement—a campaign considered by the party leaders as their highest priority.

As a result of such deliberations, further actions to reduce the entrenched ideology of male domination, encased within the traditional kinship system, were postponed. Suggestions were made that perhaps after the new organized coopera-tives had taken hold, leading in turn to a higher standard of living, political education could again be undertaken to raise the peasantry's consciousness of the importance of equality between the sexes. To do otherwise now would jeopardize the precarious economic and political gains that had already been achieved. Further-more, it would encourage more confrontation within the family, an institution that could not afford a high degree of instability, given its predominant responsibility for insuring the basic livelihood of the people.[3]

These were some of the reasons why the party members in Half Moon saw fit to strongly discourage Guo Dasao from getting a divorce or even remaining separated

[3]In other words, the party opted for male peasant loyalty at the expense of women's rights (see Andors 1983; Croll 1981; Davin 1976; and Johnson 1980).

from her husband. Obviously, the problem in this case was that such a course of action did little to challenge the self-interest of men, including the ideology of male supremacy found among many within the party.

Several active campaigns relating to the furtherance of women's equality had been carried out since the 1950s, particularly during the latter phase of the Cultural Revolution in the mid-1970s.[4] In Half Moon, one of the more successful of these was the effort to challenge the old custom of unequal pay for equal work. In 1975, the highest number of work points a woman could obtain was eight, whereas men received as many as ten. In several villages close to Half Moon, women even had their work points reduced after marriage, on the assumption that their responsibilities at home lessened their productivity in the fields.

A concerted attack on this inequality was orchestrated by the Women's Federation at the commune level. It began in many villages with wall posters protesting this reactionary thinking. They spoke especially about a highly capable and hard-working young woman who consistently finished her work more rapidly than her men co-workers doing the same task. Taking this woman as a model, political study classes, which all peasants and village workers were expected to attend, were asked to discuss her achievements and then analyze the implicit Confucian assumption that men were superior to women.

As the campaign mounted, additional targets were selected for attention. Wife beating was one. In a village down the road from Half Moon, a man known for striking his wife was hauled before a mass meeting, criticized, arrested, and eventually sent off to a labor camp for reeducation. A much broader attack focused on the issue of housework. When the Women's Federation at Half Moon took up the question, they began by asking wives to report on what happened at the end of each workday. Shared experiences bore out the expectation that on arriving home, most men would immediately head for the *kang* and light up their pipes while the wives prepared the evening meal. The obvious question was then posed: If men and women are both working, why should housework be left to the women?

By midwinter of 1975, the campaign reached a peak. During lunch break, daily reports on village loudspeakers praised one family after another for improving their backward "feudal" ways. Stories were told about how a man from a nearby village had been given the nickname "Henpecked" Yang because he did whatever his wife asked him to do without complaint. Or how "Will-do-everything" Liu was teased because he too helped with the housework. Somewhat to their own surprise, these men were held up by commune leaders as models to be emulated rather than as individuals to be ridiculed.

Significantly, the campaign had a positive effect. By the spring of 1976, in over 70 percent of the commune villages, the most productive women had begun to receive ten work points. During the campaign, a few engaged men proposed to move to their wives' villages following marriage. Women were recommended by the brigade to receive special training at commune headquarters as tractor drivers and electricians. More women were recruited into leadership positions in brigade

---

[4]Most specifically, during the "Criticize Lin Biao and Confucius Campaign."

committees. And finally, Half Moon had its first woman party secretary assigned to the village.

What was the long-term result of this political campaign? Possibly I asked this question improperly, but the answers I got were always elusive. Nevertheless, certain facts were available. When I arrived at Half Moon, few local women were involved with the Women's Federation, quite possibly because the organization was devoting its full attention to issues of family planning—not a popular topic in village households. There were no women in the local party branch. Li Guiying, the female party secretary at Half Moon during the mid-1970s, was working in a nearby factory. When asked why she had moved away, she said that she had requested the transfer; because of her lack of reading skills, she had not felt able to handle the responsibilities associated with being the village party leader. Nor was the effort to encourage new husbands to move to their brides' villages any longer mentioned. Most significant of all, the percentage of women engaged in unskilled field labor continued to grow, while men increasingly found placements in expanding sideline industries and nearby commune and state-run factories. And yet, all around me in the village, I regularly observed young men taking care of their children and assuming other tasks that had previously been the almost sole concern of women. Such sharing of family responsibilities was a real change from the past. Placing more women than men in the most menial forms of agricultural labor was not.

After the death of Mao, China's new leaders were firmly opposed to the use of mass ideological campaigns such as those associated with the Cultural Revolution. Instead, the focus shifted to "following economic laws that upgrade productivity." With this change in the party's central task, the political issue of women's inequality was largely set aside—not unlike the similar decision after the land-reform movement and the rise of collectivization. And, as in the past, social stability within the family was seen by most leaders as a necessary prerequisite to enhanced productivity. At the national level, such a decision might be seen as quite rational, although deeply held convictions of male superiority certainly continued to influence the leaders' actions. In Half Moon, the fact that the number of women involved in local-level decision making was fewer than a few short years ago suggested that traditional village patterns of male dominance were far from dormant. Equally important, when the pressure for change was reduced, old ways easily reemerged.

However, there was one question of direct relevance to women that did receive a great deal of attention in Half Moon and elsewhere: What was the optimum size of the family? An adequate answer to this question required another: Optimum for whom? At the national level, the leaders stated that China's expanding population was seriously limiting the country's economic development. Therefore, family size had to be reduced (Chen 1979).

Indeed, family planning was a vital feature of any overall strategy for economic development, and in the abstract, Half Moon villagers accepted the government's argument. But their own local experience led them to a somewhat different final conclusion. That is, the economic resources of the village and commune were still not sufficiently developed to assure them of a standard of living during their working years sufficient to allow them to give up the patterns of the past. And when they became older, without a retirement pension and with limited social security, who other than their nearby sons would assume responsibility for them? Four children might be too many, older villagers said, but at least for now, one was not enough. The contradictions within this continuing conflict between national and local interests were complex, but their resolution was of great importance if China was to be successful in its modernization effort. Given this fact, what further insights can be gained from a more in-depth look at the problem in Half Moon Village?

FAMILY PLANNING

Ma Xinxian, the older of the two female barefoot doctors, had the overall responsibility for providing birth control information and services to the village residents. In her clinic office, she kept a record of the health condition of every woman in the brigade. For those of child-bearing age, this record included the date of marriage, the method of birth control utilized, and a listing of pregnancies and deliveries. In 1979, 80 married women in the village were defined in the child-bearing category.

Unmarried women were not included in this category and, therefore, were ineligible to receive birth control devices. Of course, this practice presented the village with another problem: what to do with premarital pregnancies. Actually, such pregnancies were rather uncommon, and when they did occur, the couple was usually engaged. Such an event, though sharply criticized by local village authorities in general and Women's Federation leaders in particular, was resolved either by an immediate marriage or by an arranged abortion in a commune hospital some distance from the village.

The 80 Half Moon Village married women in the child-bearing category had selected a variety of methods for controlling births—all contraceptives being provided without charge. Condoms were available to men, but they were seldom used. As for the women, 26 chose the intrauterine device (IUD), a method strongly encouraged by Ma Xinxian, who considered it the safest, easiest, and most reliable. Eighteen used the birth control pill. One preferred a monthly chemical injection. The diaphragm was not looked on with favor by village women. Reasons given included inconvenience and problems of sanitation. Of the remaining 35 women, 17 chose sterilization after having had one or more children, and 18 were not then using any regular birth control methods, either because they did not choose to control births by such means or because they had not "given it that much thought." The latter response, in the experience of Ma Xixian, was characteristic only of younger, newly married women.

The other alternative was abortion. This practice was considered less desirable than the preventive measures mentioned previously, but was sometimes necessary given particular circumstances. Ma's records indicated that no abortions were requested in the village during the first 10 months of 1979, although several women had obtained them at the nearby district hospital the previous year. Given a newly introduced system of material incentives to reduce births, pregnant Half Moon

动员起来 把首都造成卫清洁的城市

A Women's Federation leader from commune headquarters responsible for family planning. The poster encouraged the people in the capital to improve their sanitation.

peasant women at that time could receive five *yuan* in cash and have several days off from work if they agreed to abort their unborn child. Counseling women on such matters was the responsibility of the local Women's Federation. Technical medical questions were handled by barefoot doctors in consultation with the federation. Counseling for men was undertaken either by the CYL, by leaders of the individual's work team, or by both. If the family already had three or more children, parents and even grandparents were sometimes contacted by a team leader or more senior village official. Obviously, such coordinated pressure on a given family could promote a substantial amount of conflict between household members and local authorities.

The decision to have a child was made jointly by husband and wife, with other members of the husband's family, most often the mother, being consulted as well. However, if the couple remained childless for several years, the husband and wife would eventually find themselves pressured by family elders to produce a child, preferably male. Caught between the Women's Federation and the CYL, who strongly encouraged that births be limited to one, and the older generation, who pressured the couple to have at least two, some young married villagers had difficulty deciding what action to take. It was at this point that the government's economic (and ideological) incentive strategy came into play.

In many urban areas and other more affluent sectors of China, a fairly significant reward system was put into effect to assist those couples promising to complete their family with a single birth. In Beijing, such couples often received 200 *yuan*. If they later had a second child, the money had to be returned. Usually, however, the mother was sterilized, in which case the issue was permanently resolved. Other innovative material incentives included guaranteeing the child's kindergarten enrollment, rather than placing it on the waiting list, and providing further reduction in already low health-care costs. Public praise for placing the interests of the country over that of the family was always given.

The negative sanctions applied by this new and controversial family planning policy placed a financial burden on those families who produced a third child. In Half Moon, the Women's Federation tried to persuade such a couple to have an abortion. If they refused, three repercussions followed: First, mothers would not receive any work points until 45 days after the baby was born.[5] Second, the parents had to pay for all nursery school expenses. And third, the income of both parents was reduced by 5 percent until the child reached the age of 14, this being the estimated amount that the state contributed to the upbringing of each child through food and other related subsidies. When complaints were heard, the Women's Federation was told by the government to remind the family that, given the problems of trying to modernize a country of 1 billion people, the third child of any family should be the responsibility of that family alone.

In Half Moon, the response to the new policy was varied. A few people, cognizant of the national interest, were in basic support. These individuals held the view that female and male children were of equal value. Party members, of course, were expected to support the policy, and most of them did. If they were in the party but desired more than one child, they soon found themselves under maximum pressure to revise their opinion.

On the other hand, many villagers were opposed to it. They asked: "What if something happens to the child, and the mother has been sterilized?" "What will happen to the family income?" "Who will take care of me in my old age?" "If the child is a girl, will her future husband move into our house?" Or they might say: "One child is too lonely. There will be no one for it to play with." And a mother once asked, "What will I do with my time if I have only one son or daughter?"

If the family was opposed to the policy, they could take several measures to circumvent it. Some women tried to hide the fact that they were pregnant until the latter part of the second trimester or the beginning of the third in the hope that they could escape the pressure placed on them by the Women's Federation to abort. After a child was born, the family could "forget" to register it at the district records office or could enter a protest to local and commune officials offering various

---

[5]Other village mothers with one or two babies received 45 days' leave with "pay," i.e., work points. Those few women working in the state sector received 54 days' leave with pay.

reasons why they should be exempted from the policy. Many felt that this campaign, like others before it, would eventually dissipate. Thus, for the time being, it was best simply to wait and be patient.

In nearby cities like Beijing, the new family-planning policy had begun to take hold. With a higher and more secure income, factory workers were in a better economic position to accept the one-child norm. But among the peasants of Half Moon, it would take both a continued improvement in the standard of living and a highly creative educational effort before the peasants would see any advantage of a small family over a larger one. For most Half Moon residents, neither criterion had as yet been met.

THE LATER YEARS

Growing old is never easy. But in Half Moon Village, the process was at least softened by the continuing opportunity to share in all aspects of daily life for as long as people chose and were able. The elderly were respected for their experience and knowledge, even when these attributes had limited applicability in the modern world. However, outside the home there was relatively little for them to do. Men often spent part of each day hanging around the plaza, the nonfamily center for social activity. In early spring and late fall, a favorite meeting place was an adobe wall near the village clinic. Here, they could regularly catch the warmth of the sun's rays while chatting with friends and watching younger villagers working in the fields across the road. Older women, however, did not have such freedom of movement.

A few enterprising members of the older generation regularly offered to do some work for the village. It was quite striking to walk out to the junction of the main road and the plaza as the sun was coming up in the morning and see an old man sweeping the streets of the previous day's dust. Or one might see an aged woman offering to help take care of children at the nursery—particularly if none remained at home. Although the women were not compensated for this activity, they did gain something else of considerable value—a recognition that they were still useful and wanted. In other words, respect for the elderly was not limited to the extended family but was carried into the larger community as well.

Still, for those villagers living out their later years in this supportive environment, memories of past hardships were not easily forgotten. Thus, grandparents were likely to remind their children and grandchildren not to take present-day economic security for granted. The residents were quick to acknowledge that economic improvements had occurred since the "bitter years" prior to 1949. However, they also remembered the early 1960s, following the Great Leap Forward campaign, when the combination of political and climatic disasters resulted in such poor harvests that hunger again became commonplace.

Residents also commented on the increased number of older people living in the village. This, of course, was due to the simultaneous increase in life expectancy and the lowering of the birth rate. What were the implications of such a "demographic aging process"? Given the still limited economic development of the village, even the modest contribution of older people to the family income was considered quite helpful. Women stopped working in the fields before men, usually when they reached their early 50s. As their physical strength declined, they received fewer work points. Thus, it was more advantageous to the family for them to return home and take care of the young grandchildren. A daughter-in-law—younger, stronger, and able to command more work points—was thereby freed to return to the fields. Since private production, including such tasks as feeding and selling pigs, was quite profitable in generating additional income (by as much as 15 to 20 percent), the mother could continue her contribution to the family welfare in a meaningful way.

Most peasant men, on the other hand, regularly worked in the collective sphere of the brigade well into their 60s. To the extent that they were able to retain their strength longer than women, their work points were correspondingly reduced more slowly. The men of Half Moon Village also had more jobs in the state sector by a ratio of four to one. Since this was a far more economically rewarding form of employment, these workers continued on the job for 30 years, at which time they could receive a pension guaranteeing them 70 percent of their wages for the rest of their lives.

The fact that older parents were able to continue making economic contributions to the extended family helped greatly in strengthening kin ties between generations. Furthermore, since the parents owned the house in which one or more sons resided, the latter felt an obligation in return. Daughters, on the other hand, once they married and became part of their husbands' families, did not have a similar duty, although they often felt a personal responsibility irrespective of social custom.

This same pattern carried over into the matter of inheritance. Daughters did not inherit property. On the death of a father, the house was passed on to a son, usually the eldest, who remained there. Savings were turned over to the widow, and her care was shared jointly by the sons, all of whom were expected to contribute a certain number of work points or amount of annual income for her as long as she lived.

I once asked a young woman why it was that men received an inheritance and women in the village didn't. Her answer was insightful for several reasons, not the least of which was the way in which she framed it. She responded as if her older brother were speaking rather than she. Such a way of responding illustrated rather well the continuity of traditional values in the modern setting.

I asked, "Why is it that men receive inheritance and women do not?"

"A man says: 'We take care of the parents, we give them work points while you are away from home. Maybe you come to visit the parents occasionally, but you don't have any responsibility. If the parents are ill and can't work, we will have to care for them.' "

"How do you feel about that?" I asked noncommittally.

"If women take responsibility for the parents, then they should be involved in the inheritance. But if they don't contribute, then . . ." and her voice drifted off as she reflected on what she was saying. Then she continued.

"But some women do contribute. My mother did, and on her father's death in

1965, she said about the inheritance, 'I don't want it, I don't want it.' Now I am helping my mother because she went through so many hardships to bring me up. So I think it is my responsibility to do that."

I decided not to ask whether she felt her efforts should result in her receiving an inheritance. It seemed rather inappropriate at the time.

On the death of a villager, the family immediately prepared for the funeral. A relative or local carpenter was first asked to construct a simple coffin for the body. Then the deceased, dressed in good clothes and placed on a blanket and pillow in the coffin, was taken to the central parlor of the house, where relatives and friends came and offered condolences. For those few who chose a "modern" funeral, this memorial service completed the process. The body was then removed and cremated.

However, years of lectures by local party cadres on how the superstitious beliefs associated with old burial practices had harmed the villages—most notably by removing fertile land from the use of the brigade—had not been well received by many older villagers. Neither had the idea of cremation, the alternative strongly urged by the commune leadership. In the minds of the elderly, such a practice lacked dignity and respect for the dead. Old people, especially, expressed their opposition with remarks such as, "My friend was poor most of his life, and now the family won't even give him a decent funeral." Another poignant remark came from an elderly peasant, who said softly, "It must hurt."

Because Half Moon was a relocated village, and the few ancestral plots in the area had long since been plowed up for agricultural use, the residents faced a more difficult problem than did residents of other nearby villages that still had burial grounds. In Half Moon, either the deceased were cremated or the families made arrangements for the body to be sent to kin in other locations. But in nearby villages, old rituals often continued.

On the morning of the funeral, a day or so after the death, relatives gathered outside the home of the deceased. They wore different clothes depending on their relationship to the departed. Close kin wore mourning robes of white. Women might also place a few white ribbons in their hair. Differing shapes of caps and shoes designated to outside observers the relationship of more distant kin to the deceased. Before the ceremony began, the family members and relatives might talk and even laugh. But on hearing the sound of a bowl breaking as it was thrown to the ground—the signal for the ceremony to start—all talking stopped. Straightening themselves up, the participants uttered a unified wail as they lined up for the procession to the grave site.

The eldest son—wearing white sack garments, carrying white-colored paper money, and holding a soul-calling flag—would lead the column, while a band playing mourning melodies would bring up the rear. Others carried a paper horse (for a deceased man) or a paper cow (for a woman) and more paper money, which was to be burned at the grave site for the deceased to use in the trip to the underworld.[6] As the procession passed through the village, several more bowls,

---

[6]In some areas of the country, modern-day mourners brought along paper television sets and stereos as well.

jars, or mirrors were thrown against the ground and broken. Beyond the edge of the village lay the local burial ground, its location easily distinguished by mounds of raised earth scattered in a haphazard fashion—a puzzle to present-day observers unfamiliar with the ancient practice of geomancy, a custom that assured proper placement of the grave.

On arriving at the site, mourners lowered the coffin into the freshly dug grave. The villagers then stood respectfully while the coffin was covered over, some perhaps joining in with the family of the deceased as they softly repeated a common lament in a singsong manner. After the grave was covered, offerings of eggs, cakes, and white paper money cut in an ancient shape were placed on top, and the money was burned. The procession then returned to the village to participate in a large meal hosted by the family of the deceased. After partaking of elaborate dishes of dumplings, cakes, and other special foods, the mourners disbanded and returned to their own homes. In April of each following year, at the time of the *quingming* festival, family members returned to the grave site, added some new earth, weeded or cleaned the area, and perhaps burned a little paper money and incense, thereby illustrating one more continuity in the life cycle of the village.

Given the extensive power once exercised by the elderly in the village, it would be possible to conclude that their status had diminished considerably. But such was not the case. This was due not only to the maintenance of traditional values and the continuation of the older generation's ability to contribute economically to the family welfare, but also to the collective nature of the social system, which gave specific attention and care to those who in their later years were no longer able to work. Contrasting socialist China with the capitalist West, one well-educated commune member expressed his view on the matter rather directly when he looked at me and said, "We are not so rich that we can't afford to take care of our old people."

PART TWO

CHANGING POLITICAL ECONOMY

8/"Becoming Rich Is Fine"

THE TURNING POINT

"You know, it's all right to become rich."

It was late September 1979. The person making the remark was Xiao Cai, a young woman in charge of "foreign affairs" at Red Flag. For Cai, foreign affairs meant being responsible for the activities of all foreigners who came to the commune—including me. Mostly, she met visiting delegations of agricultural specialists, tourists, and political dignitaries, arranged tours of production facilities, and planned meetings with commune leaders. She also came periodically to Half Moon Village to offer assistance in setting up interviews in neighboring villages or with leading personnel in some of the larger commune factories. On this day, I was helping her as well. For the past six months, she had been working hard to improve her spoken English by following language lessons on the local evening television broadcast. Today, I was her substitute teacher.

"What do you mean by 'becoming rich,' Xiao Cai?" I thought perhaps the phrasing of her remark in English might carry a meaning different in her mind than in mine.

"I mean that individuals and families can work hard for their own benefit. If they make money at it, that's fine. They won't be criticized any more for being selfish."

Her comment was intriguing. In contrast to what foreigners might have thought about China at this time, there was nothing unusual about expressing a desire to get rich. Of course, "becoming rich" in the Chinese sense meant achieving a comfortable and secure life rather than obtaining great wealth. Actually, the phrase "getting rich" first became popular shortly after 1949, when it was used as a slogan for rural development.

Hao Ran, in his well-known novel *The Golden Road,* took up this theme in describing the effort of peasants in a North China village to overcome their poverty during the land-reform movement. However, Hao's book, first published in 1972, was quite critical of individuals wanting to better themselves at the expense of the collective effort (see Hao 1981:115–28). So too were the authors of a study of Wandong Village, a brigade located on the southeastern edge of Beijing. Written by local university students, the report included a section subtitled "Getting Organized Is the Only Way for Poor and Lower-Middle Peasants to All Get Rich Together" (Beijing First Foreign Languages Institute 1976). So getting rich was fine, all right. The question was: how?

Now, Xiao Cai seemed to be saying that the collective orientation was less important. The fact that she was a party member and therefore knowledgeable about current debates and strategies immediately crossed my mind. Without thinking, I broached the question directly.

"You mean there has been a change in policy?"

Her response was a simple, noncommittal smile. I let the matter drop, assuming that if she had any knowledge of the subject, she was not able to discuss it with me. To learn of policy changes before they appear in the Chinese press or news reports requires contact with spokespeople considerably more senior than Xiao Cai. So I had to wait—but not very long.

A few days later, the village loudspeaker system began broadcasting a series of taped radio reports about enterprising peasants who greatly increased their family income through private entrepreneurial activity. In one broadcast, the newscaster spoke of a young man who had risen early every morning and tended his private bees before going to work in the collective fields. Significantly, the beekeeper made more money selling honey than he did working for the collective. But more revealing was what the commentator didn't say. Praising the initiative of the newly enriched peasant in earning additional money in his spare time, the speaker bypassed the other question of how beekeeping might be collectivized so that this new source of wealth could benefit a larger number of people.

Soon, newspapers from the city, though seldom found outside the brigade office, began reporting similar events. One article on the front page of the *People's Daily* was prefaced by this headline: "The Policy of Allowing Peasants to Get Rich Greatly Liberates the Productive Forces." It went on to state: "To allow some peasants to get rich, to allow some areas, some brigades to get rich first, this is an important step in accelerating the Four Modernizations in our country. It is a step to improve the relations between our Party and the peasants." Xiao Cai had kept her thoughts to herself. But it looked like others were beginning to speak out.

A short while later, on the eve of the 30th anniversary of October 1 (National Day), local radios carried a four-hour-long speech by Ye Jianying, an old and well-known party official, who offered the party's summation of the Cultural Revolution—and, by implication, Mao Zedong's leadership of it. One or two local cadres listened to the speech. A few others caught the highlights. But no one, including the villagers, appeared surprised at the final summation, which stated specifically, "The Cultural Revolution was an appalling disaster."

In the weeks that followed, the government emphasized in the press and on television that "collective effort must be linked to individual initiative." Under sound party leadership, the reports went on to say, such initiative had been tapped. But generally, the political extremism of the Cultural Revolution, offering a simplistic notion of "capitalism" and unfairly labeling people as "capitalist roaders," had brought a large decrease in individual and household sideline activities, to the detriment of China's overall economic development. Furthermore, collectively organized units often had great difficulty setting up sideline industries because of the inertia or disinterest of the government agencies responsible for approving such requests. All these statements reinforced the view, expressed in the *People's Daily*, that it was necessary to rekindle the people's enthusiasm by allowing some peasants, areas, and brigades to get rich first—and by such means to improve the deteriorating relations between the party and the people.

It was obvious to anyone following these pronouncements that a "new wind" was blowing out of the capital city. Major changes didn't occur all at once; nor did they necessarily reflect the views of just one senior leadership group. But most policy changes, many of them introduced after having been tested in different parts of the country, represented the views of Deng Xiaoping and his supporters. As Deng increasingly reestablished his influence within the party (though often behind the scenes), the new direction began to take shape. One of the key steps in this process was the effort to upgrade agricultural production and improve the standard of living of China's peasant-farmers.

AGRICULTURAL MODERNIZATION

As part of the Four Modernizations campaign, China's government had committed itself to modernizing agriculture and thereby strengthening the economy and improving the people's livelihood. It had already removed the historic class-based relations that characterized landlord and poor peasant on the one hand and industrialist and worker on the other. Privately owned factories and farms were no more. Yet, throughout much of rural China, and even in suburban communes like Red Flag, major differences between the living standards of urban workers and those of peasant-farmers still remained. What could be done to alleviate these striking differences?

One significant plan to upgrade rural livelihood was announced in December 1978, when the Third Plenum of the Eleventh CCP Central Committee approved an increase in the state procurement price of grain by approximately 20 percent, with most of the profit from these sales to be passed on to the peasant producers. Similar increases were allocated to other agricultural products. For example, the price of cotton was raised 30 percent. But the overall cost of this effort to the state was so high (over a billion *yuan* a year just subsidizing grain supplies in urban areas) that it quickly brought about a significant deficit in the state budget. An additional factor encouraging the deficit was the wage increase given to state workers to offset the rise in food costs brought about by the higher price paid to the peasantry. In this classical illustration of an inflationary spiral, the initial goal—to improve the living standard of the peasants—was partially offset by their having to pay more for those foods and other commodities purchased from the state. Nevertheless, the gain in peasant income was real.

A second strategy designed to increase both land productivity and peasant income was to further mechanize agriculture. Many stationary operations, such as pumping, chopping, grinding, crushing, and threshing, had already been mechanized. However, the mechanization of field work was much less developed. Even in technologically advanced vegetable-producing communes surrounding large cities, much of the seeding, transplanting, and harvesting in the collective sector was still done by hand.

There were several reasons for this. One was the scarcity of capital. A second was the state's concern about how to utilize the released time of a peasant work force after mechanization without incurring serious underemployment. Negative unanticipated consequences could far outweigh any resolution of the initial problem. A third reason had to do with the history of China's technological development. On American farms, agricultural machines, from cutter bars to combines, were drawn by horses long before the invention of the tractor. When the tractor finally arrived, farmers had already developed the implements to attach to it. Therefore, the transition process was relatively easy. China, on the other hand, had quite a different history of farm mechanization. As noted earlier, most villages had one or more two-wheeled walking tractors. They were seen everywhere pulling wagons along roadways, since mechanized transportation was a high-priority item for the increasingly market-oriented peasant farmers. But few were found in the fields where they were also needed. Why? Because the design and extensive manufacture of appropriate farm implements to go with the tractor had never been adequately developed.

Nor was the problem simply one of importing or copying machines used elsewhere. In much of China, small terraced fields, surface irrigation, interplanting, and multiple cropping with transplanting created problems that required solutions drawn from the people's own conditions and experience (Hinton 1982:112–15). Only in relatively large expanses of semiflat land with limited population density could large American or European tractors and seeding and harvesting equipment be effectively utilized. For most of China, a much simpler intermediate-level technology geared to the particular geographical conditions was more appropriate.

Although the government gave little consistent support to this type of agricultural mechanization, it did try to stimulate production by lowering the state's sale price of existing agricultural products such as farm machinery and fertilizer. However, this plan, first put into effect in late 1978, was soon withdrawn. The expected benefits in increased production and sales did not materialize rapidly enough to offset the high initial cost to the state, which by this time was facing a serious budgetary crisis.

A third strategy designed to enhance agricultural productivity was to reduce bureaucratic control over economic planning and distribution in favor of an increased use of markets and floating prices. A closely related effort reinforced the importance of individual bonuses as a form of economic incentive in the workplace. And finally, in some parts of the country, small "work groups" *(zuoye zu)* of three to five families were established that could assume responsibility for "contracting from the brigade land, seed grains, and tools for cultivation"—as long as they contributed the agreed-upon amount of production *(baogan zhu)* to the state through the appropriate accounting unit.[1]

This was the alternative the Red Flag Commune leader Yu Shanshan had implicitly referred to when he had spoken of a single blooming flower encouraging bureaucracy.[2] To motivate the peasants to higher productivity—especially in poor

---

[1]This latter strategy was developed in the spring of 1978 and formalized in December at the same Third Plenum CCP Central Committee meeting that had approved the higher state procurement price of grain to increase peasant income (Domes 1982:255–56).

[2]See Chapter 2.

or backward villages—the link between one's actual output and one's income needed to be strengthened and the emphasis on the collective downgraded. By this means, it was felt that China's rural villagers could free themselves from some of the stifling bureaucratic controls that had so limited agricultural productivity in the past.

THE INDIVIDUAL, THE COLLECTIVE, AND THE STATE

What was the response of Half Moon residents to these new ideas? Any suggestion that work groups be broken up into smaller units and land "contracted out" was rejected as not being applicable in their context. Since the village had already chosen to hold its private plots in common (in opposition to proposals put forward by higher party officials), the idea of dividing up the larger brigade land wasn't even discussed.[3]

However, the proposal to maximize incentives by using individual bonuses and reestablishing peasant markets did stimulate considerable discussion. Local factory workers strongly supported the idea of bonuses, but like the issue of getting rich, implicit in the process was the question of how—in this case, how should bonuses be allocated.

The 300 workers at Red Flag's large commune-run machine-repair shop located near the administrative headquarters had a particularly difficult time deciding how to resolve that question. The shop, in addition to repairing tractors and other types of farm machinery, manufactured simple threshing machines and specially designed axles for sale to the state. When the shop leaders first introduced the principle of bonuses, the workers supported it. However, in discussing how to distribute the bonuses from the surplus income (profit) generated by the workers, they faced a dilemma.

Everyone knew it was much harder to derive a surplus from machine repairing than from manufacturing. But those in the manufacturing division represented less than one-third of the total work force. Should bonuses be limited to that smaller group? No, because if that happened, everyone would want to work in the manufacturing shop and no one in repair. After much further discussion, the factory members finally decided to divide the surplus income drawn from the manufacturing sector among all workers in the shop. Those in repair shouldn't be penalized because the nature of their responsibilities precluded them from generating surplus income.

Then the workers turned to the question of how to evaluate the productive value of each worker. Again, in the manufacturing sector, the evaluation was completed with little difficulty, since men and women worked closely together and each worker's productivity level was known to the other. In the repair shop, where the people were more isolated from one another and tasks more varied, the decision

---

[3]Actually, at this time, government efforts to strengthen individual initiative by reducing the collective input were primarily focused on poorer, more isolated villages and communes and on those whose local leadership was known to be weak. In affluent, more highly mechanized, well-developed suburban communes like Red Flag, the contract system was considered less necessary and, therefore, was less used (Lippit 1982:147).

Half Moon Village workers at a local factory.

was made to establish, for each form of work, quotas from which bonuses could be determined. For example, a standard of 50 hours was decided on for the overhaul of a tractor. If the individual regularly completed the overhaul in 45 hours or less (and the quality of performance was satisfactory), the savings in labor power represented a "profit" and therefore should be reflected in a higher bonus for that particular worker. Most repair workers, however, received the same bonus. Overall, it was an intriguing solution to a difficult problem—utilizing the strength of the bonus system in stimulating productivity while combining individual and collective incentives into one package.

The individual incentive policy was also successfully implemented in much larger manufacturing centers, such as an automobile assembly plant in Beijing. One villager from Half Moon worked in such a factory, living in a worker's dormitory for most of the week and returning home on weekends or whenever he had time off. One day, I asked him whether bonuses were stimulating production at his plant.

"The new system really does some good. Before, when you went to the factory, nobody was too active at learning. One old worker told me that he always felt ashamed if he didn't know how to do something. But today, a lot of young people don't care. They say, 'If you don't know how to do something you won't have to do it.' Or: 'The more you know, the harder you have to work. The less you know, the less you have to work.' But in our factory, the work isn't even up to the capitalist standard."

"What do you mean?" I asked.

"I mean, here you get the same salary regardless of the amount of work you do. Until now, seniority has been the only real factor determining pay increase. The specific job you do hasn't counted. Some people like me, who try to learn as much as they can, end up working harder while others just sit on their tails doing nothing. And yet, we both get about the same income. Isn't that a form of exploitation? That's why I like the new system. Everyone has to take a test before receiving a raise and be evaluated before they get a bonus. That's the way it should be. So this bonus is doing some good. People are paying more attention and working harder. And everyone benefits."

Inquiring about the reemergence of peasant markets, I also found general support for this new policy. The market closest to Half Moon was just outside the commune border in the old market town, about a half hour away by bicycle. Markets had never been established within Red Flag's boundaries because there were too few goods that local villagers didn't already have. The market was particularly useful when local distribution was poor and when peasant-farmers could trade with town and urban residents. City workers with cash wanted to purchase fresh products from the countryside. Peasants not only needed the money but also enjoyed the respite from field work. However, in Red Flag, where most villagers earned over 1 *yuan* or more per day, some villagers opposed spending much time at the market.

Ma Haimen was one of these. "For many people, going to the market is really a waste of labor power. Say your hens lay 20 eggs and you want to sell them at the market. The city [state-controlled] price may be 10 *fen* [100 *fen* equals 1 *yuan]* per egg, and you can sell fresh ones for 15 *fen* per egg. That only brings you 5 *fen* per egg while you stand there all day. You aren't even going to earn the 1 *yuan* you would earn working in the fields or in a sideline. So, in this case, the market isn't going to do any good at all. Furthermore, there aren't enough goods to sell anyway."

The commune leader Yu Shanshan added one additional perspective on the reemergence of the market system at Red Flag. "Under current conditions, peasant markets play an important economic role in that brigade farmers are a bridge to the city. It is impossible for state-run commercial networks to satisfy all the people's needs. So local markets facilitate small production and compensate for the short-comings of the state commercial network. Still, there is a need to strengthen supervision. State-owned stores should be able to influence market prices. If you don't have economic controls, the state sector will be in trouble. Sometimes prices in the peasant market are higher than in the state sector. Then the state stores raise their price, which can encourage an upward-spiraling competition. When that happens, the masses really curse somebody."

When viewed in combination with one another, changes such as the proposed revision of the brigade's collective orientation, the reemergence of the market, and the emphasis on individual material incentive highlighted another dimension of the new economic policy, one that set it apart from the expressed goals of earlier periods. This new dimension was the recognition that these steps would eventually heighten economic inequalities existing between individuals, between villages within the commune, and in the country at large. Given this recognition, the government mounted—in the press, on television, and through various party channels—a major ideological campaign against "egalitarianism," emphasizing that under socialism, people should receive "according to their work." That is, one's income should be proportional to one's contribution to the production process. Quoting Marx (1875:14), the government suggested that only in a classless (communist) society where major inequalities between its members had disappeared and where the social wealth had been fully developed should the people "contribute according to their ability" and "receive according to their need."

Of course, this proposal was hardly new; in its utopian form it could be traced back to political philosophers considerably before Marx. Furthermore, this overall goal involved not just a redistribution of wealth from private to collective and state ownership, but also the political, economic, and social development of a society in which the laboring people—peasant-farmers, industrial workers, technicians, teachers, and others—could eventually gain control over the important institutions that governed their lives. Where was Red Flag Commune in this transition process? Certainly, economic livelihood had improved greatly, particularly when compared with that of China's more isolated rural populace. But the development of political institutions able to strengthen democratic decision making by the people was severely limited, to say the very least.

Shortly before I left Half Moon, Ma Haimen, the vice brigade leader, said that in a forthcoming election of the local administrative committee all candidates, both party and nonparty, were to be placed on the same ballot. Those with the highest number of votes would become the new members. No longer, he said, were separate party and nonparty slates to be presented. If these and similar political experiments continued, eventually resulting in the establishment of regularized voting procedures, the electoral aspect of the democratic process would certainly be strengthened. If, however, government bureaucracy at the national and local level became more pervasive, even this tentative, decentralized, grass-roots democracy would not develop, and other more direct forms of participation in decision making would not even be explored.

When one looks back on the experience of the past several decades, it is clear that China's leaders had sought to achieve two key goals: one was to insure that the people became ideologically committed to the new social order. The second was to train teachers, scientists, and other intellectuals who could build a technically developed, highly productive society able to substantially improve the living standard of its people within an egalitarian framework. During Mao's leadership, he emphasized that these two qualities should be nurtured within each individual, with "redness" guiding "expertness." Since, in his view, the existing society did not adequately provide this nurturance, he tried to change its structure so that it could. This effort took many forms. In education, for example, it included an insistence that students and teachers live with and learn from the peasants and workers and that the latter's skills, capabilities, and opportunities be emphasized.

This same philosophy guided the self-reliant building of the middle school near Half Moon Village while frustrating the local principal and teachers who were no longer able to follow their regular course of instruction. This same political ideal first led Zhang Yanzi to commit her life to helping build a socialist society in the Northeast and, later, to turn away in discouragement, accepting help through the back door that she had earlier rejected. Indeed, through the course of this period, the commitment to being "red" became mired in factionalism defined as purity, while the effort to develop "experts" deteriorated into a denouncement of educational standards in general. And the youth, in whose name much of the struggle was fought, were left distrusting many of their leaders and, in some cases, the cause of socialism itself. Now, China was turning in a new direction, seeking its rural development through a political approach that linked economic benefit more directly to the individual family and the smaller work team while still maintaining a collective form of ownership.

On my last morning in Half Moon Village, I found it difficult to envision the future of those I had come to know and respect. Rising early, I went down to the plaza for a final look around the village. Young students, clustered in small groups, had already begun their trek along the main road toward school. At the other end of the village, Jiang Lijiang stood at his usual location by the brigade office door, watching over the work teams out in the fields. Several team members, recognizing me and knowing that I was about to leave, waved good-bye.

Turning back toward the Wang house to finish packing, I saw off in the distance Zhang Yanzi firmly seated on her red tractor. I stopped and watched as the machine moved slowly down a path toward a field beyond. Crossing the road, Zhang passed an elderly woman walking toward the district store. Tied around the old woman's head was a faded blue kerchief, and below that she wore a worn work jacket, baggy pants carefully patched, and tiny canvas shoes covering her deformed feet. In her fingers she held a small long-handled shovel. Every few feet she leaned forward and deftly scooped up from the roadway some animal manure, which was then expertly tossed into a shoulder basket strapped to her back. Once the basket was full, she would return home and enrich the soil of her family garden, in much the same way as her mother and grandmother had done before her. Standing quietly at the edge of the village, I thought about the scene before me: Zhang and the modern tractor in the field and the old woman on the road. China had changed immensely in 30 years. And yet, much remained to be done.

9/A Decade of Change

by Norman Chance and Fred Engst[1]

ECONOMIC REFORM

Sweeping changes begun in the late 1970s continued in suburban Beijing through-out the following decade. As free markets expanded, peasant-farmers from Half Moon and other villages began taking their foodstuffs and wares directly into the city instead of remaining on the outskirts, as had been the previous pattern. In the early 1980s, under Deng Xiaoping's leadership, a new "responsibility system" *(zeren zhi)* was introduced in which separate households, and even individuals, could contract with production teams and brigades to produce their grain, veget-ables, and other agricultural goods on specific plots of brigade land divided up for that purpose. After providing the contracted amount of grain to the brigade and the state, they could keep the rest for themselves. Long-term leasing of village fields was also allowed in the hope that this would increase the incentive to improve the land. Not surprisingly, events such as these soon changed the nature of commune organization throughout much of China.

Efforts to decentralize production also reduced the number of cadres responsible for economic management. Political and administrative functions of the communes decreased. In 1981, responsibilities for civil and social affairs such as residency registration, public security, schools, and health facilities still remained under commune jurisdiction. But the revised Chinese constitution of 1982 made it abun-dantly clear that these administrative responsibilities were to be turned over to the township *(xiang)*, the political unit of government that was below the county *(xian)* and that had largely been superseded by the communes in 1958.[2]

As for the early success of the responsibility system, official government figures for 1982 stated that between 60 and 70 percent of the brigades in the county where Red Flag Commune was located had broken up the land into smaller economic units

---

[1]Much of the following data concerning social and economic changes occurring in the Beijing suburbs and Half Moon Village in the 1980s is drawn from research undertaken by Fred Engst between 1987 and 1989.

[2]This decision eventually resulted in Red Flag Commune's reverting back to its pre-1958 designa-tion as a large state farm.

in which more modest-sized work groups and households (including old lineages) negotiated contracts with production teams or brigades. It was hoped that with decollectivization, peasant-farmers would form spontaneous volunteer cooperatives similar to the lower-level cooperatives of the 1950s. However, in Half Moon Village as well as many other areas in and outside of Beijing Municipality, that did not happen.

The residents of Half Moon first learned they were expected to privatize collectively held land and to implement the responsibility system when their leaders were contacted by Beijing officials in 1980. Opposition was strong, particularly when it came to breaking up the 450 *mu* on which they grew their grain. They recognized that in poorer areas of China, dismantling the collectives had appeal, especially where bureaucratic party leaders had stifled local initiative and stagnated productive labor. But for Half Moon villagers, along with others in Red Flag Commune, decollectivizing the grainfields was considered a formalistic response that disregarded their specific social and economic conditions. In this farming area where mechanization was relatively advanced, any decision to divide the land into smaller segments would require that large-scale agricultural machinery, such as wheat-harvesting combines, be abandoned. Having worked hard to purchase this collectively owned machinery, and experiencing the benefits of a mechanized wheat harvest, the villagers had little interest in reverting back to manual labor.

Fear was also expressed over the class "polarization" (*jie ji fen hua*) that would surely result from this reform program. For implementing the responsibility system meant not only that some people would get rich first, but also that others would fall further and further behind, possibly culminating in a return to the harsh class exploitation of earlier years.[3] Party cadre too were afraid that such a move would reduce that aspect of their power derived from directing resources and arranging jobs. And no one liked being told by Beijing Municipal authorities how to organize their economic life. Thus, in response to Beijing's initial request, the residents of Half Moon Village did nothing.

Ignoring a similar order to implement the responsibility system the following year, Half Moon's leaders eventually became the focus of criticism by city authorities, as did other village leaders in Red Flag and elsewhere who had also chosen to passively resist privatization. Finally, after one dissident villager wrote a letter to the Beijing authorities and asked why his local leaders had refused to implement the responsibility system, city officials sent an investigative team to delve into the problem more fully. When the officials arrived in Half Moon, they inquired of its leaders whether the cropland had been broken up into family-sized units. Not surprisingly, the response contained a certain degree of ambiguity.

"Yes, of course we have implemented the responsibility system. This cropland is used by the Dong family down the road, and that land over there is used by another family."

But when the officials asked whether the villagers had actually planted their *own* crops, the party leader's answer was, of necessity, more precise.

---

[3]Fear of class polarization was a common response throughout rural China at this time (see, for example, Zweig 1983 and Anagnost 1989).

"Well, not exactly. You see, after accepting the responsibility system, the people decided it was better to plant the crops together and then harvest them together!"

When told by the city investigative team that they had to implement the new policy, Half Moon's leaders proposed that the villagers' own views be sought on the matter. The result of that proposal was overwhelming support for continuing the collective utilization of the cropland. Only two villagers expressed interest in breaking it up—at which point the other residents had a good idea who in their midst had written the letter to Beijing. The event also clearly illustrated the age-old strategy used by peasants to resist bureaucratic decisions to which they were opposed: lie low and wait for "a new wind to blow."

Shortly thereafter, leaders from Evergreen Commune, located in the western suburbs of Beijing, went even further and publicly defended the view that *all* of their agricultural land should remain collectivized. In an article in the *China Daily*, they stated that though they too had accepted the responsibility system in principle, "Getting rich collectively" remained their primary slogan. A highly productive vegetable-producing commune, Evergreen had 14 production brigades, each specializing in a single product. The specialization of production, they said, plus the large-scale division of land, was conducive to further mechanization. The management of machinery was also specialized, as were the various sideline industries. In the view of the Evergreen Commune leaders, this specialization and the large scale production required an economic decision-making body of sufficient size and power that "could only be accomplished by a collective system"—a system that in their case was able to support three well-equipped hospitals, provide free medical care and education for all its members, and assume full responsibility for all senior citizens who had no family to care for them. The article concluded: "The collective system is a natural and inevitable product when the scale of production and mechanization has reached a certain stage. The system practiced at Evergreen may well point to the future of China's agricultural institutions" (Huang 1983:4).

Several years later a sharp drop in grain production forced the central government to declare that the agriculturally advanced farmers in the Beijing suburbs and elsewhere would be allowed to maintain their cropland as a collective endeavor. The term given to this arrangement was "scale farming" *(guimo jingying)*. By defining scale farming as a special form of the responsibility system, the government was able to declare that the new policy had been accepted in these areas. For their part, Half Moon's suburban farmers were willing to have their effort called by whatever name the government liked as long as they could maintain their cropland as a collective enterprise.[4]

[4]In some instances, villages sought to keep all their lands as a cooperative enterprise. Referred to as the "Four Unities" *(si tongyi),* this arrangement called for unified planning, unified financing, unified management, and unified technology and machine work. Although the land was contracted out, all beans and other vegetables, corn, and wheat were planted together. The best seed and fertilizer were then bought by the village to be used later on. All plowing, harrowing, fertilizing, planting, and spraying were also done collectively right up through the harvest.

Differences between collective and decollectivized land-use patterns were strikingly evident from the air. On a trip from Beijing to Shanghai in 1983, William Hinton (1983a:43–44) described the contrast

(continued)

While struggling to keep their grainland intact, Half Moon's peasant-farmers had diverse views on Deng Xiaoping's economic reforms. Some simply perceived the changes as reflecting China's central leadership's shift away from the socialist precepts of the Maoist era, the economic reforms being necessary to meet the revised modernization goals of the country's new ruling elite. Others saw them as a way of combatting the negative aspects of past experience, making the government less bureaucratic and more responsive to the needs of the people. Still others saw the market as helping to resolve the constant infighting that had plagued the highly centralized planning process of earlier years. Since the market was impersonal, why not let the value of new goods be decided by consumer demand rather than by bureaucrat fiat? Finally, more than a few were drawn to the prospect of "getting rich" in the expectation that they would be among the first to benefit from this new policy. And indeed, for the first few years of the reform movement, a large number of Half Moon's urban villagers did improve their living standard quite substantially.

This new wealth was achieved through a combination of factors. Particularly significant for the vegetable-producing farmers of Half Moon was the 20 to 30 percent increase in the vegetable price set by the government in the late 1970s and early 1980s. In addition, Beijing had been designated by the central government as a major center for economic and cultural development. Through such effort, the industrial infrastructure of the city would be upgraded, along with adding desperately needed new and improved housing for urban workers. The tourist industry was also to be enhanced, thereby bringing into the country much-needed foreign currency. The result of this decision was a huge infusion of cash into the city, culminating in numerous expanded roadways, factories, and high-rise apartments and hotels, all requiring new construction materials, goods, and services. Suburban sideline and state-run industries able to fulfill such requirements grew rapidly. Still, for most of Half Moon's agriculturally based families, vegetable production and its transportation to nearby urban markets remained their key source of new wealth. Being perishable, vegetables had to be grown near the city. Given the new inflated price and the village's location close to the capital center, the residents of Half Moon and other nearby districts were ideally situated to reap a considerable benefit.

With mounting pressure put on them by Beijing Municipal authorities, and with the price of cabbages, tomatoes, peppers, and other vegetables soaring, Half Moon's farmers eventually decided to break up their approximately 200 *mu* of vegetable-producing fields. The land was then allocated, based on family size, to individual households, each household receiving between one and two *mu* per capita. The vegetable income per household was influenced by the amount of garden land held, climatic conditions during the growing season, the labor input, and the fees that had to be paid to the village for services rendered. These services included providing thin plastic sheeting for greenhouses and dispensing fertilizer,

---

vividly: "While flying over the municipal area in the fall you will see large fields—10, 20, 30, 50 acres—all uniformly planted to wheat in accord with some measure of central planning. But as soon as the plane flies out over Hopei the character of the land use changes dramatically. Suddenly you see nothing but the most haphazard and incredible pattern of small strips of different colors on fields that clearly, a few years ago, were farmed as a unit. Many of these strips are no more than a yard wide, too narrow for a cart to even traverse them. And this pattern continues right down across the north China plain into the mountains of Shantung and beyond."

The new affluence of Half Moon Village is reflected in the modern exterior of the Wang house.

chemical sprays, and similar agricultural products that village leaders, with their back-door connections, could obtain far more cheaply than could individual households. Service fees also paid the wages of village leaders. Under this agreement, hard-working members of a large family could make as much as several thousand *yuan* a year—a very significant increase over the previous period.

However, grain production was another matter. Since grain was a basic commodity, its price remained under tight economic control by the central government, an action that made grain less desirable to grow than vegetables, with their rapidly inflating value.[5] Still, Half Moon's agricultural residents were required to produce a certain quota of grain for the state, thereby enabling the state to assure that enough wheat, corn, and rice would be available to supply the basic food needs of urban workers. In addition to the state grain quota, the village was responsible for its own food consumption. It could not buy subsidized grain from the state. Only those with an urban permit could. To buy grain on the free market would be too expensive. Thus, the villagers needed to maintain their own crop production. However, there was a problem with this. Whereas the size of the village quota had not changed in years, the need for additional housing, fishponds, and the like had reduced the available land base on which the crop was grown. Forced to grow grain on less land when higher profits could be obtained from selling vegetables, these suburban farmers faced an obvious dilemma: how could they continue to enhance their income when they were forced to grow less-profitable grain?

[5]After 1987, grain prices were periodically raised.

The answer was not long in coming. Under the responsibility system, families were able to negotiate contracts whereby land assigned to them could be rented to another village member, enabling the latter to obtain a larger agricultural base from which greater potential profits could be made. Since more land needed more laborers, those contracting this resource were also allowed to employ field workers. An analogous strategy for Half Moon and other suburban farmers that used "scale farming" as their method of operation was to rent their land to a "farm manager" (*nongye jingli*), who could then hire peasants from poorer provinces surrounding Beijing to come and work the still collectivized grainfields. Such an arrangement was particularly appealing in suburban Beijing, where increasing numbers of peasant-farmers were seeking jobs in expanding local, district, and state-run industries.

As soon as the plan was approved by the government's central leadership, hundreds of thousands of peasants from poorer regions of North China began arriving in Beijing's agricultural suburbs to help with the grain harvest. In the slack winter season, approximately 20 percent or so stayed on, fulfilling other needed tasks for the local villagers. In each instance, farm managers assumed the overall responsibility for hiring and supervising these migrant workers. Although economically advantageous to the village residents and their managers, the arrangement did raise once again the age-old issue of peasant exploitation. Were China's suburban farmers now getting rich off the backs of their poorer rural counterparts? This concern gained further substance when critics learned about the food and housing offered these temporary laborers.

"It looks like a prison labor camp to me," commented one visitor on seeing Half Moon's migrant worker dormitories. "After spending all day in the fields, these poor peasants return to their dorms in the evening only to be doled out a bare minimum of food—lots of grain but not many vegetables. Once the harvest is over, they are paid a small wage by the manager and then head back to Henan, Hebei, or whatever province they came from. It's highly exploitative."

In the more urban areas of Beijing, day laborer job markets also began appearing at this time. Crowding the trains and buses, rural peasants would arrive in the city seeking work in construction or similar non-skilled endeavors. Contractors, trying to keep their costs down, were quick to hire them. Once these temporary workers had saved enough money, they returned to their home villages—although some, of course, remained. Because these rural-based peasants were willing to work for much lower wages than city residents, the latter regularly called on the government to close the job markets down.[6]

As the government reduced its emphasis on central planning, thereby stimulating greater local initiative, the residents of Half Moon began seeking additional

---

[6]After the suppression of the Tiananmen Square protest in June 1989, the government did crack down on such markets. An important reason was that some of the violence and destruction occurring in Beijing during the protest had been committed by these highly frustrated day laborers. Angry that the acute rate of inflation and other economic problems in their villages had forced them to seek work in an exploitative environment far from home, they took out their anger on the government by joining thousands of other city residents in blocking army convoys coming into the city and by destroying military equipment.

ways to enhance their income. In 1983, imbued with a new entrepreneurial spirit and recognizing the increased demand for bricks in the booming Beijing construction industry, several villagers proposed that a kiln be built on 50 *mu* of village-held land. As cropland, the soil was not very good. Yet its clay-like properties were fine for the production of bricks. Since its present use as a grainfield brought little profit, why not follow the government's lead and turn the land into a collectively run brick factory that would bring new wealth to the village? However, Party Secretary Jiang Lijiang, recognizing the scheme would require a large loan, urged that the proposal be delayed so that more careful consideration could be given to exploring its implications. Opposing Jiang's conservative stance, the brick kiln proponents sought support from district party officials outside the village.

Shortly thereafter, Jiang Lijiang was urged by the district leadership to consider reassignment to a nearby small factory that was facing a number of unresolved difficulties. Responding that he would think it over, he was transferred anyway, at which point Half Moon Village found itself with a new party leader—who, it turned out, was far more supportive of the kiln proposal. Within a surprisingly short time, a loan was negotiated with the state for 100,000 *yuan,* and construction began.[7] A year later, the kiln was in full operation. Unfortunately, the success of the enterprise was only temporary. Much to the disappointment of the kiln supporters, it turned out that the soil needed to make the bricks was only three to four feet deep. Now the village had a 100,000-*yuan* loan to repay and a 50-*mu* hole of unusable land. At that point, district leaders called the villagers together and informed them that Jiang Lijiang was to be transferred back to Half Moon Village, and together they would have to deal with the problem of the new debt!

On his return, Jiang quickly closed the kiln. Searching around for other economic enterprises that might replace the failed operation, Jiang eventually used his back-door connections to obtain a contact with a Beijing candy-making factory eager to enlarge its export-oriented business. After establishing a shop in the village and with the help of a few city technicians to assist in the initial start-up, Half Moon was able to hire 20 local villagers and begin production. It was a great success. It also brought Secretary Jiang new recognition, since such an achievement required considerable *guanxi.* When he followed that effort with a second contract to make fire-retardant paint spray used in construction, his status grew even more—for by these means, it was projected that the 100,000-*yuan* village loan could be paid off by the early 1990s.

The brick kiln, candy factory, and fire-retardant products were not the only entrepreneurial activities undertaken in Half Moon Village at this time. Other, more individualized economic endeavors appeared on the scene as well. One early venture involved the transport of vegetables to the city. Not having the time or interest to sit in a booth and wait for a sale, farmers were considerably attracted to the prospect of having someone else transport their vegetable products to market. Thus, those few households or individuals able to purchase a small tractor or truck

---

[7]State bank-credit policies encouraged this type of entrepreneurial activity by offering tax holidays and liberal loans to new businesses while denying or severely limiting credit to older, collective endeavors.

Unloading vegetables at a wholesale market. The transportation of such produce has become an important entrepreneural activity for many of Beijing's suburban villagers.

from the village were assured of receiving an income considerably higher than that achieved by their earlier collective labor.

In Half Moon, the village leaders organized just such a transportation service, hiring a trucker to take the tomatoes, peppers, or other products to market. Each household wishing to participate was charged a certain amount per pound of vegetable transported. Other charges included a small amount for fuel, wages, and what it cost the driver to sell the goods in the city. Of course, with sufficient funds and a vehicle, any household could set up its own competing business, purchasing vegetables from local families and transporting them to nearby wholesale markets on their own. In either instance, once the produce arrived at the market, it was resold to a peddler who, after setting up a stand on a neighborhood street corner, offered it again to those passing by, for up to twice the original price. These peddlers, selling 50 kilograms of vegetables a day at five *fen* per kilogram, could do quite well for themselves—making as much as a field hand might earn in an equivalent day's work.

Other new private businesses included the establishment of small family-run convenience stores. By 1984 several of these enterprises, located in family court-yards, were selling candies, cookies, soy sauce, liquor, toilet paper, cigarettes, and similar items. But before long, so many families had set up similar enterprises that the competition eventually forced the closing of all but the most successful of them. And of these, none were able to support more than a single household member.

Looking back on these dramatic changes, Chu Meiying, the Half Moon Village accountant whose three older sisters all had jobs in state-run factories, commented: "What we are doing now is capitalism. That's what we were warned about before. And Mao said, if we do this, we will go back to the old society, we will suffer again, and we will be oppressed just like in the old days. That will happen if we let the revisionists come to power. But look. We are not suffering. We are doing fine. So we no longer need to worry about what Mao said."

RISING DISCONTENT

Chu Meiying's statement summarizes rather well the perspective of the affluent sector of Half Moon Village. Coming from a family whose members all had secure state employment, she could easily say that life was fine. And indeed, for her family, it was. She, for example, together with her three sisters and brothers-in-law, had been able to build a highly attractive home for her parents. Though lacking urban conveniences such as an indoor toilet, hot water, or central heating, it was well constructed, with colorful designs decorating the smooth cement floor and large, well-placed windows located on the outer walls—quite a fine and generous gift for an elderly couple who in their youth had faced the threat of starvation.

Still, for the two-thirds of Half Moon's residents who worked in agriculture, the Chus' affluence and that of similarly advantaged families was looked at with both criticism and envy. As agricultural residents with a rural residency "permit" (hukou), farmers had no long-term economic guarantees. Furthermore, any food or other commodities they wished to purchase had to be obtained at non-subsidized prices. Since state workers, such as the three sisters in the Chu family, were nonagricultural residents, they not only were able to buy subsidized grain at cheap prices, but also could get cooking oil and similar food items that were often in short supply.[8]

Discrimination against Half Moon farmers took other forms as well. When a factory sought new workers, it was most likely to hire ones who already had urban residency permits. Why? Because urban workers were seen as needing employment, whereas rural people could care for their own needs. As a consequence, the children of male urban workers and rural women were required to retain their mother's rural residency status. Needless to say, such marriages were not very common.

Discrimination also was practiced against farm youths applying for admission to high schools, technical schools, and colleges. In the 1970s, qualified students from Half Moon and other villages had been able to attend a nearby middle school. But following privatization, the school was closed. When a local school official was

---

[8]The one key item they couldn't get was adequate housing. For years Beijing had faced a chronic housing shortage, with people crammed into small, overcrowded rooms. Half Moon's long-term agricultural residents, by contrast, generally had far better housing. Able to build their own homes in the countryside, they had more square footage per person—perhaps as much as three times that of a city dweller. Thus, if one could become a state-employed urban resident with a home in a village like Half Moon, this clearly represented "the best of both worlds."

asked why, he responded: "We didn't have enough qualified teachers. And since we couldn't guarantee the quality of the education, we disbanded the school." The strategy was that for improved educational quality, consolidation was required. But for Half Moon children living a considerable distance from the new consolidated school, the opportunity to continue their education was diminished. Equally frustrating was the policy that to attend a technical school or college, rural high school graduates now had to receive a higher grade on the entrance examinations than did their urban counterparts. The government's justification was that if agricultural residents graduated from college, they would be assigned state jobs and thus become urban residents, exacerbating the already overcrowded urban job market. Of course, if the parents had sufficient contacts and money, they might be able to place their children in higher-quality schools by offering a bribe to a principal or teacher. Administrative cadres had considerable power in the schools, but their wages were low. Given the rising problem of inflation, accepting a bribe was one way for cadres to prevent their income from eroding.

Bribery, of course, had a long history in China. But in contrast to the previous three decades, it grew enormously during the 1980s. In 1979, three party officials from the district encompassing Half Moon Village had used public funds to obtain wood to build a house. When caught, they were quickly removed from their positions of leadership and punished. But 10 years later, such activities went on all the time with little fear of punishment. In 1979, a man wanted a cigarette or a meal to transport goods from one location to another. A decade later, a similar effort required a large payment of *yuan*. Now, if one raised chickens, it was necessary to know someone to buy the low-state-priced chicken feed. Every market transaction seemed to be tied to personal connections. Nor was it just a matter of obtaining feed for one's chickens. Since feed was in such short supply, fulfilling your own needs could well mean that someone else would likely have to do without.

Corruption became more pronounced in other spheres as well. When the health inspector came to look over Half Moon's new candy factory, he stated that the workers' locker room was too far away from the production line. The health code called for the two to be adjacent to one another, without the workers having to go outside to reach their work stations. He then indicated that though he was willing to overlook this problem, it was necessary that each factory worker receive a health checkup—primarily for hepatitis. The doctor's examination fee was 10 *yuan* per person. When the villagers complained bitterly at the high cost, the health inspector commented, "Well, you pay me something, and then we won't have to bother with the health checkup!"

Toward the end of the 1980s, the problems inherent in the contradictory strategy of privatizing production and encouraging market relations while continuing largely intact the bureaucratic state control were becoming increasingly apparent. In 1985, the output of China's grain and cotton production had plummeted, forcing the country to again import grain. Steadily rising inflation, combined with low, state-controlled grain prices, had forced millions of peasants to seek work in the cities, even though their agricultural production was desperately needed. Once there, those unable to find regular jobs brought to the fore problems of unemployment, homelessness, prostitution, and other manifestations of an underclass that had long been abhorred.

At this same time, government officials and new party leaders were raising the level of corruption to unprecedented heights by taking advantage of the dual-price system to purchase commodities at the state-controlled price and then selling them at the going market price.[9] Nepotism too had brought increased wealth to government officials—including those in high government positions. Although laws forbade such officeholders from participating in lucrative businesses such as import-export trade, their children often did, and some, including those of Deng Xiaoping and the party general secretary Zhao Ziyang, became quite wealthy in the process. With high-cadre families enriching themselves so grandly, lesser ones quickly followed, wining, dining, and traveling with little regard to cost or need. So too, the policy of decentralization allowed provinces, counties, and cities to set their own course of action, negotiating trade within and outside the country with little concern for the nation's larger interest. A flood of foreign commodities—including extravagantly priced automobiles, many from Japan—entered the country, quickly draining the nation's foreign currency reserves and undercutting locally made products. In a 1986 protest, students marched in Beijing and other cities, raising slogans about the new Japanese economic imperialism as well as demanding that the state address the needs of higher education.

As economic problems mounted, the government found itself having to temporarily halt construction projects, reestablish price controls, and recentralize decision making to keep from losing complete control of the economy. This in turn exacerbated other problems such as unemployment. Peasant-farmers too felt this economic squeeze as greater controls were placed on their produce. Other unanticipated consequences followed as well. In 1984, when grain production appeared to be at its highest ever, the state decided to raise the protein level in the people's diet. Numerous animal-feed factories were set up, based on the assumption that there would be a continuing large surplus of grain. But the following year, the amount of grain available dropped precipitously, causing a sharp increase in the free market price of corn. Unable to deal with this price rise, new rural animal-feed factories soon went bankrupt.[10]

Between 1984 and 1988, the agricultural crisis grew in intensity—the population increasing by 61.4 million while grain input fell by 13.3 billion kilograms (Smith 1989a). Faced with a cash flow problem, the government eventually was forced to begin paying for requisitioned grain with government IOUs. Farmers retaliated by cutting back on pig and poultry production, in some instances choosing to slaughter them rather than sell them at the government's low procurement prices. Egg and meat rationing were reintroduced throughout the country. In 1988, Beijing residents were allowed only one kilogram of meat and 2.5 kilograms of eggs at state-subsidized stores. Those wishing to eat more meat had to pay a much higher price in the free market. Actually, Beijing was the last of China's cities to

---

[9]The famous dissident astrophysicist Fang Lizhi referred to this form of profiteering as "official turnaround," describing it as "the use of official power and connections to procure commodities or other resources at low prices in the state-run sector of the economy, then turning around to sell them at huge mark-ups within the private sector" (Fang 1989:3–4).

[10]Actually, the large grain increase in 1984 was due more to the process of decollectivization than to an expansion in production. For that was the year in which the collectively stored grain (along with other assets) was dispersed to brigade villagers and then placed on the open market.

implement rationing, its leaders waiting until after the party had adjourned its congress before making the announcement.

As the problems magnified, residents of Half Moon began looking more critically at the economic reforms put into effect over the past decade. For many, increased inflation and reduced social services had diminished their lives economically, while individual entrepreneurialism and mounting corruption had weakened their identification with the collective. Now, education for their children had to be paid for by the family. This, along with the household's need for more labor input in vegetable gardening, had a negative impact on class enrollment. Having done away with the welfare fund, the village no longer had money to assist elderly residents. The delivery of health services too had changed, for with the demise of the collective, families had to pay the privatized barefoot doctors directly for medical treatment. For those in good health, the loss of a socialized medical-care program was not a concern. As one young villager expressed it: "I'm not sick. Why should I have to pay for someone else's illness?" But for those faced with a serious problem, the result could be devastating.

Several years ago, the daughter of an elderly woman from Half Moon Village was diagnosed with cancer. The resulting operation cost the family 1,000 *yuan*. Since the daughter worked in the fields and had a rural residency permit, she lacked any health benefits. Both mother and daughter were distraught. When the mother was asked what she was going to do, the older woman responded: "What can I do? It's just my bad fortune, that's all." She made no reference to the earlier collective period, when the cost of health care was shared jointly with other village members. Rather, she spoke of how one son had died in infancy and another shortly after he was married. Now, only her daughter was left, and it appeared she would not have long to live. If the mother had been employed by the state, her work unit would have taken responsibility for her medical care. But as an elderly peasant woman with one sick daughter and no sons, she was on her own with nowhere to turn.

If fatalism continued to be called upon by older villagers to explain their plight, such a response was less characteristic of younger farmers. They, when asked "Are you in favor of the reform movement?" were likely to say "yes." But when asked "Do you like what is happening?" They often said "no." The reforms were liked, but not the consequences of reform. The national party leader Zhao Ziyang once said he couldn't understand how people carrying a rice bowl could still be cursing him on the street (that is, "Why are you cursing me when you have enough to eat?"). The point, of course, was that some rice bowls had become a great deal larger than others. Indeed, it was stated on occasion that corrupt senior-level officials were eating out of "golden rice bowls." After 30 years of socialism, the people had come to take for granted its egalitarian principles. When they saw that crooked officials and a growing privileged elite were the primary beneficiaries of the reforms, they became very angry. Corruption had become so deep, so pervasive, so enormous that it touched every aspect of people's lives. Thus, in Half Moon, although a few agreed with Chu Meiying's view that everything was fine, many felt otherwise. And for at least some, Mao Zedong's earlier remarks on revisionism and suffering began to take on new meaning.

In 1988, when asked to explain the reasons behind this epidemic of corruption, an articulate local party member responded at some length.

> Some people feel the nature of the party and the state has changed. The change first appeared in the late 1960s and 1970s when the power and authority, rather than representing the interests of the people, came to represent those in power. This process took some time to unfold. But now it is quite clear what Mao meant when he warned us about the danger of capitalist roaders. We in the party get a lot more information than the ordinary people through the party channels. We witness the various behavior of party leaders during the two-line struggle in the last 30 years. When the "exaggeration wind" came down in 1958, Mao had to personally write letters to all of us in the party to put a stop to this. But it was of no use. It became clear now that some of our leaders those days were instigating the exaggeration wind to discredit Mao. You don't know how hard it was for us to figure out what was going on. Mao tried time and time again to weed out the capitalist roaders, but he failed. Now, people don't know what to do.
>
> The students in Beijing strongly oppose Deng Xiaoping's leadership. Some even feel that it will take a new revolution to resolve the problem, and others look to Western models for possible solutions. The workers are also outraged, but leaders who can direct their anger into political action are few in number. For those living in the countryside, the situation is quite different. Being less aware of the sweep of events taking place in the urban areas, they focus their attention on how these changes affect their day-to-day lives. When they do think about leaders like Deng, Mao becomes their point of reference. Mao was tall. Deng is short. Mao sent his son to the front lines in the Korean war. Where did Deng send his son? To the United States. During the hunger of the three difficult years after the Great Leap Forward, Mao didn't eat meat. But now look what party leaders are doing when they ask us to tighten our belt. People talk about the need for a new leadership, but they don't see from where it will come.
>
> There is a tendency among us Chinese to wait for our saviors. Some people say, "Since Mao came along many years ago and saved China from the mess it was in, someone else will come along someday and save us from the mess we are in today." There is another tendency among us Chinese and that is we are a very patient people. But if we get pushed too far, we act violently. It's like a clay cooking pot. It takes a long time for it to heat up, but once it starts to boil, it will boil for a long time after removing it from the stove.

Throughout this monologue, the party member carefully refrained from stating his own views on these events. However, it was quite clear that he was deeply concerned about his country, its leaders, and the problems it was having to face.

While Half Moon's residents were reflecting on how the economic reforms of the 1980s had influenced them, other villagers working near or in Beijing City were facing a somewhat different set of problems. Over the course of a single decade, the city had undergone an incredible period of change, its urban core expanding inexorably out toward the once rural suburbs. Especially noticeable were the large number of high-rise apartment buildings, offices, and highways that had sprung up in recent years, practically doubling the center city's overall size. Its growth could also be detected by observing the expanding congestion of the major highways. At certain times, it took longer to travel from the south end of the city to the north by car than by bicycle. Every day during rush hour, the two urban beltways turned into large parking lots—a grid-locked pattern requiring hours to clear. Most of the growth in traffic was due to the greater number of trucks—a striking sign of heightened economic activity. Trucks had all but replaced horse-carts, although an increasing number of motorcycles also were competing for space on the road.

If horse-carts had disappeared, bicycles were still used to transport food and commodities from the suburbs into the city proper. On Beijing's highways, groups of men regularly rode bicycles loaded with bales of cotton, stacks of brooms, or buckets of eggs. These were the peddlers, who, after purchasing goods from a location where they could be obtained cheaply, sold them somewhere else for a higher price. In some instances, a bicycle trip could take the peddler several days to bring his goods into the city, whereas on another occasion, he might be fortunate enough to negotiate a ride from an empty truck going his way.

Along with road congestion, Beijing's atmosphere had become highly polluted. Gone was the clean and crisp air of earlier years. On a windless day, arriving in Beijing was sometimes akin to entering a gas chamber. The pitch-black smoke from the coal furnaces in winterized apartment buildings, fumes from cars and trucks that were in desperate need of tune-ups, the fall burning of cornstalks and the spring burning of wheat straw by nearby farmers preparing to clear their fields for plowing, and the year-round smoke from industrial pollution had made much of the city air seemingly unbearable. Yet suburban residents, taking advantage of improved public transportation, regularly sought opportunities to work in Beijing's more urban surroundings. For along with the possibility of gaining greater economic security,

A long line of peddlers on bicycles waiting at a wholesale market to obtain vegetables for resale.

they enjoyed shopping in the well-stocked stores, making use of improved services, and finding employment in less demanding jobs.

Another feature of urban life that influenced suburban villages like Half Moon was the influx of Western movies, television, books, and magazines. Store displays in the commercial district reflected a Western format. Clothes were modeled after Western fashions. Traditional Chinese songs and plays were all but drowned out by Hong Kong pop music and disco tunes, all of which began appearing on the city's outskirts as well. Sexually oriented portraiture too had begun to challenge traditional Chinese morality. Bookstores commonly displayed posters of pretty girls. The walls of homes and offices had similar posters of scantily dressed Western models. The most popular calendar posters, which once offered scenes of nature, now highlighted women's bodies. Sex novels and magazines, always available from underground sources, were sold on Beijing street corners. Beauty contests of young women dressed in two-piece swimsuits appeared on national television, attracting millions of viewers. Female body-building competitions attracted similar large audiences looking for erotic thrills. VCRs began showing up in homes—including those of affluent Half Moon villagers.

Still, an increased interest in consumerism and the acceptance of Western-oriented popular culture should not be taken to mean that the people were entirely happy with their new existence. Life, it seemed, was not as hard as it was irritating. On a trip to a state-run store, one frequently faced a grumpy salesperson. Going to work by public transportation required elbowing others away to get on an over-crowded bus. Nor were the bus drivers happy with their jobs, a fact they readily made known to their passengers. To keep the drivers from striking, the city government gave them a series of incremental raises. Since a driver could make much more money elsewhere, driving a taxi for instance, the bus company was continually faced with having to find replacements. It seemed as though the only way to preserve the work force was to prevent the drivers from transferring to other jobs. Eventually, in keeping with that goal, the city threatened to fine any state-run enterprise that hired an urban driver. Given these pressures, the drivers quickly took their grievances out on the passengers, refusing to stop if too many people were waiting or closing the door before the people had an opportunity to get in. Others angered prospective passengers, who had waited patiently for long periods in designated lines, by first picking up those at the end of the line. With this kind of provocation, it wasn't long before bus commuters began venting their grievances as soon as they arrived at their own work site.

Illustrative of these tensions was a conversation overheard at a Beijing bus stop in 1987 during a student demonstration. After waiting for over an hour and frustrated by the four or five buses that had passed without stopping, two would-be passengers discussed the nature of the problem.

"Obviously, the drivers are not happy with their jobs, and they are taking it out on us," commented one worker.

"Of course they're not happy. But there are plenty of others too," responded the other. "Look at the students, they're always stirring up trouble. The problem with them is that they care only about their own fate," he continued. "If they raised slogans that concerned the workers in the city, high inflation for instance, the students would have a lot more of a following."

Actually, college and university students played a significant role in recent Chinese history. On May 4, 1919, they led nationwide demonstrations against the Allied powers' decision in the Versailles Treaty to give Germany's special rights in Shandong Province to Japan instead of returning them to China. In March 1926, thousands more marched to Beijing's Tiananmen Square in support of the country's National Army and to protest Japanese imperialist intervention in the Northeast. Following a series of speeches, a small vanguard of students moved toward the government headquarters, a petition listing their concerns raised above their heads. Without warning, guards opened fire, killing 47 and wounding many. The reaction of city residents ranged from open anger to sympathy for the students to fear that any expression of nationalism might cause them difficulty or harm. For its part, the government described the demonstrators as "rioters" who were "morally responsible for their own deaths." Lu Xun, China's foremost short-story writer of the time, wrote in response: "This is not the conclusion of an incident but a new beginning. Lies written in ink can never hide truth written in blood!"

Years later, students marched again in support of the 1956 "Hundred Flowers Campaign," which sought to encourage a broader range of political expression and involvement in the building of China's socialist society. During the Cultural Revolution of the 1960s, they played a leading role in Mao's effort to rid the party of those people "taking the capitalist road." In 1979, responding to Deng Xiaoping's call for open criticism of Mao's earlier policies, they posted their views on Beijing's "democracy wall"—until the criticisms went beyond those approved by Deng. At this point, the movement's prominent leaders, such as Wei Jingsheng and Wang Xizhe, were arrested and, after a series of highly publicized trials, received long prison sentences.[11] Feeling manipulated and betrayed by Deng, some students in Beijing and elsewhere lost what remaining faith they had in the party and began actively exploring Western models of political governance. This feeling of disillusionment coincided with the opportunity for China's brightest (and politically well-placed) students to continue their educations in Europe and North America—an experience that further enhanced their view of the need for substantial economic and political change.

In late 1986 and early 1987, students again demonstrated in Beijing and 30 other cities to protest poor campus living conditions, an inflexible curriculum, dissatisfaction with job assignments following graduation, the high rate of inflation, unfair Japanese trade practices, the need for greater political democratization, and more freedom of the press. Since these issues stirred little interest among the larger populace, the government's initial reaction was lenient. Nevertheless, after placing legal restrictions on all "unauthorized public activities," the government arrested student leaders and brought the protests to a halt.

---

[11]Although the Western press often portrayed the movement as pro-capitalist and pro-liberal, the student leaders actually bridged the political spectrum; Wang Xizhe, for example, drawing on classical Marxist thinking, had demanded that workers be allowed to actively participate in decision making in both production and governance.

By April and May 1989, the movement had risen once more. Although the size of this student protest eventually was as large as that occurring at the beginning of the Cultural Revolution, its basic nature was very different. Whereas the earlier movement had been launched from the top, under the direction of Mao, this student effort was initiated from below with little, if any, initial involvement of high-level party or government leaders. Furthermore, the students remained strongly unified, instead of dividing into factions as had occurred during the 1960s. Finally, by focusing on issues of corruption and inflation as well as democracy, they quickly drew the interest of Chinese intellectuals, workers, and even suburban farmers. It was, in the minds of the students, a massive effort to achieve a "Second Liberation." For Deng Xiaoping and his associates, it was perceived quite differently—"as an anti-government riot led by counterrevolutionaries" intent on changing China's basic political system. And for millions of workers and others who eventually joined the protest, it was a profound political statement informing the nation's leaders that they had lost their mandate to govern.

PROTEST AT TIANANMEN SQUARE

The protest began on April 15, following the death of the former party general secretary Hu Yaobang, whom the students perceived as the one senior party leader sympathetic to their demands for greater freedom of speech and their opposition to official corruption. Two years earlier, Hu had been charged with allowing China to succumb to "bourgeois liberalism" and had been forced to resign in disgrace. He had been replaced by Zhao Ziyang. Comparing Deng Xiaoping with Hu Yaobang, the students concluded succinctly, "The wrong man died."

After Hu's funeral, three Beijing students engaged in a ritual not unlike that enacted at Tiananmen Square 63 years earlier. Walking to an entrance of the Great Hall of the People, they carried above their heads a petition calling for free speech and an end to corruption within the government. Kneeling down in front of the door, they waited. Eventually, Chia Ling, the senior student leader in charge of the protest at the square, along with many others, broke into tears. It was clear that on that day their plea would not be heard. Soon, however, liberal teachers, journalists, and other intellectuals in the city did respond, actively speaking out in support of the demonstrators. As the protest gathered momentum, the party issued its first serious warning, stating in a *People's Daily* editorial of April 26 that the student movement was a "planned conspiracy, the nature of which is to negate the leadership of the Party and the socialist system." In response, the students demanded that they be allowed to form an autonomous student organization, that the personal wealth of senior government and party officials be made public, and that the students have an opportunity to meet "on an equal basis" with government leaders to press their grievances. After their demands were rejected, students and supporters again marched through the streets, this time carrying a new banner that stated: "To be patriotic is not a crime."

Then, on May 4, the 70th anniversary of the 1919 May 4th Movement, nearly 200,000 students and other citizens, in a massive demonstration of their strength, returned to the center of Beijing. May 4 also happened to be the date scheduled for the opening of the Asian Development Bank's (ADB) annual conference to be held at the Great Hall of the People, adjacent to Tiananmen Square. While thousands of protestors stood outside, 2,000 bankers and officials from 47 countries (including Taiwan) met in an opening ceremony. In his speech of greeting to the ADB, Party General Secretary Zhao Ziyang made reference to the student protest, stating that the party would open a dialogue with the students—a remark that surprised many in the audience, since it publicly challenged the views of other top leaders, including Li Peng, China's Prime Minister, who strongly opposed the student demands. At this point it was clear that a serious split had occurred among the country's senior leaders.

Shortly thereafter, 300 journalists from 15 state-controlled media centers undertook their own demonstration, criticizing the numerous political controls placed on their activities. Joining the students, they carried banners—"Workers of the Capital Press"—and shouted slogans such as "We are no longer mouthpieces for the government," and "Protect the Constitution Article 35 for press freedom." Soon, protests began springing up in other cities, including Shanghai, where 10,000 students marched to the People's Square, receiving strong support from onlookers along the way.

As the crisis deepened, Beijing students again attempted to enter into a dialogue with government officials to seek recognition for their newly established autonomous student association. This association, which included in its membership representatives of the various universities in the city, was democratically structured, with all its elected leaders serving as activists in the movement. A second student committee, again elected by students, was responsible for directing the activities planned for Tiananmen Square. Drawing on the principle of democratic centralism, the students in the square agreed that after a full debate, the minority would be bound by the decision of the majority. Thus, if the majority voted to remain in the square, the minority were expected to remain as well.

In this same month, a Beijing organizing committee for an independent union was formed. The leaders of this new organization were to be democratically elected, and its members would take part of their own free will. Instead of simply serving as a welfare organization, the union was to be an arena where workers could put forward their views on economic and political matters. It would have the right to monitor the decisions of the Chinese Communist Party. Furthermore, in state-owned and collective firms and businesses, the union would be able to use "all appropriate and legal means . . . to ensure that the workers are really the masters of the firms." And finally, the organization would be able to guarantee the legal rights of its members in the constitutional and legal spheres. The founding document was signed by the Provisional Committee of the Beijing Independent Worker's Union on May 21, 1989.

While students and workers were planning their strategies, China's top leaders were attempting to resolve problems within their leadership. Some, such as Li Peng and the country's president, Yang Shangkun, wanted to move quickly and firmly against the students, whereas others, such as Zhao Ziyang, wanted a dialogue.

Zhao, closely tied to the policies of economic reform, was aware that his eventual success as a leader required the support of China's young, educated elite. But by agreeing with the student demand for a dialogue in the open forum of the Asian Development Bank's annual meeting (and elsewhere), he quickly found himself opposed by older, conservative leaders—including his earlier mentor, Deng Xiao-ping.

On May 15 and 16, in a meeting of crucial importance, China's key leaders were to join the Soviet Party leader, Mikhail Gorbachev, at the Great Hall of the People to discuss improving relations between their two countries. In a move timed specifically to embarrass the Chinese government, hundreds of students had begun a hunger strike three days earlier. As the strike progressed, it rapidly gained a great deal of sympathy among city residents. Workers from the Capital Iron and Steel Factory turned out in large numbers. Other participating groups included Beijing's Petrochemical Company, the Capital Hospital, Xidan Supermarket Workers, Beijing Autoworkers Union, All-China Federation of Trade Unions, the Pipe Music Instrument Factory, civilian employees of the PLA, the People's Bank of China, and various hotel and restaurant employees. As thousands marched through the streets, doctors and nurses came to the square to give medical assistance to those in need. Factory workers sent large amounts of food and other essentials. Finally, on May 20, after a brief visit to the students by Zhao Ziyang and Li Peng—in which Zhao commented: "I came too late. I can't do anything anymore"—martial law was declared by the government. Early that morning, PLA troops were ordered into the city to take the square, only to find their way blocked by millions of residents who had poured into the streets in protest.

By the end of the month, large numbers of troops were still bivouacked at the edge of the city. Under the shadow of this military force, the movement began to dissipate, as students became fearful of what the future might hold. Deciding to end the hunger strike, leaders nevertheless suggested that some students, including those who had recently arrived in Beijing, remain in the square, while urging others from local colleges and universities to leave and organize additional support on campuses, at shops, in local factories, and elsewhere. At this time, students from the Beijing Central Art's School, recognizing the need for a dramatic new protest symbol, constructed on their campus a tall statue of a woman holding a lamp in her hands. Calling it the "goddess of democracy," the students brought the statue to the square and, after uncovering it, dedicated it to the hunger strikers.[12]

By early June, the People's Liberation Army had tried on several occasions to enter the city, only to be blocked at its outskirts by large barricades put up on the highways by Beijing citizens. This effort, one of the most significant of the whole citywide protest movement, drew together thousands of suburban workers, day and unemployed laborers, and even nearby farmers. Buses were moved and placed at the center of intersections, the gaps then filled with trucks and cars. Within a short

---

[12]Modeled in part on America's Statue of Liberty, it symbolized a democratic commitment to end corruption and privilege in China. It was not meant to represent a desire for Western-style democracy, as was sometimes reported in the American press.

time, all access roads to the city had been closed, thousands of people remaining on guard to be sure no soldiers could get through. Recognizing that any forward movement on their part would result in the loss of civilian lives, the soldiers stopped. Some fraternized with the protestors while others sat stoically, waiting for further orders. Occasionally a youth would come by with the latest news obtained from student motorcyclists who, while dodging the PLA, were serving as liaison personnel, carrying messages between the square and the campuses. Other protestors turned on their shortwave radios and listened to broadcasts from Britain's BBC or the United States' Voice of America.

In Tiananmen Square on the afternoon of June 3, students gathered to sing the Internationale, an inspirational anthem of the working class, along with protest songs from other countries, including America's "We Shall Overcome," just as they had done in the previous days and weeks. Speaking over the loudspeaker, student leaders reported on the events of the day and on plans for the morrow. A young professor stood up and announced the formation of a new People's University, which would begin that evening. After dark, reports began circulating that around 10:30, soldiers had begun firing on city residents in an effort to reach the west side of the Great Hall of the People. Shortly thereafter, 8,000 helmeted troops—carrying satchels but without visible weapons—charged out of the Great Hall and down the street toward the square. Immediately they were met by a large number of people who completely filled the roadway with their bodies. These people in turn were followed by thousands of others, eventually blocking any further forward movement by the soldiers.[13]

Throughout this time, occasional gunfire was heard on the street, but it wasn't until several hours after midnight that heavy firing from automatic weapons and tanks informed Beijing's residents that a full-fledged assault was in progress. Waking from their sleep, foreign visitors in high-rise hotels close to center city were able to observe armored personnel carriers advancing along the streets, followed by PLA troops. As the tanks crushed one barrier after another, troops coming from both east and west lingered behind, shooting automatic weapons indiscriminately at the people as they pushed forward, killing many. Those in the back of the crowds, thinking that the soldiers were perhaps firing into the air, continued to press on, trapping those in front. Finally arriving at Tiananmen Square, the army tanks ran over the last remaining barricades and secured the area. The approximately 4,500 students remaining in the square then began negotiating with the soldiers. Many eventually left by the southern entrance, although a few were run over by tanks in what was quite possibly an accident. Others may have been killed after refusing to leave, but no exact account of casualties, either in the square or outside, was ever determined.

On June 17, almost two weeks after the massacre, the lead editorial in the *China Daily* stated: "The Chinese authorities have recorded a major victory in putting down the anti-government riot which showed its extremely damaging nature in the

---

[13]These events have been portrayed in considerable detail in the press, in filmed television footage, and in numerous photographs taken by both Chinese and foreign newspeople. One firsthand account by an American observer of what happened in Beijing during the protest is contained in a book by William Hinton (1990), from which several of the events described above are drawn.

first days of this month in Beijing and some other cities of the country. . . . The extremists among the students and the hooligans on the streets deviated so far from the interests of the people, and their damage to the peaceful life of the capital and attack on the people's army developed so seriously that the authorities' use of force became inevitable." At the same time, National Chinese television showed dramatic footage of Beijing "hooligans" throwing gasoline bombs and setting military tanks on fire, seemingly as the troops were entering the city. The implication was that "criminal elements" had first attacked the PLA, who had then been forced to respond in kind. In fact, as later became known, the broadcasters had reversed the film footage. The Beijing residents, angrily attacking the armed personnel carriers, had done so after the tanks had brought death and destruction to the city, not before.

Reporting on the event from the perspective of the students, Chia Ling (1989:10), the 23-year-old Tiananmen Square protest leader, tape-recorded an emotional appeal while hiding underground: "Countrymen! The regime is out of its mind. The Beijing massacre has become a nationwide slaughter. . . . The tighter the mindless fascist suppression, the sooner the true people's republic will be born. Down with the fascists. Down with military rule. The people shall triumph. Long live the republic!"

In the countryside, however, the response to the tragedy in Beijing was far more subdued.

VILLAGE RESPONSE

A little over a month after the protest had been brought to a close by the PLA, the event continued to be a regular topic of conversation by the people of Half Moon. One issue that received considerable attention was the accident that had occurred while an army convoy was passing along the main thoroughfare between the village and the nearby market town. Turning incorrectly, one of the tanks slipped off the side of the road and became stuck in the mud of the adjacent shoulder. Not allowed to stop, the rest of the convoy continued on its way toward the city, leaving the vehicle mired down in the soft earth. Soon, residents came trekking out to the road to see the tank and the damage that had occurred.

After a while, an older peasant, familiar with military vehicles, walked over to the tank and began discussing how its engine could be taken apart so that it would no longer work. Urged on by others standing along the road, he eventually dismantled it. Several weeks later, security investigators from the PLA arrived and began asking who had sabotaged the tank. When given the individual's name by a local leader, the old man was arrested, taken away, and thoroughly interrogated. During the inquiry, several villagers spoke about the old man, stating to the security officers that he was considered to be somewhat retarded mentally and, therefore, not accountable for his actions. Eventually, the man was released and returned to his village.

Stories also circulated among the residents about students from a nearby village who had taken action against the PLA, including barricading highways not far from Half Moon. Comments on this event brought mixed reactions. Based on their past knowledge and experience, most villagers found it inconceivable that the PLA would fire on the protestors. Even during the height of the Cultural Revolution, the army had gone unarmed into the colleges and universities, where the worst fighting had occurred. But when several factory workers reported that the army had fired on crowds at street corners, the tenor of the conversations began to change.

Still, not all the reports were critical of the army. Some told of army truck drivers who refused to enter the city or, if they came across a wooden barricade, declined to remove them. In another instance, a driver, finding that his tire had been punctured, simply sat in his truck, without making any effort to fix it. People who had been in touch with friends in the city spoke of the afternoon of June 4, when 20 or 30 trucks were burned in just one location, the pavement under them spotted with an accumulation of twisted metal, melted tires, and gasoline stains. A little later, when the body of a young man was carried on the back of a pedicab past people standing at a street corner, a nearby group of PLA soldiers, moved to tears, removed their caps and began saluting the onlookers. Finally, after they were ordered by an officer to continue their march toward the city's center, one angry onlooker told the soldiers that after they left, he was going to burn a truck himself! Without a protest of any kind, the soldiers left, after which all the remaining army trucks in the area were burned to the ground.

As the weeks passed by, the tragic events in Beijing slowly slipped into the background of daily life at Half Moon. Some villagers maintained their outspoken criticism of the party and the army. Others disagreed, feeling that the students had brought the action on themselves. Repeating the commentary of the television newscasters, they emphasized that Beijing students and citizens had no right to block the army from trying to maintain order in the city. But all acknowledged that since the demonstrations were over, everyone should go back to work—and further-more, it was useless to argue with people who had guns.

However, for villagers working in state factories, putting aside the happenings of the past month was not so easy. For on returning to their jobs, they were all required to make a report stating what they had been doing during the demonstration and whether they had been an organizer, a participant, or just an observer. A few workers had been asked to organize counterdemonstrations against the students, for which they were to be paid 10 *yuan* a day. Most had refused or called in sick. Those who had been active participants in the demonstrations simply lied about their actions, knowing full well that if they were caught, they would lose their jobs.

In reflecting back over the events of May and June, Jiang Lijiang, the party secretary, was quite prepared to express his view—which, of course, was the official perspective of the party. Pleased that no villagers from Half Moon had been directly involved in the protest, he stated: "All the people in Half Moon are law-abiding citizens. We don't have any troublemakers here. No one over 40 got involved. A few younger ones did, but they didn't do any damage. In a nearby village, there was a problem. Three students got arrested. At the beginning the students were right to protest against corruption. But they went too far. Here, we only care about production. Our fire-retardant factory was going to open in June with 20 new jobs, but because of the rebellion, we couldn't start."

When asked about the old man from the nearby village who had dismantled the tank, Jiang responded: "Over 250 trucks passed by Half Moon Village without a single interruption. Most of the people around here were simply bystanders having fun watching what was going on. That old man, he didn't know what he was doing. It is true that some unemployed workers and peasants from other places did cause some difficulties. But none from around here. One reason we don't have any trouble is that we report any strangers coming to the village. If any demonstrator showed up, we'd know it right away. People say that one student heard on a Voice of America broadcast a report of Deng Xiaoping's bank account. He taped it and then replayed it for his friends. He shouldn't listen to the Voice of America. He should listen to the party. If I had a son in college, you'd be sure I'd call him back home."

Jiang Lijiang, as the party secretary, was the official village spokesperson for Half Moon. Therefore, he was able to converse with outsiders quite easily about such matters. Others had to be more cautious. Over much of the past 10 years, foreigners had been able to develop quite close friendships with Chinese intellectuals and, occasionally, even with workers and peasant-farmers. But since the events of Tiananmen Square, these associations have been fraught with difficulty, in some instances bringing the threat of serious punishment to those Chinese perceived by the authorities as opposed to the government and its policies. Thus, except for people such as Jiang Lijiang, it is likely that we will have to wait until some future time to hear the views of other Half Moon villagers.

BUREAUCRACY, PRIVATIZATION, AND DEMOCRACY

There is a story circulating in Beijing about the planned economy in the Soviet Union. It is said that at one time in that country, those with trucks and cars drove on the left, whereas the people of most other nations of the world drove on the right. After a good deal of discussion, the government decided that the country should join the majority and drive on the right too. But since the Soviet Union was a planned economy, it was important to do things in stages. So, a governmental directive announced that in the first year, all Soviet trucks should drive on the right, and this was to be followed in the second year by other vehicles!

The parallel is obvious. In China, the transition from a planned economy to a market-oriented one is occurring in stages, of which the two-track pricing system is the most obvious. But while the government price remains relatively constant, the market price keeps rising because of inflation. Furthermore, widespread corruption by officials able to purchase commodities at the state price and sell them at the market price has created intense friction between those who have more and those who have less. And this conflict is heightened by the fact that much of the corruption is concentrated among bureaucratic leaders running the central, regional, and local party and government.

Thus, from Chinese intellectuals living overseas, one regularly hears arguments that the only way to get rid of this corruption is to either return to a centralized economy or replace it with a market-driven one such as is found in the capitalist West. "Since most Chinese have no wish to return to a fully controlled economy," it is proposed, "why not opt for a rationalized market approach? Competition can resolve both the problem of the 'big pot' (waste in government subsidies) and the 'iron rice bowl' (paying laborers 'unwilling' to work). If managers don't make profits or workers don't produce the goods, they can be replaced by those who can."

Challenging these advocates of privatization, others suggest that such a perspective overlooks several crucial problems. It is argued that in the urban sector, one major difficulty is the extraordinary emphasis China's leaders have placed on nonproductive investment such as housing, offices, and, to some extent, hotels. By diverting financial resources in this manner, while at the same time allowing the import of immense amounts of foreign consumer goods, the country has seriously depleted its vast reserves and has hamstrung its local production.

Another major problem has been the extreme fragmentation of farmland and the corresponding deemphasis on agricultural mechanization. Although such a strategy has encouraged individual initiative and has brought an increased standard of living to some, it also has made the long-term rise in labor productivity far more difficult. Seeing no way out of this dilemma, many able peasant-farmers now seek work elsewhere, leaving the less able to work the land. These latter individuals, in turn, are less productive, thereby encouraging a slow downward spiral.

Still another set of issues concerns the management of China's industrial and farm enterprises. If a fully market-oriented economy took hold, who would assume control? Would existing bureaucratic managers and leaders be willing to turn their power over to a new managerial elite residing outside the party? More likely, the party and government bureaucracy would do everything possible to protect their existing power base from such a take-over.

This dilemma highlights a basic contradiction underlying China's recent economic reform movement, a contradiction we have already seen played out at the local level in Half Moon Village. For the reforms initiated in the early 1980s quickly shifted important economic decision-making powers in that village from party cadres to the increasingly privatized peasant-farmers and workers. That is, not only did local farmers assume greater control over their own agricultural production, but in vegetable production they bypassed the government completely. And as for grain, though they did have to provide the state with a certain quota, what remained could be sold on the open market too.

What then was left for local leaders to control? In Half Moon, they were still quite influential in determining access to and control over land and its distribution. They were responsible for hiring a farm manager who employed migrant laborers to do the manual work needed to produce the grain crop. They obtained fertilizer, small machinery, and other means of production for the village's vegetable and sideline industrial output. They played an important patronage role in determining local job assignments in new sidelines such as the candy and fire-retardant materials factories. And they carried overall responsibility for implementing the family-planning program.[14] But that was largely it—quite a contrast to 10 years earlier,

---

[14] By 1989, Half Moon Village had 60 one-child families, a substantial increase in a few short years. However, because of a quirk in the family-planning directive, families who were renting houses in the village and who were neither agricultural nor urban residents (i.e., they were private entrepreneurs) were not bound by the one-child policy and could have as many children as they wanted. These people were called "underground residents"!

when Jiang Lijiang had tried to cajole Half Moon's peasant-farmers, in a village-wide meeting, to finish spreading the collective manure piles before the arrival of the fall freeze-up.

A different but somewhat comparable process occurred in Beijing and other state-run urban industries where local managers were given more responsibility for fiscal authority, thereby diminishing the power of large centralized planning ministries. The managers could also use a share of the profits to invest in new equipment, give out larger bonuses, and the like, thereby assuming additional decision-making powers once held exclusively by more-distant bureaucratic entities. Thus, in this instance, the reform nurtured a new managerial class that began to challenge the party bureaucracy.

As a result of these experiences, it is not at all surprising that many government and party officials at all levels, increasingly concerned about their own futures, steadfastly refused to consider any further turn toward a more capitalist, market-oriented economy. They were also aware that China's urban population, most of whom were from the working class, resented the new affluence being flaunted before their eyes. Therefore, by the late 1980s, factory managers were still not able to hire or fire employees as they saw fit. Three-fourths of all raw materials and machinery inputs remained in the hands of government planning agencies, while state banks continued to monopolize most industrial credit (Smith 1989a). And in November 1989, after the June protest movement, the New China News Agency announced that a nationwide crackdown on nonstate enterprises had removed more than 1 million rural industrial collectives and 2.2 million private enterprises because of inefficiency, tax evasion, smuggling, and profiteering. In a separate report, the government stated that it could continue to support a closely supervised growth of the private sector as long as the sector became prosperous "through honest labor and lawful dealings."

As the contradictory trends contained in these efforts continued to magnify, Deng Xiaoping and other senior party leaders became increasingly fearful that they might eventually lose control over the national economy. Wanting to privatize, they could only introduce halfway measures to do so. Managers were granted more freedom, but they still could not fire workers as they saw fit. Peasants were allowed to control the land they farmed, but they could not own the land outright. At the same time, the government rejected two deeply ingrained tenets of Maoist socialism: first, that collective enrichment should be a fundamental principle of all economic and social development; and second, that highly advanced areas should serve as distribution points for assistance to those less developed. If "building on the best" was stressed throughout the 1980s, redistributing the wealth from these areas (through taxation or other means) in order to fund the building of a new economic infrastructure in the poorer regions was not. Instead, increasing corruption drained off much of the profit that could have gone toward reducing the inequalities long existent between the industrial and the agricultural sector, the worker and the peasant.[15]

---

[15]In March 1990, for example, Ye Xuanping, the senior leader of China's southern Guangdong Province, one of the country's wealthiest, rejected the central government's request to increase the province's allocation to the state, although a temporary contribution was approved.

Thus, while rejecting several fundamental features of both capitalism and socialism, the country's leaders did concentrate their attention on what the nation had excelled at for centuries—state bureaucracy.[16] As long as market-driven reforms didn't too severely threaten the privileged position of the bureaucracy, they were allowed to continue. Then, as these developments began to jeopardize leadership, senior government officials quickly reverted back to a central planning approach—but without socialism's other distinguishing features of economic enhancement through collective endeavors and of sharing the wealth with those less able to develop on their own. Finally, not knowing how to proceed economically, and with mass discontent building among the people, the reform coalition began splitting apart, the managerial class of "moderates" opting for a course of action different from that advocated by bureaucratic, conservative, "hard-line" octogenarians. The distinctions were minor, however, for both sought power at the expense of the people.

Also, both factions were completely united in wanting to block the emergence of any autonomous worker movement such as had sprung up during the spring protest of 1989. In contrast to its relatively subdued harassment and arrests of students and intellectuals, the government's crackdown on the workers was harsh. Some were severely beaten to obtain further information on the nature of the independent union and its leadership, while others directly involved in the destruction of military and other property were executed. By contrast, no intellectuals or students faced such extreme punishment. Willing to tolerate at least some dissent from students, the government was highly fearful of any independent organizing by its labor force.

Efforts by workers, students, and intellectuals to develop closer political ties in opposition to the government also were limited by their sharply differing social and economic statuses. Students, coming mostly from economically advantaged and politically well-placed families, tended to look at workers with some disdain and thus downplayed problems the latter were having to face.[17] Additionally, they were dissatisfied that their wages would be only roughly on a par with those of factory workers. They did, however, take a generally positive view toward many of the government's economic reforms of the 1980s. Workers, on the other hand, faced with increased inflation and with threats of future layoffs, speedups, and the like, saw these economic reforms in a far more negative light. As long as corruption didn't threaten their incomes, they were willing to look the other way. But as their standard of living dropped, the growing corruption among bureaucratic officials became a target of their increased frustration and anger.

So too, the concept of "democracy" was viewed quite differently by intellectuals and students than it was by workers and farmers. For the latter, democracy was

[16]Richard Smith has expressed this with particular succinctness: "Their own reproduction both as a dominant class and as individuals depends on the state's control of the economy and their control, in turn, of the state" (Smith 1989b:31).

[17]In September 1989, when students who had escaped from China met in Paris to form a new democratic political organization committed to establishing a Western form of democracy, a multiparty system, and private ownership, they didn't raise issues of workers' interests or social justice until two students from the United States reminded them of the omission (Chan and Unger 1990:80).

concerned with economic freedom from the controls and restraints placed on them by the bureaucracy, whether of the party or of the government. Intellectuals, however, tended to be divided on the matter, some feeling that the country should have as its leaders those chosen by popular vote, while others were drawn to the "new authoritarianism." This latter political model, drawing its inspiration from Taiwan, South Korea, Singapore, and Hong Kong, stressed prosperity without democracy, electoral politics being put aside until the distant future.

Implicit in this proposal is the assumption that by emphasizing privatization and a market-driven economy, China too can achieve a similar prosperity. However, those four nations that were able to break out of Third World poverty were small, were on the Asian periphery, and were the beneficiaries of two large Asian wars financed by America. There is little reason to assume that a market-driven economic system will enable China to repeat the process. Much more probable is a return to a neo-colonial status with small islands of prosperity and corruption on the coasts and with stagnation in the hinterland—a sure formula for future revolutionary up-heavals.

Glossary

Baigang: A strong white liquor often used in celebrations.

Baogan zhu: A "package-type" contract system in which land and tools are allotted to peasants on a long-term basis in return for fulfilling an agreed-upon quota of agricultural produce.

Baojia: An administrative system that originated in ancient China. The KMT government reintroduced it in the 1930s. In the KMT version, the *jia* was made up of 10 households, and the *bao* was made up of 10 *jia*. The Japanese preserved this system during their occupation.

Cadre: An official representing an administrative institution, the government, and/or the party.

Danwei: A work unit to which an individual is assigned.

"Dong kou bu dong shou": A phrase referring to cadres and others who spend their time talking but seldom using their hands; that is, "big mouth and lazy hands."

Gaozhuang: A complaint lodged to the authorities for bad behavior.

Guanxi: Personal connections that enable individuals to gain special benefits for themselves, their families, and their friends.

Huasheng: Peanut. Sometimes used as wedding food for good luck. *Hua* in Chinese also means "variety," and *sheng* means "birth," hence the association "give birth to various sexes of children."

Hukou: A residency status registered with the local government. A rural resident cannot legally move into the city without changing his or her residency status—a very difficult process.

Jiaozi: A popular kind of dumpling, often stuffed with vegetables or meat and eaten on special occasions, particularly during Spring Festival (Chinese New Year).

Jin: 1 *jin* equals 0.5 kilogram, or 1.1 pounds.

Jin jiaoqu: A municipal district lying just outside an urban center.

Kang: A large raised platform, made of earth or brick, that serves as a bed at night and a sitting area during the day and can be heated during the winter.

Lao: Old or older.

Li: 0.5 kilometer, or 0.3107 mile.

Lianzou: An old penal principle under which a whole family, clan, or neighborhood group could be held accountable for a serious crime committed by a given member.

Man yue: A celebration of a newborn child's first month of life attended by all nearby relatives and friends of the family.

"Men dang hu dui": Literally, "matching doors and windows." The phrase means that families of young marital candidates should be similar in personal, social, and economic background.

Mu: 1 *mu* equals 0.0666 hectare, or 0.1647 acre.

Nao dongfang: A traditional wedding-night ritual that includes teasing the couple in various ways, some of which may carry sexual connotations.

Pinyin (or hanyu pinyin): The official (Han) Chinese system of spelling using the roman alphabet.

Quingming: Annual day (April 5 or 6) during which people pay respect at the graves of deceased relatives. Such events often include a variety of ritual activities.

San cong si de: The "three obediences and four virtues," which required a woman to first follow the lead of her father, then her husband, and on her husband's death, her sons, and to be virtuous in morality, proper speech, modesty, and diligent work.

Shangshan Xiaxiang: The "Up to the Mountains and Down to the Countryside" campaign undertaken between 1956 and 1979, in which millions of urban middle school graduates were called on to assist in developing China's rural areas. The movement also resolved problems of urban unemployment.

Shehui diaocha: A social investigation or field research study.

Shuxiang: A horoscope utilized to determine one's fortune.

Wubao: The "five guarantees," a form of social security provided by the collective for childless elderly and disabled people. The guarantees included housing, food, clothing, medical care, and burial expenses.

Xian: A county.

Xiang: A township, the administrative duties of which were largely taken over by China's communes in 1958. Today, townships are being reinstated as an important level of rural governmental organization.

Xiao: Little or small. Often used as a nickname for someone younger than the speaker.

Xiegi: A malevolent ether or wind that can bring sickness or misfortune.

Yuan: A form of Chinese currency. 100 *fen* (cents) is equivalent to 1 *yuan*. In 1979, 1 *yuan* equaled approximately 58 cents (United States).

Yuan jiaoqu: A remote suburban district outside an urban center.

Zao: A date (fruit). The sound is the same as that meaning "early." An association is sometimes made between the two so that *zao* is understood to mean "get a son early."

Zeren zhi: The "responsibility system" introduced in 1980 whereby separate households (and individuals) could establish contracts with production teams and brigades to produce agricultural foods on brigade land divided up for that purpose.

Zou houmen: The practice of obtaining exceptional, unfair, or illegal favors for one's self or others by resorting to personal contacts. Referred to as "going through the back door."

Zuo yuezi: Literally "sitting month," a custom in which mother and child remain inside the house for the first month of the child's life so that they may be protected from harmful agents, natural or supernatural.

Zuoye zu: A small working group or production unit.

Bibliography

Anagnost, Ann
1989 "Prosperity and Counterprosperity: The Moral Discourse on Wealth in Post-Mao China." In A. Dirlik and M. Meiser, *Marxism and the Chinese Experience*. Armonk, N.Y.: M. E. Sharpe.

Andors, Phyllis
1983 *The Unfinished Liberation of Chinese Women, 1949–1980*. Bloomington: Indiana University Press.

Baker, Hugh D. R.
1979 *Chinese Family and Kinship*. New York: Columbia University Press.

Balazs, Etienne
1954 "Tradition and Revolution in China." In E. Balazs, *Chinese Civilization and Bureaucracy*. New Haven, Conn.: Yale University Press.

Baum, Richard, and F. C. Teiwes
1968 *Ssu-Ching: The Socialist Education Movement in 1962–66*. Berkeley: University of California Press.

Beijing First Foreign Languages Institute
1976 "The History of Wandong Village." Beijing. Mimeograph.

Bennett, Gordon
1978 *Huadong: The Story of a Chinese People's Commune*. Boulder, Colo.: Westview Press.

Bernstein, Thomas P.
1977 *Up to the Mountains and Down to the Villages: The Transfer of Youth from Urban to Rural China*. New Haven, Conn.: Yale University Press.

Bianco, Lucien
1971 *The Origins of the Chinese Revolution*. Stanford, Calif.: Stanford University Press.

Blecher, Marc
1986 *China: Politics, Economics, and Society*. Boulder, Colo.: Lynne Rienner.

Chan, Anita, Richard Madsen, and Jonathan Unger
1984 *Chen Village: The Recent History of a Peasant Community in Mao's China*. Berkeley: University of California Press.

Chan, Anita, and Jonathan Unger
1990 "China after Tiananmen." *The Nation* 250(3):79–81.

Chance, Norman A.
1973 "China's Socialist Development and the Dialectical Process." *Perspectives in Social Change and Development* 8:1–12.

Chen, Jack
1973 *A Year in Upper Felicity*. New York: Macmillan.

Chen Muhua
1979 "To Realize the Four Modernizations, Is It Necessary to Control Population Increase in a Planned Way?" *People's Daily (Renmin Ribao)*, August 11.

Chesneaux, Jean
1973 *Peasant Revolts in China: 1840–1949*. London: Norton.

Chia Ling
1989 "Tiananmen Square Massacre." *Asian Outlook* 24(4):10–13.

Croll, Elizabeth
1981 *The Politics of Marriage in Contemporary China*. London: Oxford University Press.

Crook, Isabel, and David Crook
1959 *Revolution in a Chinese Village: Ten Mile Inn*. London: Routledge and Kegan Paul.
1966 *The First Years of Yangyi Commune*. London: Routledge and Kegan Paul.
1979 *Ten Mile Inn*. New York: Pantheon.

Davin, Delia
1976 *Women-Work: Women and the Party in Revolutionary China*. London: Oxford University Press.

Diamond, Norma
1969 *K'un Shen: A Taiwan Village*. New York: Holt, Rinehart and Winston.
1975 "Collectivization, Kinship, and the Status of Women in Rural China." In Rayna Reiter, ed., *Toward an Anthropology of Women*. New York: Monthly Review Press.

Domes, Jurgen
1982 "New Policies in the Communes: Notes on Rural Societal Structures in China, 1976–1981." *Journal of Asian Studies* 41(2):253–67.

Fang Lizhi
1989 "China's Despair and China's Hope." *New York Review of Books*, February 2.

Fei Hsiao-Tung [Fei Xiaodong]
1939 *Peasant Life in China*. London: Routledge and Kegan Paul.
1980 "Toward a People's Anthropology." *Human Organization* 39:115–19.

Fei Hsiao-Tung, Wu Wen-Chiao, and Lin Yueh-Hwa [Fei Xiaodong, Wu Wenzao, and Lin Yuehua]
1973 "Commentary." *Current Anthropology* 14:482.

Fried, Morton H.
1953 *The Fabric of Chinese Society: A Study of Social Life in a Chinese County Seat*. New York: Praeger.

Frolic, B. Michael
1978 "Reflections on the Chinese Model of Development." *Social Forces* 57(2):384–418.

Gallin, Bernard
1966 *Hsin Hsing, Taiwan: A Chinese Village*. Berkeley: University of California Press.

Gamble, Sidney
1954 *Ting Hsien: A North China Rural Community*. New York: Institute of Pacific Relations.

Gurley, John G.
1971 "Capitalist and Maoist Economic Development." In E. Freedman and M. Selden, eds., *America's Asia: Dissenting Essays on Asian-American Relations*. New York: Vintage Books.

Hao Ran (Liang Jinguang)
1981 *The Golden Road*. Translated by Carma Hinton and Chris Gilmartin from the 1972 Chinese edition. Beijing: Foreign Languages Press.

Hinton, Carma, and Richard Gordon
1986 *One Village in China: A Trilogy*. New York: Long Bow Group. (Films available through New Day Films, New York.)

Hinton, William
1966 *Fanshen: A Documentary of Revolutionary Change in a Chinese Village*. New York: Vintage Books.
1970 *Iron Oxen: A Documentary of Revolution in Chinese Farming*. New York: Vintage Books.
1982 "Village in Transition." In Mark Selden and Victor Lippit, eds., *The Transition to Socialism in China*. Armonk, N.Y.: M. E. Sharpe.
1983 *Shenfan: Continuing Revolution in a Chinese Village*. New York: Random House.
1983a "A Trip to Fengyang County: Investigating China's New Family Contract System." *Monthly Review* 35:6.
1990 *The Great Reversal: The Privatization of China, 1978–1989*. New York: Monthly Review Press.

Howard, Pat
1988 *Breaking the Iron Rice Bowl*. Armonk, N.Y.: M. E. Sharpe.

Hsu, Francis L. K.
1979 "Traditional Culture in Contemporary China." In Godwin C. Chu and Francis L. K. Hsu, eds., *Moving a Mountain: Cultural Change in China*. Honolulu: University Press of Hawaii.
1981 *Americans and Chinese: Passages to Difference*. 3d ed. Honolulu: University Press of Hawaii.

Hu Hsien-Chin
1944 "The Chinese Concept of Face." *American Anthropologist*. 46:45–64.

Huang Shu-min
1989 *The Spiral Road: Change in a Chinese Village through the Eyes of a Community Party Leader*. Boulder: Westview Press.

Huang Yasheng
1983 "Collective State Brings Wealth to Vegetable Farmers." *China Daily*, August 2.

Johnson, Kay Ann
1980 "Women in the People's Republic of China." In Sylvia A. Chipp and Justin J. Green, eds., *Asian Women*. University Park: Pennsylvania State University Press.

Leys, Simon
1977 *Chinese Shadows*. New York: Viking.

Liang, Heng, and Judith Shapiro
1982 *Son of the Revolution*. New York: Knopf.

Lin Yueh-Hwa
1947 *The Golden Wing: A Sociological Study of Chinese Familism*. New York: Oxford University Press.

Lippit, Victor
1982 "Socialist Development in China." In Mark Selden and Victor Lippit, eds., *The Transition to Socialism in China*. Armonk, N.Y.: M. E. Sharpe.

McGough, James P.
1979 *Fei Hstao t'ung: Dilemma of a Chinese Intellectual*. Armonk, N.Y.: M. E. Sharpe.

Mao Zedong
1949 "Report to the Second Plenary Session of the Seventh Central Committee of the CCP." *Selected Works of Mao Tse-tung.* 1969 ed. 4:361–75. Peking: Foreign Language Press.
1955 "On the Question of Agricultural Cooperation." *Selected Readings of Mao Tse-tung.* 1971 ed. Peking: Foreign Language Press.
1956 "On the Ten Great Relationships." Speech to the Political Bureau of the Central Committee. Printed in *Peking Review,* January 1, 1977.
1977 *A Critique of Soviet Economics.* Translated by Moss Roberts. New York: Monthly Review Press.
1978 *Socialist Upsurge in the Countryside.* Ed. from abridged edition, 1955. Peking: Foreign Language Press.

Marx, Karl
1875 *Critique of the Gotha Programme.* 1972 Chinese trans. Peking: Foreign Language Press.

Myers, Ramon H.
1970 *The Chinese Peasant Economy: Agricultural Development in Hopei and Shantung, 1890–1949.* Cambridge, Mass.: Harvard University Press.

Myrdal, Jan
1963 *Report From a Chinese Village.* New York: Penguin.

Nee, Victor, and James Peck, eds.
1975 *China's Uninterrupted Revolution.* New York: Pantheon.

Oksenberg, Michel
1982 "Economic Policy-Making in China: Summer 1981." *China Quarterly* 9:165–94.

Parish, William L., and Martin K. Whyte
1978 *Village and Family in Contemporary China.* Chicago: University of Chicago Press.

Peng Zhen
1982 "Report on the Revised Draft of the Constitution of the People's Republic of China." *People's Daily (Renmin Ribao),* December 6.

Potter, Sulamith Heins, and Jack M. Potter
1989 *China's Peasants: The Anthropology of a Revolution.* New York: Cambridge University Press.

Priutt, Ida
1979 *Old Madame Yin: A Memoir of Peking Life, 1926–1938.* Stanford, Calif.: Stanford University Press.

Schell, Orville
1977 *In the People's Republic of China: An American's First-Hand View of Living and Working in China.* New York: Random House.

Selden, Mark
1982 "Cooperation and Conflict: Cooperative and Collective Formation in China's Countryside." In Mark Selden and Victor Lippit, eds., *The Transition to Socialism in China.* Armonk, N.Y.: M. E. Sharpe.

Shirk, Susan L.
1982 *Competitive Comrades: Career Incentives and Student Strategies.* Berkeley: University of California Press.

Shue, Vivienne
1980 *Peasant China in Transition*. Berkeley: University of California Press.

Siu, Helen
1989 *Agents and Victims in South China*. New Haven: Yale University Press.

Siu, Helen, and Zeida Stern
1983 *Mao's Harvest: Voices from China's New Generation*. New York: Oxford University Press.

Skinner, William G.
1978 "Vegetable Supply and Marketing in Chinese Cities." *China Quarterly* 76:733–93.

Smith, Arthur
1899 *Village in China*. Reprint, 1970. Boston: Little Brown.

Smith, Richard
1989a "Class Structure and Economic Development: The Contradictions of Market Socialism in China." Ph.D. diss., University of California at Los Angeles.
1989b "Contradictions of the Economic Reform: Neither Market nor Socialism." *Against the Current*, September/October.

Stavrianos, L.
1975 "The Mandarin View of China." *The Nation*, February 6.

Stover, Leon, and Takeko Stover
1976 *China: An Anthropological Perspective*. Pacific Palisades: Goodyear.

Tsou Tang, Marc Blecher, and Mitch Meisner
1982 "National Agricultural Policy: The Dazhai Model and Local Change in the Post-Mao Era." In Mark Selden and Victor Lippit, eds., *The Transition to Socialism in China*. Armonk, N.Y.: M. E. Sharpe.

Unger, Jonathan
1982 *Education Under Mao: Class and Competition in Canton Schools, 1960–1980*. New York: Columbia University Press.

Vermeer, E. B.
1982 "Income Differentials in Rural China." *China Quarterly* 89:1–33.

Whyte, Martin K., and Burton Pasternak
1980 "Sociology and Anthropology." In A. Thurston and J. Parker, eds., *Humanistic and Social Science Research in China*. New York: Social Science Research Council.

Wiens, Thomas
1981 "The Economics of Municipal Vegetable Supply in China." In Donald L. Plunkett and Halset L. Beemer, Jr., eds., *Vegetable Farming Systems in China*. Boulder: Westview Press.

Wolf, Margery
1968 *The House of Lin*. New York: Appleton-Century-Crofts.
1970 "Child Training and the Chinese Family." In Maurice Freedman, ed., *Family and Kinship in Chinese Society*. Stanford, Calif.: Stanford University Press.
1974 "Chinese Women: Old Skills in a New Context." In M. Zimbalist Rosaldo and Louise Lamphere, eds., *Women, Culture, and Society*. Stanford, Calif.: Stanford University Press.

Yang, C. K.
1959 *Chinese Communist Society: The Family and the Village*. Cambridge, Mass.: M.I.T. Press.

Yang, Martin C.
1945 *A Chinese Village: Taitou, Shantung Province*. New York: Columbia University Press.

Zweig, David
1983 "National Elites, Rural Bureaucrats, and Peasants: Limits on Commune Reform in China." In Ronald A. Morse, ed., *The Limits of Reform in China*. Boulder: Westview Press.

Index